We heard from the chairman of the Federal Reserve that unless we act the financial system of this country and perhaps the world will melt down.... There was complete silence for twenty seconds. The oxygen left the room. Chairman Bernanke said, "If we don't do this tomorrow, there won't be an economy on Monday."

Senate Banking Committee Chairman Christopher Dodd on a meeting of legislative leaders with Bernanke and Secretary Paulson in Speaker Nancy Pelosi's office on September 17, 2008 (interview with Charlie Rose, November 26, 2008)

These bad loans have created a chain reaction and last week our credit markets froze – even some Main Street non-financial companies had trouble financing their normal business operations. If that situation were to persist, it would threaten all parts of our economy.... We must now take further, decisive action to fundamentally and comprehensively address the root cause of this turmoil. And that root cause is the housing correction which has resulted in illiquid mortgage-related assets that are choking off the flow of credit which is so vitally important to our economy. We must address this underlying problem, and restore confidence in our financial markets and financial institutions so they can perform their mission of supporting future prosperity and growth.

Treasury Secretary Henry Paulson to the Senate Banking Committee, September 23, 2008

"I do try to put a lot of weight on what people are saying," Watt said, referring to the overwhelming opposition of his constituents. "But in this case, I think a lot of people don't know exactly why a bailout is necessary.... On this issue, we [Congress] have heard the top two economic authorities in the world tell us we're on the verge of a calamitous event."

Mel Watt, North Carolina congressman, *Winston-Salem Journal*, September 30, 2008

You never want a serious crisis to go to waste.

Rahm Emanuel, president-elect Barack Obama's chief of staff, *Wall Street Journal*, November 21, 2009

Central Banking in a Democracy

The Federal Reserve System, which has been Congress' agent for the control of money since 1913, has a mixed reputation. Its errors have been huge. It was the principal cause of the Great Depression of the 1930s and the inflation of the 1970s, and participated in the massive bailouts of financial institutions at taxpayers' expense during the recent Great Recession.

This book is a study of the causes of the Fed's errors, with lessons for an improved monetary authority, beginning with an examination of the history of central banks, in which it is found that their performance depended on their incentives, as is to be expected of economic agents. An implication of these findings is that the Fed's failings must be traced to its institutional independence, particularly of the public welfare. Consequently, its policies have been dictated by special interests: financial institutions who desire public support without meaningful regulation, as well as presidents and those portions of Congress desiring growing government financed by inflation.

Monetary stability (which used to be thought the primary purpose of central banks) requires responsibility, meaning punishment for failure, instead of a remote and irresponsible (to the public) agency such as the Fed. It requires either private money motivated by profit or Congress disciplined by the electoral system as before 1913. Change involving the least disturbance to the system suggests the latter.

John H. Wood is Reynolds Professor of Economics at Wake Forest University, Winston-Salem, North Carolina, USA.

Routledge explorations in economic history
Edited by Lars Magnusson
Uppsala University, Sweden

Central Banking in a Democracy

The Federal Reserve and its alternatives

John H. Wood

Routledge
Taylor & Francis Group

LONDON AND NEW YORK

First published 2015
by Routledge

2 Park Square, Milton Park, Abingdon, Oxfordshire OX14 4RN
52 Vanderbilt Avenue, New York, NY 10017

Routledge is an imprint of the Taylor & Francis Group, an informa business

First issued in paperback 2019

British Library Cataloguing in Publication Data
A catalogue record for this book is available from the British Library

Library of Congress Cataloging in Publication Data
Wood, John H. (John Harold)
Central banking in a democracy: the Federal Reserve and its alternatives/
John H. Wood.
   pages cm
   1. Board of Governors of the Federal Reserve System (U.S.)
   2. Monetary policy–United States. 3. Banks and banking,
   Central–United States. I. Title.
   HG2565.W65 2014
   332.1'10973–dc23   2014013319

ISBN: 978-1-138-01639-2 (hbk)
ISBN: 978-0-367-86968-7 (pbk)

Typeset in Times New Roman
by Wearset Ltd, Boldon, Tyne and Wear

To Sue, Jim, and Ann

Contents

Plates

Figures

Tables

Data sources

Sources of data for figures and in the text are:

Balke, N.S. and R.J. Gordon. 1984. "Historical data," in R.J. Gordon, ed., *The American Business Cycle*. University of Chicago Press.

Cannan, E. 1925. *The Paper Pound of 1797–1821*. P.S. King & Son.

Federal Deposit Insurance Corporation. *FDIC Quarterly*.

Federal Reserve Board. 1943. 1976. *Banking and Monetary Statistics, 1914–41* and *1941–70*.

———. 1959. *All-Bank Statistics. United States, 1896–1955*.

———. Data releases. *Economic Research and Data*.

Federal Reserve Bank of St. Louis. *Economic Data*.

———. *National Economic Trends*.

Friedman, M. and A.J. Schwartz. 1963. *A Monetary History of the United States, 1857–1960*. Princeton University Press.

Jastram, R.W. 1977. *The Golden Constant*. Wiley.

Levin, F.J. and A. Meulendyke. 1979. "Monetary policy and open market operations in 1978," *Federal Reserve Bank of New York Quarterly Review*, spring.

President's Council of Economic Advisors. *Economic Report of the President*. Annual.

Sutch, Richard, *et al.*, eds. 2006. *Historical Statistics of the United States: Earliest Times to the Present*. Cambridge University Press.

Preface

On December 16, 2013, during the celebration of the centennial of the Federal Reserve Act, former Fed Chairman Paul Volcker (1979–87) recollected the illustrious history of the institution. It had repeatedly met the need for responses to "economic and financial disturbances ... that only an institution equipped with authority and judgment could timely act upon." (He passed over the fact that the Fed had been a cause of many of those disturbances, such as the inflation of the 1970s and the bubble of the 2000s.)

> Now I think no one can claim that every year in every circumstance in every crisis the Fed got its policies exactly right. But what is beyond debate is that this institution has served the country well.... Strong action, sometimes testing the limits of its legal authority [has] rested on a sense of integrity – integrity that it achieved and maintained over the years, in the sense that it was able to act free of partisan and political passions. [The] organization ... has come to command and maintain respect over the years ... to the point that the phrase "Don't fight the Fed" has become close to an axiom in the financial marketplace. [T]he confidence in the ability of our century-old central bank to cut through intellectual and political debate to act in the public interest ... is essential not only to the strengths of our banking system and our financial markets, but I believe, to the effective governance of this country.

Former Chairman Alan Greenspan (1987–2006) agreed, gave an example in the Fed's response to the stock crash of October 1987, and attributed its successes to the unmatched "grouping of people of expertise in virtually every subject matter you can conceive of" (Board of Governors of the Federal Reserve System/About the Fed/Federal Reserve System/Centennial).

Volcker and Greenspan's pride in the Fed's expertise and goodwill is justified. The quality of its economics staff, for example, equals those of leading research universities and is the envy of other government agencies, who refer to it as Club Fed. Yours truly has enjoyed many pleasant and productive times at the Fed, beginning when I was a beneficiary of a generous graduate-student stipend from the Federal Reserve Bank of Chicago, where I shared offices with

Ed Feige and Bill Poole during successive summers, and had the opportunity to observe Director of Research George Mitchell, soon to be a governor at the Federal Reserve Board; then as an economist at the Board's Flow-of-Funds Section with Steve Taylor, Mike Grove, Neva Van Peski, and Pat Hendershott, and present at the beginning of the Fed's econometric model with Frank deLeeuw and Director of Research Dan Brill; later visiting the Federal Reserve Bank of Philadelphia and rubbing shoulders with Dave Eastburn, Mark Willis, Lee Hoskins, and Ed Boehne; the Federal Reserve Bank of Dallas with Harvey Rosenblum, Dale Osborne, Joe Burns, and Cara Lown; and the Chicago Fed again, with George Kaufman and Randy Merris.

We can agree about the quality of the Fed as an institution. When we look at its effects, however, we cannot escape the conclusion that its morale is a direct function of its intellectual and political distance from those affected by its policies. That there is some understanding of this is indicated by the frequency of Chairman Ben Bernanke's (2006–14) defensive assertions that the Fed's massive support of selected Wall Street institutions is really in the interests of Main Street. He also regularly, including at the centennial celebration, points to (undocumented) increases in transparency and accountability because the "legitimacy" of the Fed's "tough decisions … rests on the understanding and support of the broader American public, whose interests we are working to serve." Yet he keeps in his office, as light-hearted evidence of the Fed's determination to fight inflation, one of the 2×4s mailed by home builders to the Fed in protest of the high interest rates of the early 1980s – selectively forgetting that the inflation was the Fed's doing and maintaining its psychological barrier against the possibility of genuine criticism.

1 Introduction

The Federal Reserve's 2013 centenary would have been a suitable occasion to run a check on our central bank, grade its performance, and decide whether and how it might be improved. That duty would seem to have been especially compelling in light of recent decisions by Fed officials to alter the structure and purposes of the institution with which they have been entrusted, and the widespread public dissatisfaction with those decisions. In earlier eras, national monetary institutions were adopted, revised, or rejected after vigorous political debates over their purposes and the prospects of achieving them.

Those debates are past. The Fed is criticized, and changes around the edges are discussed – such as regular audits, a smaller policy role for Reserve Bank presidents, and formal monetary rules – but the fundamental nature of the institution is safe – from Congress, at least, although we do not know what new revisions in purposes and methods the Fed itself will decide. Opposition to the Fed's existence is limited to the few and marginal. Congressman Ron Paul (*End the Fed*) has received much publicity but little support, and the theory of competitive money, which dispenses with the need for an officially imposed central bank, is well developed but ignored by most economists.[1]

There has always been a good deal of sophisticated discussion of the theory and history of money and banking. We know that the central bank determines the price level, and that the Fed's commitment to its stability has been episodic, at best. We know the history of banking crises, including the roles of central banks and regulatory restrictions in bringing them about – the Great Depression and the Great Recession are two examples – and then making them worse by obstructing market adjustments. The recent bailouts of large financial institutions continued past practices. Only the New York–Washington political-financial corridor is happy with the success of the Fed and Treasury in preventing a recurrence of the Great Depression, as they like to say.

We are assured and reassured that the Fed has learned, and will do better next time, and legislation is repeatedly aimed at preventing future crises and their embarrassing and damaging official reactions (Bernanke 2002; Feldstein 2010). Yet the pattern continues (Schwartz 1992; Kaufman 1996; Miron 2009a). Neither theory nor experience has been enough. It's time we considered incentives. In particular, we need to ask what makes the Fed operate against the interests of society. An answer requires an examination of the influences to which it is subject, beginning with the nature of the organization. Revealing the bottom line of this study at the outset, members of the Fed do not bear the public costs of their decisions. The Federal Reserve was created as an independent monetary authority to keep money out of politics and above the popular mood, but its structure subordinates its actions to the interests of particular groups and their emergencies, real or imagined. The electoral fortunes of members of Congress and the President are directly affected by economic conditions and their fiscal policies, especially taxes, but in the Fed they created a buffer to deflect blame for their policies.

Economists typically try to explain behavior by models in which information, other constraints, and benefits are specified, for example, income, prices, and utility for consumers who buy the goods that maximize those utilities subject to the constraints of their incomes and prices. Managers are assumed to maximize firm values subject to production possibilities and relative prices. All this is forgotten when it comes to public policy. Official agencies, including central banks, are simply assumed to do "the right thing" as defined in terms of an economic model, such as a constant rate of money growth as recommended by Milton Friedman, or a trade-off between inflation and output according to Keynesians or the Taylor rule (Friedman 1960; Samuelson and Solow 1960; Taylor 1993). Mistakes and bad outcomes simply bring renewals of advice to do better, without changing the institution's incentives in ways that make better behavior more likely. There is a large literature on the theory and practice of public choice, but it finds little place in discussions of monetary policy (Niskanen 1971).

After all, why should the Fed follow any of the recommended monetary rules when its officials would enjoy none of their benefits even if they shared the monetary theories implied, which is unlikely in view of their indifference to economists' abstractions. If economists wish to explain the Fed in the manner of other groups, they must take account of the Fed's view of the world – what it knows best, especially the financial sector – and its interests, especially its survival. The latter depends on Congress, which likes easy money to finance the national debt, the President, who likes monetary stimuli, and the financial interests for whom the Fed was founded and are its chief supporters.

The behavior resulting from these influences is complex. Sometimes Congress and the Executive exert considerable control over the Fed and sometimes apparently leave it alone, lending some credence to the fiction of an independent agency. Would Congress have been so ready to provide the expensive bailouts of the unpopular financial firms in 2008 if it had not been able to hide behind an expert agency which announced that "the sky is falling," that is, if it had been directly responsible for monetary policy? The alleged emergency was represented – and accepted – as a great surprise on Capitol Hill even though the growing problems of financial firms, and the entire system, had been discussed for years. The opening quotations of the book tell the mood of Congress, the Fed, the Treasury, and the administration. The chairman and the secretary, backed by the President, urged the congressional leadership to act quickly, without debate, and got their way.

If decisions had been in the hands of a responsible and accountable body from the beginning, they might have been better informed, more thoughtful, less infused with panic, and most of all, considered the probable costs and benefits. Would you, dear reader, have willingly transferred your wealth to the investment bankers? Not if you were represented by most of the letters and polls (see the statement by congressman Watts). Yet isn't their realization supposed to be the strength of democracy? Instead, in the Federal Reserve, we have realized the fears of Jefferson and Jackson.

The Fed was slightly modified after the Great Depression of 1929–33, and during the Great Inflation of the 1970s, but the institution was not changed in any fundamental way that might have improved its decision processes.[2] However, when conditions settle down and there is time for reflection on the mistakes leading up to and during the Great Recession, a new Congress will have a chance to reconsider the Fed. Will the new law, if there is one, simply advise an unchanged Fed, as in the past, to "do better next time," or will it try to erect a monetary structure with incentives necessary to decisions that promote the public's stability and prosperity. The panic-driven Wall Street Reform and Consumer Protection (Dodd–Frank) Act certainly made no such attempt.

The separation of the fortunes of the public and the Federal Reserve make it unlikely that the Fed's decisions will take account of the ordinary citizen. The separation was most unfortunate during the Great Depression, when survival of the central financial institutions, including Number One, was the Fed's first objective, and again during the Great Recession. If the public's pain is not felt by policymakers, the latter lack the incentive to act. It does no good to say "Don't forget Main Street" – no matter how many times – if there are no costs of neglect and the rewards are elsewhere. The Fed's demonstrated first priorities – the finance of the federal debt and the interests of those "too connected to fail" – are explained, even dictated, by the incentives inherent in its structure.

This book is among other things a history of the connections between the structures and decisions of American monetary authorities, suggesting, I hope, lessons for the organization of the Fed's replacement. It is part compression and part extension of my *History of Central Banking in Great Britain and the United States* and *A History of Macroeconomic Policy in the United States*, which included sympathetic studies of monetary policy, including examinations of the influences on central bankers and an explanation of their atheoretical decision processes that offend economists. I argued that economists' criticisms were often misplaced because practitioners are not guided by academic theories. Central bankers' preoccupations with the details of the financial markets rather than the wider economy is a case in point, and is unsurprising in light of their backgrounds, environments, and political pressures that are unaffected by changes in their composition, including recent increases in the number of professional economists at the Fed. These preoccupations help explain why the differences between the monetary policies of the Great Recession and the Great Depression were insignificant.

Monetary theories provide valuable insights into the effects of policies, but those policies are decided by the officials of institutions – we might say the institutionalized. Douglas North (1990: 3) wrote that "Institutions are the rules of the game in a society or, more formally, are the humanly devised constraints that shape human interaction." In particular, they shape monetary policy. Theories of money and prices may be important, as are the personalities and education of central bankers, but if we hope to understand their decisions, we must also know the incentives and constraints to which their institutions are subject.

We have learned much from the classic analyses of the effects of institutions on the accumulation and preservation of knowledge and practice in Elinor Ostrom's *Governing the Commons: The Evolution of Institutions for Collective Action* (1990), and Edmund Burke's *Reflections on the Revolution in France* (1790), both of which can teach us about the Fed. Ostrom considered "similarities among enduring, self-governing 'common pool resources'," that is, dealing with scarcity in less-than-routine governmental circumstances. First, they were all confronted by uncertain and complex environments, most often erratic rainfall, although the principles were the same for the other cases. Second, in contrast to the uncertainty of environments, the populations remained stable and predictable for long periods. "Individuals have shared a past and expect to share a future. It is important for individuals to maintain their reputations as reliable members of the community." They "live side by side [and] expect their children and grandchildren to inherit their land." This is comparable to politicians' often expressed concern for "our children and grandchildren." Third,

> extensive norms have evolved [which] narrowly define 'proper' behavior [and] make it feasible for individuals to live in close interdependence ... without excessive conflicts. Further, a reputation for keeping promises, honest dealings, and reliability in one arena is a valuable asset. Prudent, long-term self-interest reinforces the acceptance of the norms of proper behavior.
>
> (Ostrom 1990: 88–89)

"Reputation" and "reliability" are just as necessary to bank regulation and effective monetary policy, of course. So why haven't we had them? The answer is suggested in this book, in institutional incentives, in the disconnect between administrative agencies like the Fed and the public.

Fourth, "the most notable similarity," Ostrom wrote, "is the sheer perseverance of" these systems and institutions. They "meet [the] criterion of institutional robustness, in that the rules have been devised and modified over time according to a set of collective-choice and constitutional-choice rules." Nothing could be further from this evolutionary process than the "creation" ("out of nothing") of organizations like the Fed by reformist governments and concentrated interests (Ostrom 1990: 89; Shepsle 1989).

Ostrom's discussion suggests a fifth similarity in the choice and enforcement of rules by those involved and affected, which is violated by the Fed (and other government agencies) because they do not bear the costs of harmful policies. Their incentives are embedded not in the public's welfare but in their own. Their independence (of the public) and expertise (special knowledge) violate all the criteria of commitment, reputation, and reliability that make institutions work.

A famous exposition of the benefits of the known and traditional was Burke's (1790: 274–275) warnings of the dangers of the novelties of the French Revolution:

> Rage and phrenzy will pull down more in half an hour than prudence, deliberation, and foresight can build up in an hundred years. The errors and defects of old establishments are visible and palpable. It calls for little ability to point them out; and where absolute power is given, it requires but a word wholly to abolish the vice and establishment together.... To make every thing the reverse of what they have seen is ... easy.... No difficulties occur in what has never been tried. Criticism is almost baffled in discovering the defects of what has not existed...
>
> At once to preserve and to reform is quite another thing. When the useful parts of an old establishment are kept, and what is superadded is to be fitted to what is retained, a vigorous mind, steady persevering attention, various powers of comparison and combination, and the resources of an understanding fruitful in expedients are to be exercised; they are to be exercised in a continued conflict with the combined force of opposite vices; with the obstinacy that rejects all improvement, and the levity that is fatigued and disgusted with every thing of which it is not in possession. But you may object – "A process of this kind is slow. It is not fit for an assembly which glorifies in performing in a few months the work of ages. Such a mode of reforming possibly might take up many years." Without question it might; and it ought. It is one of the excellences of a method in which time is among the assistants, that its operation is slow and in some cases almost imperceptible.

The public "is better served by custom than understanding," Friedrich Hayek (1979: 157) wrote, along the same lines, because it has "learnt to do the right thing without comprehending why it was the right thing." There is "more 'intelligence' incorporated in the system of rules of conduct than in man's thoughts about his surroundings." "To avoid therefore the evils of inconstancy ... ten thousand times worse than those of obstinacy," Burke (1790: 192) advised, a man should approach existing defects of the state

> with due caution; ... he should never dream of beginning its reformation by its subversion; ... he should approach the faults of the state as ... the wounds of a father, with pious awe and trembling solicitude. By this wise prejudice we are taught to look with horror on those children of their country who are prompt rashly to hack that aged parent in pieces, and put him into a kettle of magicians in hopes that by their poisonous weeds and wild incantations they may regenerate the paternal constitution and renovate their father's life.

The novelty of the Federal Reserve's structure and powers, with the extravagant claims of its founders, was a case in point. It was more a printing press than a bank, its powers were limited only by political self-restraint, often meaning not at all, its stated purpose to provide an elastic currency was ambiguous, dangerous if taken literally, and the President's statement that it was "a democracy of credit," directed by "a public board of disinterested officers of the Government," reflected the loose thinking upon which the institution was founded. Congressman Carter Glass, the legislative "founder of the Fed," called it "an altruistic institution, a part of Government itself, representing the American people, with powers such as no man would dare misuse," although six years later, as Wilson's Secretary of the Treasury, he pressured the Fed into continuing easy money war finance into the postwar period. Its shocks to the system did not end with the creation of the Fed, whose irresponsibility has allowed it to fly into sudden and frequent policy innovations that have made it the most watched and feared institution in the world.

The 20 years after 1913 were financial and economic catastrophes, including, but not limited to the Great Depression and the end of the monetary system that the Fed was created to support. Almost as unfortunate was the recent episode of monetary policy before and during the Great Recession which indicates that the Fed has not learned from its mistakes. How could it, we may ask, with no incentives to learn? This book reviews the Fed and its predecessors, with emphasis on the connections between their structures and performance, in the hope that we will learn something useful for the construction of a central bank or other monetary arrangements that might defend the value of the currency as well as before 1913. After retaining its value the preceding century, the 1913 dollar lost 96 percent of its purchasing power over the next 100 years.

An overview of the structures and performances of central banks in the past may be a helpful introduction to the more detailed discussions of later chapters. It is necessary to begin with the Bank of England, upon which the first US central banks were patterned, and whose pre-1914 practices still supply most of the theory of central banking. The evolution of the Bank's monetary policy consisted primarily of learning to support the payments system, that is, of assuring sufficient cash to carry on the nation's business. The Bank enjoyed public privileges but was a private firm which learned that its survival depended on the survival of others.

The first and second Banks of the United States (1791–1811 and 1816–36) were also founded by government, under private ownership, as sources of finance and fiscal services. They generally performed well, and might be regarded as embryonic central banks, but their 20-year charters were not renewed. State banks disliked their competition and borrowers were dissatisfied with their caution. The second Bank of the United States also suffered from the general movement away from government monopolies that was supported by Jacksonian democracy. Most important, perhaps, their charters expired in peacetime, when the financial needs of government were minimal.

Whether they were necessary, as Alexander Hamilton claimed, or even helpful, which Thomas Jefferson doubted, has not been settled. At any rate their capacity for harm was limited by competition and the gold standard.

There was no formal central bank in the United States between the 1830s and 1913, but the Treasury, the money-market banks, and their clearing houses filled most of the void. The Independent Treasury Act of 1846 required the Treasury to avoid banks and to pay and receive in coin, although in liberal interpretations of the law the Treasury tended to smooth currency flows. The Independent Treasury System was as novel as the Fed, but its power over money was much less. Clearing houses also helped stabilize the financial system with credit to illiquid but solvent banks, and Congress' oversight of the Treasury made monetary policy more sensitive to the electorate than in other periods. The frequency of panics raised the call for a more elastic currency even though the main culprit was the system of thousands of small local banks that was forced by anti-branching laws.

The first purpose of the Federal Reserve Act as given in its Preamble was to preserve the payments system by furnishing an elastic currency. The price level was left to the gold standard. The Fed's monetary powers derived from its ability to print money, specifically to create bank reserves in the process of supplying credit. The Fed was made politically acceptable by its sponsorship by the progressive Wilson government, its benefits to the money-center banks, especially a guaranteed line of credit, and the ability of banks to stay outside the Federal Reserve System.

The immediate effects of the Fed included the most volatile period in the history of the American economy and the death of the gold standard. Its extensive powers were used by the executive and Congress to finance World War I, more than doubling money and prices in the process, without realizing that the gold standard required an eventual reversal of the dollar's depreciation, which brought the Great Depression of 1929–33. The Fed also failed in its primary responsibility of maintaining the payments system when money fell by one-third and parts of the economy were reduced to barter. We were given the reverse of an elastic currency.

The United States departed from the gold standard's restraints in 1933, and the Treasury assumed control of monetary policy. The Fed was eventually allowed to resume day-to-day monetary control, although the importance of the 1951 Treasury–Fed accord is exaggerated. Perennial congressional deficits continued to be financed by the Fed under political pressure that is sometimes rationalized by economists' theories of beneficial inflation.

The public's reaction to inflation at the end of the 1970s, with the return of congressional support and the relaxation of executive pressure on the Fed, allowed two decades of reduced inflation. This was disturbed in the new millennium by the housing bubble and the Fed's return to stop–go monetary policies that produced the financial crisis of 2008. The Fed's responses to the crisis contradicted all that might have been learned from the monetary policies and regulatory mistakes of the preceding decades, but were dictated by the narrow vision and political influences of its structure. Instead of focusing on the integrity of the payments system, the Fed supplied unprecedented largesse to politically favored firms and low interest rates for record federal deficits.

This policy expanded what had become standard. Bank bailouts were common in the 1970s and 1980s, although with regrets and promises, sometimes incorporated in law, that they would not be repeated. Nevertheless, the pressures of interests on an unaccountable body able to print money have been irresistible. Fed officials continue to cry illiquidity (the unavailability of cash to solvent firms) whenever an insolvent, allegedly too-large-to-fail, firm has difficulty borrowing.

"It certainly is a tragically comical situation that the financiers who have landed the British people in this gigantic muddle should decide who should bear the burden," Beatrice Webb wrote in her *Diary* on August 23, 1931, as the British government negotiated an American loan, conditional on budget cuts, to defend the pound. After the Great Recession, as much as after the Great Depression, the agencies most responsible for the problems are entrusted with their solutions.

The accumulation of the Fed's errors, from the Great Depression to the Great Recession, with no indication of learning, would seem to be sufficient reason for changes beyond good advice. It should call for a system that generates and uses information in more productive and less destabilizing ways. Beyond this, it should be realized that even the goals specified in the Federal Reserve Act have been abandoned. For support of the payments system the Fed has substituted the allocation of resources. It has chosen to use its power to print money to support selected failed firms and activities.

Genuine incentives require accountability, which means shared suffering. In our system of government this requires more direct involvement by Congress in monetary policy, as before 1913. That period was unsatisfactory because of the frequency of panics, but the wrong changes were made. The Federal Reserve Act produced a novel, incentive-free, jerry-rigged structure with unclear lines of authority more than usually, even for a government agency, susceptible to political manipulation. A fundamental argument of this book was stated by Milton Friedman. Anna Schwartz (2009; see Hess 2012), wrote

> It may be of some surprise that ... Friedman, a believer in limited government, proposed subordinating the Fed to the Treasury department not as an ideal but as an improvement of existing arrangements. He contended that it would result in a single locus of power over monetary and fiscal policies, and would establish accountability for mistakes in policy that otherwise leave each institution free to blame the other for policy errors.

Friedman (1962) wrote:

> [B]elief in the rule of law rather than of men ... is hard to reconcile ... with the approval of an independent central bank in any meaningful way. True, it is impossible to dispense fully with the rule of men. No law can be specified so precisely as to avoid problems of interpretation or to cover every explicit case. But the kind of limited discretion left by even the best of laws in the

hands of those administering them is a far cry indeed from the kind of far-reaching powers that the laws establishing central banks generally place in the hands of a small number of men.

When the world changes, and problems unimagined by the law-makers confront the monetary authority, as will happen from time to time, it is essential in a democracy that the public be consulted. Then maybe the legal commitment to a reserve ratio will not be enforced at the expense of massive deflation and unemployment, as in 1929–33, nor apparently casual spur-of-the-moment wealth transfers from the public to risk-taking financial institutions, as in 2008.

Of course intelligent decisions in emergencies, as at other times, require the public's representatives to do their job. A well-run monetary system requires that Congress take the Constitution's assignment "to regulate the currency" seriously, which means first of all a meaningful incentive structure. Only if policymakers suffer from their mistakes, which requires more responsibility to the electorate than applies to the current so-called expert administrators, can good policies be expected. That means significant change in the institutions of American monetary policy. This study examines the relations between past monetary institutions and their policies in the search of lessons for change. There is reason for optimism because of the performance of earlier institutions that were richer in incentives in the public interest, in profits and losses and electoral rewards and punishments.

The book is organized as follows. Chapters 2–5 review the structures and monetary policies of British and American central banks from the Bank of England in 1694 to the end of the last century. The Bank of England and the first and second Banks of the United States were private, profit-dependent institutions with special government privileges and responsibilities. There was no question of them being independent of either government or markets. Their *raisons d'être* were sources of government finance, which, however, were limited by a combination of the gold standard and market forces. The Independent Treasury System evolved into joint congressional–Treasury responsibility for monetary policy. All of these institutions were less than perfect in their contributions to monetary stability, but their damage was limited by dependence on – sensitivity to – the public and its representatives, whose attentions to monetary policy were close and continuous. The Federal Reserve, on the other hand, was founded with a much-vaunted but ill-defined independence, which turned into a cover for inflationary finance of government debt and subsidization of its political patrons.

Chapter 6 relates the continuation of these practices, enabled by the lack of learning, before, during, and since the Great Recession, after Chapter 7 reviews the Fed's dilution of bank regulation for the same reasons – its adverse incentives – as its monetary failures. The last chapter draws lessons from our history for the development of a better structure of American monetary policy that must be founded on genuine incentives. Two necessities are emphasized: those in charge – meaning Congress in any system – must be knowledgeable and responsible; and there must be no serious shocks of transition. The first means no "independent" buffers between decision-makers and the public. The second argues against a quick return to a gold standard, although that could be allowed to grow. Our monetary system can easily be improved – technically, that is. Politically is another matter.

Notes

1 White (1984), Klein (1974), Hayek (1990). Paul chaired a hearing of the subcommittee on Domestic Monetary Policy, *The Federal Reserve System: Mend It or End It* (May 8, 2012), but none of the proposals considered made it to the House floor.
2 The Banking Act of 1935 and Congress' impositions of targets in the 1970s are discussed in Chapters 4 and 5.

2 Early central banks

The early central banks of Great Britain and the United States were profit-seeking private institutions, albeit with government privileges, whose fortunes were tied to those of other banks and of the economy in general. They were much less powerful than modern (post-1914) central banks unconstrained by the gold standard or other market and even political forces, and had to respond to events subject to their limited powers in ways they hoped would be conducive to their own and the general prosperity. Their decision-making, in other words, could not be as remote from markets and the public as that of modern central banks.

The gold standard and the Bank of England, 1694–1914

Investors in the *Governor and Company of the Bank of England* were granted a corporate charter in exchange for a loan to a government at war. Its central banking – bankers' bank and lender of last resort – functions developed alongside its private goals as the banking system grew. It kept a good part of the country's gold reserve, came to be held responsible for the smooth functioning of the payments system, and developed many of the principles of central banking as they are understood today. Its survival, unlike that of its legally entrenched successors, depended on learning the right lessons. This did not include bailing out insolvent firms, which it could not afford and the Treasury was not inclined to help. Although not formally nationalized until 1945, the Bank effectively became a public institution during World War I.

The monetary standard

To understand central banking in the United States, we must begin with the Bank of England, the gold standard, and the rule of law. The Bank provided the pattern for the first American central banks and its policies evolved under the gold standard, the monetary system into which the Bank and the Fed were born. The functions of money – the means of payment and the standard of value – have been performed by commodities most of recorded history. Gold, silver, and copper coins had long been England's money when the Bank was founded. In the eighth century, King Offa of Mercia, in what is now the English midlands, adopted Charlemagne's currency in which 240 pennyweight silver coins weighed a pound (livre, £). Over the next 700 years, the silver and gold contents of the pound currency were reduced by half, largely during the wars of Edward III (1327–77) and the Great Debasement of Henry VIII (1509–47) and Edward VI (1547–53) (Feavearyear 1931: app. 1).

Stability was restored under Mary (1553–58) and Elizabeth I (1558–1603), and gold became the fixed standard from 1717 (officially from 1819) until 1931, except during the war suspensions of 1797–1819 and 1914–25.[1] This long period of stable money corresponded with a Parliament of land and commercial interests based on property rights and contracts, dependent on the stability of money's purchasing power. The use of money was encouraged by An Act for Encouraging of Coinage, which repealed mint charges (seignorage) in 1666. The price index in Table 2.1 shows the dramatically different inflation experiences of commodity (silver and gold) and fiat standards. The inflations of the sixteenth and seventeenth centuries, arising from the New World's precious metals and then the growth of credit, look small to us but were thought substantial at the time (Ramsey 1971; Feavearyear 1931: ch. 6).

Except for debasements, official monetary policies were limited. The price level – the inverse of the purchasing power of a unit (weight) of money (gold or silver) – was governed by money's cost of production. Governments encouraged money in their jurisdictions by subsidizing production of the precious metals and encouraging exports of other goods. This policy of mercantilism was condemned as wasteful by Adam Smith, but defended by J.M. Keynes as one of the few monetary policies available (Smith 1776: Bk. IV; Keynes 1936: ch. 23).

The first 100 years of the Bank

The seventeenth-century banking system, if so it can be called, was rudimentary, consisting primarily of goldsmiths issuing transferable claims/notes on deposits of the precious metals. Economic statistician and entrepreneur William Petty

Table 2.1 British cost of living

Decade beginning	Index[a]	%Δp.a.
800	50	
1500	100	0.14
1600	457	1.53
1700	568	0.21
1830	1,102	0.51
1930	1,067	−0.03
2000	34,806	5.10

Source: Brown and Hopkins (1946); Mitchell (2007).

Note
a Average of decade beginning the year shown.

was one of those who urged a large corporate bank that would "almost double the effect of our coined money" by notes and checks secured by fractional reserves.[2]

Such proposals were unsuccessful partly because of the king's distrust of money interests. On the other side, banks were subject to the depredations of needy monarchs. This had been demonstrated by Charles I's "stop" of the mint in 1640. It served as a safe depository but he directed it to refuse withdrawals. Referring to this incident, Samuel Pepys wrote in his *Diary* on August 17, 1666, that "The unsafe condition of a bank under a monarch, and the little safety to a Monarch to have any City or Corporacion alone ... to have so great a wealth or credit ... makes it hard to have a bank here." It had to wait for the coincidence of a government "in desperate want of money" and the improved security of property that came with limited government (Bagehot 1873: 90).

The alliance against Louis XIV's France depended on English finance, but years of profligacy and repudiations by the Stuart kings had weakened the government's credit. They raised taxes "as far as they dared," borrowed from "everyone who would lend," and resorted to tontines and lotteries. "Finally, and almost as a last resort," in 1694, they endowed a group of investors called the Governor and Company of the Bank of England with a corporate charter in exchange for a low-interest loan (Feavearyear 1931: 125).

The ability of the government to borrow even with this inducement was made possible by the constitutional changes arising from the Glorious Revolution of 1688. The replacement of James II by William and Mary was followed by a shift of financial control to Parliament, that is, from the king's purse to a national budget. The old system was deemed unsatisfactory for the liberties and safety of the king's subjects. To keep the king poor risked security and public services, but voting him sufficient resources had run into the profligacy of Charles II (1660–85) and the oppression of his financially more prudent younger brother, James II (1685–88). A similar conflict had contributed to the civil war of the 1640s between king and Parliament.

After 1688, the king was assured of revenue for his personal needs while the expenses of government, including war finance, were managed by Parliament. The other side of the contract was the protection of property. The commitment of property owners to supply revenues on a continuing basis relieved the king of the necessity of casting about for funds during crises. The Glorious Revolution has been seen as a triumph of property, with government converted from predator to protector. The cost of protection was the land tax (North and Weingast 1989).

To ensure that the Bank would not be a means of the government's circumvention of the legislature, the Tunnage Act, so-called because the loan was secured by "Rates and duties upon Tunnage of Ships and Vessels, and upon Beer, Ale and other Liquors," required its government loans to be approved by Parliament and prohibited its purchase of Crown lands, to which monarchs had resorted for funds. The Charter was more concerned with restraints on the new institution than with clearly setting out its powers (Anderson and Cottrell 1974:

40). Time has demonstrated the futility of attempts to prevent governments' abuse of banks.

The Bank's management was entrusted to a governor, a deputy governor, and 24 directors, most of whom "were substantial City merchants and members of the leading City companies" (Acres 1931: 21; Clapham 1944 i: 17–27). The typical new director, Walter Bagehot wrote, was "a well-conducted young man who has begun to attend to business, and who seems likely to be fairly sensible and fairly efficient twenty years later" – such as Samuel Thornton (1754–1838), the eldest brother of Henry (see below) and a partner in his father's merchant firm headquartered in Hull and engaged in the Baltic trade. He became a Bank director in 1780, was deputy-governor 1797–9, and governor 1799–1801, after which he reverted to his directorship until 1836, 56 years in all, except four years due to rotation. John Pearse (1759–1836), one of those interviewed by the Bullion Committee, was a clothier and supplier to the army, a Bank director from 1790, deputy-governor and governor 1808–12, and director again 1812–28. Thornton and Pearse were vocal supporters, in and out of Parliament, of Pitt's administration at a time the government relied on the Bank (Bagehot 1873: 200; Acres 1931: 621–622; *Dictionary of National Biography*).

An annual one-third turnover of directors was mandated, but the eight who stepped aside were normally taken from the youngsters who had not "passed the chair" (been governor), and most returned the next year. The deputy governor was selected from the directors primarily on the basis of seniority, and usually succeeded the governor. Both were elected for one year and nearly always served two consecutive terms.

Term limits and rotation were rejected by the directors in 1694, but imposed by Parliament in 1697 to discourage the perpetuation of cliques, which it evidently feared more than inexperience. It might have thought the latter would be offset by the senior advisory body, the Committee of the Treasury, composed of former governors.

Bagehot, on the other hand, thought the Bank's mistakes were due more to a lack of knowledge that might be corrected by training and experience. Running the bank was a part-time (for the directors) or temporary (for the deputy-governor and governor) job held by merchants. These shortcomings might be alleviated, Bagehot thought, by a permanent chief executive, or at least a permanent deputy who was a professional banker. Immediate changes after Bagehot defied his recommendations. Director rotation was eliminated, and not until after World War I did long-serving governors and deputy governors, with permanent senior staffs, become standard (Bagehot 1873: ch. 8; Sayers 1976: ch. 22; Wood 2005: 280–282). It is doubtful that Bagehot would have been pleased with the results. The powers and changed incentives that came with becoming a government department trumped any advances in knowledge or expertise.

The Bank's original charter was valid to August 1, 1705, with expiration requiring 12 months' notice and repayment of the loan. The loan was never repaid. Britain was at war, or preparing for war, almost continuously to 1815, and the Bank's charter was renewed, with loans to the government, seven times between 1697 and 1800, the last for 33 years. Its privileges were also expanded by the government's promises that it would charter no other banking corporation (1697) and the prohibition of note issues by associations of more than six persons (1708) (McCulloch 1858; Richards 1934).

L.S. Pressnell's *Country Banking in the Industrial Revolution* (1956) suggested that the occasion of these market restrictions "may well have been a rash of financial failures in the two or three years preceding.... It long outlasted any reasonableness, however; by the time it was abolished by the legislation of 1826 and 1833 it had done much harm by depriving the country of a banking system" needed during "a period of rapid economic growth" (5–6).

The limits on bank size retarded specialization, and

> credit remained largely a subsidiary or auxiliary occupation. Even when large numbers of country banks began to appear in the second half of the eighteenth century, many self-styled bankers were engaged extensively in non-banking enterprises. Equally, quasi-banking functions were performed by many who never called themselves bankers.

The Bank of England, which could have been called the Bank of London, failed to use its ability to establish branches and thereby promote its notes outside the metropolis (Pressnell 1956: 6, 12; Ashton 1948: 100–101). This experience fits into the history of financial legislation dominated by hasty official reactions to crises – such as the Bubble Act of 1720, the New Deal securities and banking acts of the Great Depression, and the Wall Street Reform and Consumer Protection (Dodd–Frank) Act of 2010 – which themselves were results of government interferences.[3]

The Bank's legal privileges were increasingly contested as the economy developed. Its charges for managing the government's finances were thought excessive, bankers objected to its monopoly of corporate banking, and its conduct during crises left much to be desired (Clapham 1944: ch. 7). Yet during the debate over the charter renewal of 1781, the prime minister, Lord North, defended the Bank as,

> from long habit and the usage of many years,... a part of the constitution; all the money business of the Exchequer being done at the Bank, and as experience had proved, with much greater advantage to the public than when it had formerly been done at the Exchequer.
>
> (*Parliamentary History* June 13, 1781)

The Bank of England was not created as a central bank. The term would have been meaningless before the development of a banking system. However, normally capable and conservative management earned it reputations for safety and efficiency, and the Bristol banker Vincent Stuckey was able to say: "My customers give their money to me, and look to me for it; I do the same to the Bank" (House of Commons 1832: Q1145). By the end of the eighteenth century, the Bank had become a central bank, although it was slow to appreciate its position.

After the Bank rationed credit to protect its reserve during the credit crunches of 1793 and 1797, leading to the ruin of many overextended banks, Sir Francis Baring, founder of the merchant bank, observed that it was the country's "*dernier resort*" (1797: 20).

Suspension and resumption, 1797–1821

Britain's long war with France beginning in 1793 meant government pressures for Bank finance, sometimes in violation of its charter. The practice was assisted by the secrecy of the Bank's accounts, although the deterioration of its reserves was known or at least suspected. An invasion scare in 1797 caused the Bank, with the government's approval, to suspend the redemption of its liabilities for gold. Resumption was discussed when the Bank's reserve recovered later in the year, but Baring and the majority were opposed as long as there was less than full confidence in its performance.

> My chief reason is that credit ought never to be subject to convulsions; a change even from good to better ought not to be made until there is almost a certainty of ... preserving it in that position; for a retrograde motion in public credit is productive of consequences which are incalculable. With this principle in view, I am averse to the Bank re-assuming their payments generally during the war whilst there is a possibility of their being obliged to suspend them again.
>
> (Baring 1797: 69)

The inconvertibility of Bank liabilities was accompanied by a rise in prices, which critics blamed on the Bank's easy credit. Figure 2.1 compares the rise and fall in prices during this episode with other British and American suspensions and resumptions. The experience inspired some of the most fruitful intellectual exchanges in the history of monetary theory. Banker Henry Thornton's *Enquiry into the Nature and Effects of the Paper Credit of Great Britain* (1802) examined the causes of the inflation enabled by the suspension, and David Ricardo's first appearance in print, in the *Morning Chronicle* of August 29, 1809, addressed the 20-percent depreciation of the currency from its official, pre-suspension, gold value (*Works* iii: 17). Edwin Cannan called it *The Paper Pound* when he compared the finances of the Napoleonic Wars and World War I. Ricardo calculated the pound's depreciation from its market rates of exchange with Hamburg, which had not suspended. Although price indexes were in the future, he understood that a currency's domestic and foreign depreciations moved in tandem, and were caused by increases in money following from the Bank's easy credit.

Thornton and Ricardo were not alone in tracing inflation to the Bank of England's actions under government pressure. Merchant banker and speculator Walter Boyd, who had lost heavily in government loans, wrote an open letter to the prime minister in 1801:

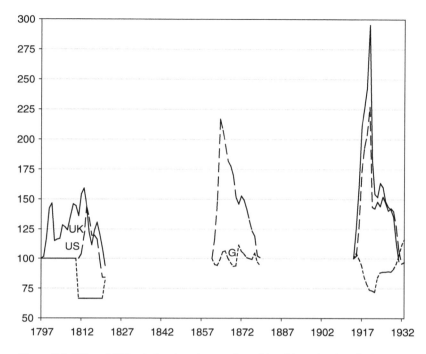

Figure 2.1 US and UK wholesale prices and world gold production during suspensions and resumptions, all indexed to 100 (source: Jastram, 1977).

Indeed it is not to be supposed that a corporation whose profits chiefly arise from the circulation of its Notes, and which is exclusively directed by persons participating in the profits, has been, or could possibly be, proof against the temptation which license [i.e., suspension] they have enjoyed since February 1797 has afforded.

(Boyd 1801; Viner 1937: 125–126, 133)

Those seeking to monitor the Bank were hampered by its secrecy. Its published accounts were incomplete and irregular, requiring "an Oedipus to decipher them," actuary William Morgan complained. His estimates of the Bank's loans to the government indicated that "its principal purpose had been to enable a minister to lavish the public revenue much faster than it could ever be collected; and to furnish him with the means of engaging in the most extravagant and ruinous expense before his prodigality could be submitted to the deliberation of Parliament."[4] The eventual publication of the Bank's accounts validated its critics (Cannan 1925: xliii–xlvi).

In 1810, Bank officials denied to a parliamentary inquiry – the Bullion Committee – that suspension had changed its lending. The Bank could not be a cause of inflation, they said, because they had continued to lend on real bills, i.e., secured by goods and good names. The fallacies of this argument had been explained in Thornton's *Enquiry*. Money could not be tied to, or limited by, goods without fixing their prices, which varied with money (1802: 244). Claims that the Federal Reserve has been guided by the real-bills doctrine are examined in Chapter 4.

A logical defense of its practice would have been that the Bank was merely doing its duty, what central banks have always done – finance governments, especially in wartime. More surprising than the increase in its lending, "with such motives to excess," economic historian Thomas Tooke observed, was that "there was so trifling an increase" (1838 i: 283). This might be explained either by the fact that the Bank directors knew more about the effects of their lending than they let on, and wished to limit inflation, or they were unsure when the war would end and convertibility resume. John Clapham pointed out in his history of the Bank (1944 ii: 25) that it had demonstrated in peacetime that it knew how to protect its reserve by rationing discounts, but "had no intention of stinting the Chancellor" in wartime.

The Bullion Committee was led by distinguished economists. In addition to Thornton, Francis Horner had been an economic correspondent for the *Edinburgh Review* (partially reprinted in Horner, *Economic Writings* [1802–6]) and William Huskisson was the government's foremost economic spokesman, who wrote the often reprinted *Question Concerning the Depreciation of Our Currency*. They applied their monetary theory – also Ricardo's – to the inflation. Their *Report* supported the view that it was due to the Bank of England's "liberality of ... loans to private individuals [and] to the service of Government for the support of the Army," and recommended its correction by an early return to convertibility (Cannan 1925: 67).

The *Report* was overwhelmingly rejected by Parliament. Rejection was necessary to "winning the war," declared a former secretary of war, by allowing the continuation of "that system of currency" which had so far enabled "us to confine [Napoleon's] violence to the continent." The prime minister said its adoption would amount to a declaration that the country should not "continue those foreign exertions which they had hitherto considered indispensable to the security of the country. [They] would disgrace themselves forever by becoming the voluntary instruments of their country's ruin" (*Parliamentary Debates*, May 7–8, 1811; Fetter 1965: 53–64). Napoleon was at his peak and the British army under Wellington in Spain (the Peninsular War) was the sole regular force on the Continent opposing him.

The Bank's defenders called attention to the lack of correlation between the value and quantity of money. Government spokesman Nicholas Vansittart pointed out that the rise in gold's price between 1810 and 1813 had not been accompanied by an increase in the Bank's circulation, and the price fell between August 1813 and October 1814 while the circulation rose (the French armies suffered a series of defeats beginning in June 1813). Furthermore, Cannan (1925: xxvii) added, the "violent fluctuations ... in the year of Waterloo could certainly not be attributed to changes in the note circulation." Wesley Mitchell (1903:

188) described a similar sensitivity of the value of government paper ("green-backs") to military fortunes during another suspension that accompanied the American Civil War:

> fluctuations in the premium on gold were so much more rapid and violent than the changes in the volume of the circulating medium that not even academic economists would regard the quantity theory as an adequate explanation of all the phenomena.

The apparent exceptions to the quantity theory of money are explained by realizing that the value of money, as of any asset, is affected by its expectation. For example, Napoleon's 1813 losses improved the chances of early resumption, which was understood by the "Continental Merchant" who testified to the Bullion Committee that "ultimate results are anticipated by the speculation of individuals" (Cannan 1925: xliii).

Resumption received more serious consideration after the war. The authorities "were, generally speaking, in favour of a return to cash payments on the old basis – some day" (Feavearyear 1931: 204). Progress was uneven as the Bank shrank from forcing the necessary deflation (Fetter 1965: 79). By an Act of 1803, the convertibility of Bank notes was scheduled to resume six months after the war's end. In 1814, this was moved back to July 5, 1815, then to 1816, then 1818 (House of Commons 1819: 3).

While those wishing to return to the old standard hesitated, others proposed fundamental changes of three kinds: devaluation under the old standard; fiat money; and a more efficient gold standard with or without devaluation (Viner 1937: ch. 4). The Bullion Committee, this time speaking for the majority, called devaluation a "breach of public faith and dereliction of a primary duty of Government" (Cannan 1925: 68). Looking back from 1821, after the depression, Ricardo said privately that if inflation has gone far enough and long enough, the balance of justice, considering the parties entering into contracts at high prices, perhaps in the belief that the old par would not be resumed, would be on the side of devaluation (*Works* ix: 72).

Gold is not the best way to stable prices, anyway, said the proponents of paper money. Birmingham banker and reformer Thomas Attwood believed that

> depreciation of the currency is beneficial to a country in every way that it can be considered. It is only injurious to … holders of monied obligations, who ought to be bought up, or compromised with, by the public, rather than suffer the national welfare to be arrested by a crippling of the circulation.
>
> (1817: 163)

A decade after resumption he wrote: "More injustice had been done to, and more misery had been endured by, the productive classes" during each of the contractions of 1819–22 and 1825–8 "than would have been done to or endured by the fundowners if the Government had abolished the whole national debt at once" (Attwood 1828: 94).

Ricardo agreed that gold was only a step in money's development:

> A well regulated paper currency is so great an improvement in commerce that I should greatly regret if prejudice should induce us to return to a system of less utility. The introduction of the precious metals for the purposes of money may with truth be considered as one of the most important steps towards the improvement of commerce and the arts of civilised life; but it is no less true that with the advancement of knowledge and science we discover that it would be another improvement to banish them again from the employment to which, during a less-enlightened period, they had been so advantageously applied.
>
> (Ricardo 1816: 65)

Keynes expressed a similar sentiment a century later, when during another resumption he urged gold's dismissal as "a barbarous relic" (1923: 172). Ricardo was more cautious than Keynes, fearing that money and inflation might be unbounded without the discipline of convertibility. He conceded that "gold and silver are ... subject to greater variations than it is desirable a standard should be subject to. They are, however, the best with which we are acquainted" (1816: 62). So tradition – a monetary system that had at least been consistent with growth – and distrust of unrestrained governments and banks meant a return to the old system after Waterloo, as after the American Civil War and World War I (Figure 2.1).

Eventually, in the Resumption Act of May 1819, Parliament forced the Bank's hand by setting a path to par: from 81 shillings (a pound consisted of 20 shillings) per ounce of gold, payable for not less than 60 ounces on February 1, 1820, to 79.5 on October 1, and 77.875 (par) on May 1, 1821. Full convertibility would resume on May 1, 1823, when the Bank was to redeem its notes on demand in the coin of the realm. The Bank complained, supported by merchants and bankers alarmed by the planned deflation. The governor warned the House of Commons Resumption Committee against a fixed timetable: "It is very difficult to say when the Bank could with propriety resume its cash payments, it must always be judged of by experience" (Bank of England 1819).

The Bank's hesitation to force resumption after Waterloo differed from its position after World War I, when it would lead the push for a return to gold at the prewar rate, and impose as tight a monetary policy as the government would stand. "I would rather see Finance less proud and Industry more content," the beleaguered Chancellor of the Exchequer Winston Churchill told an advisor in 1925. The long-serving Governor Montagu Norman (1920–44), on the other hand, thought that complaints of unemployment "were greatly exaggerated and ... much more psychological than real," especially when compared with the "advantages of the external position [the exchange rate in particular]" that are "in the long-run greatly to the interest of finance and commerce." He deplored policy by "counting noses." The policy that Norman defended before the Macmillan Committee in 1931 had earlier occasioned Keynes' criticism that "In the long run we are all dead" (House of Commons 1931: Q3328–33; Chernow 1990: 475; Keynes 1923: 65).

On the earlier occasion, the government was backed by the prestigious Ricardo, who persuaded the House of Commons that although the "question [of resumption] was one of immense importance in principle,... the manner of bringing it about was trivial, and not deserving half an hour's consideration.... The difficulty was only that of raising the currency 3 per cent in value." "Professed alarms" at the move were due, he said, "to the indiscrete language of the Bank" (*Parliamentary Debates*, May 24, 1819; Ricardo, *Works* v: 9–17; Hilton 1977: 47).

In the event, resumption involved considerable deflation, unemployment, and unrest (as in the 1920s). The price of gold dropped precipitously, along with the Bank's notes and deposits, and gold flowed into the Bank. Early in 1821, with a record reserve, the Bank was able to resume. Full convertibility had been achieved in less than two years instead of four, and the value of the currency had risen to par in less time than that. Money and prices fell by a third between 1819 and 1822, and unemployment soared. On August 16, 1819, 15 people were killed and hundreds injured in the so-called Peterloo Massacre in St. Peter's Field, Manchester, when a public protest was disbursed by a cavalry charge reminiscent of the Battle of Waterloo.

Ricardo was blamed for what was popularly believed to have been consequences of his resumption plan, and it was rumored that he recanted on his deathbed (Sayers 1953). He rejected these charges in the House of Commons. All would have gone smoothly if the Bank had reduced its circulation "cautiously." "[T]hey had not a sufficient degree of talent for the management of so vast a machine as that with which they were intrusted," Ricardo told the House on June 12, 1822.

He might have been correct about the Bank's incompetence, but his discrete plan was deficient in its neglect of arbitrage. As the "continental merchant" would have known, the knowledge that prices are to change on a certain date advances their realization. Controlled change is immensely difficult, and cautions us about central bank assurances of "smooth" exits.

Boom and bust, 1822–5

The economy turned up, spurred by investment in the newly independent countries of South America, and the Bank joined the crowd in its first post-resumption credit expansion (Page 1919: 69–72). Its gold reserve, which had reached £13.8 million in February 1824, fell to £3.6 million in August 1825. This was practically the country's entire reserve, for "there was but little gold in the provinces.... Add to this the fact that many of the country banks as well as their customers were heavily involved in the purchase of shares in bubble flotations, and it becomes clear," Feavearyear (1931: 219) wrote, "that the situation was at least as full of danger as that of 1793 or 1797." The prime minister condemned the "general spirit of speculation which was going beyond all bounds, and was likely to bring the greatest mischief on numerous individuals." He urged them to reflect what would be the situation of the public if (not to speak of actual war) … any embarrassing event were to occur. Their lordships would recollect that when commercial embarrassment occurred during the late war, bankers and merchants came forward and applied to parliament for aid, which they obtained by issues of Exchequer bills [government securities used as currency]. He wished it, however, to be clearly understood that those persons who now engaged in Joint-Stock Companies, or other enterprises, entered on those speculations at their peril and risk. He thought it was his duty to declare that he never would advise the introduction of any bill for their relief; on the contrary, if such a measure were proposed, he would oppose it, and he hoped that parliament would resist any measure of that kind.

(Lord Liverpool *Parliamentary Debates*: March 25, 1825)

This was the reverse of the Greenspan Put, but the warning was ineffective. Although it recognized an impending crisis in September, the Bank did not raise its rate until December. However, its restriction of credit in November had significant effects. News "that the Bank was returning a considerable portion of the bills sent for discount by even the largest houses" provoked runs on the country banks. "On Sunday, the 27th, partners of the London houses were fetched from church to supply gold to their desperate provincial customers.... In three weeks sixty-one country banks and six important London houses ceased payment" (Feavearyear 1931: 220–221). The Bank's own position was desperate. On December 15, it turned to the government for help either in Exchequer bills or an authorization to stop payment.

The Bank and the financial markets had been warned by the prime minister in March, and on November 29, by *The Times*:

As for relief from the King's Government, we can tell the speculating people and their great foster-mother in Threadneedle Street, that they will meet with none – no, not a particle – of the species of relief which they look for. The King's ministers know very well the causes of the evil, and the extent of it, and its natural and appropriate remedy, and we may venture to forewarn the men of paper that no such help as they are seeking will be contributed by the State.

As promised, the government refused the Bank, advising it to be ready to "pay out to the last penny." A Bank director (Jeremiah Harman) recollected the incident for the Committee of 1832:

Q: Did any communication take place between the Bank and the Government respecting an Order in Council to restrain payment in gold at that period? *A:* Yes, it was suggested by the Bank.

Q: What answer did His Majesty's Government give to that? *A:* They resisted it from first to last.

Q: It was stated by the late Mr. Huskisson … that he as a member of the Administration at that time suggested to the Bank that if their gold was exhausted, they should place a paper against their door stating that they had not gold to pay with, but might expect to have gold to recommence payment in a short period; do you recollect such a suggestion? *A:* There was such a suggestion.

Q: What would, in your opinion, have been the consequences of that paper placed against the door of the Bank, without preparation to support commercial and financial credit? *A:* I hardly know how to contemplate it.

(House of Commons 1832: Q2217–32)

Thrown on its own resources, Harman told the Committee, the Bank lent assistance by

> means, and in modes that we never had adopted before; we took in stock as security, we purchased exchequer bills, we made advances on exchequer bills, we not only discounted outright, but we made advances on deposit bills of exchange to an immense amount; in short by every possible means consistent with the safety of the Bank; and we were not upon some occasions over nice.

The Bank worked overtime to produce new notes and sent agents into the country to lend them, raising its discounts in a few weeks from £5 million to £15 million. The panic stopped, the drain of gold from the Bank slowed, and by spring had turned around.

The joint-stock banks

There was no official inquiry into the crisis because its causes were agreed (Feavearyear 1931: 223). The Bank had been slow to respond, but the main fault was the banking system. The hundreds of small issuers had been too susceptible to the mood of speculation and too weak to survive the collapse. In 1826, legislation opened the door to joint-stock banks of issue as long as they did not have offices within 65 miles of London. The Bank did not get the charter extension it wanted – that would wait until the current charter had almost lapsed – but it was encouraged to open provincial branches.

In 1822, the government opened negotiations with the Bank to allow corporate competitors in exchange for an extension of its charter and legal tender status for its notes. Although the directors agreed after some hesitation, the government did not proceed, "mainly because of the strong opposition in Parliament to the renewal of the Bank's charter." Legal sanction was given to joint-stock banks without concessions to the Bank, and some soon rivaled it in size (Acres 1931 ii: 41; Thomas 1934: 49).

Another reason for the deterioration of the Bank's political position was Thomas Joplin's (1822) observation that in contesting the establishment of joint-stock banks the Bank of England claimed a monopoly it did not possess. The Act of 1708 prohibited companies of more than six partners from issuing "bills or notes payable on demand," but said nothing about banks of deposit (Feavearyear 1931: 223; Thomas 1934: 72–73).

Finding a monetary rule

The end of war threatened the Bank's privileges. With a balanced budget and good credit, the government was no longer dependent on the Bank, and the public did not hold it in high regard. It had reinforced, instead of restrained, booms and contractions. In its hoarding of reserves during the crisis of 1825, until compelled by the government to act, "the Bank behaved as unwisely as it was possible to behave" (Bagehot 1873: 190).

In 1833, almost at the last minute, the Bank's charter was renewed until 1844, on condition of improved transparency and the Bank's assurance that it had found a rule for stabilizing credit (Wood 2005: 69–70). Fluctuations continued, however, and the debate over the Bank's monopoly of the currency grew warmer. Opponents argued that a competitive note issue possessed mutual restraint, whereas a monopoly issuer was dangerous because it could do what it liked. During an 1841 parliamentary inquiry, Robert Peel suggested to J.W. Gilbart, general manager of the London and Westminster Bank, that a single issuer guided by "constant reference to the state of the exchanges" provided "greater security ... than many issuers, none of whom, according to your own statement, pay the slightest regard to the state of the exchanges."

Gilbart disagreed. "What then supplies the check?" Multiple issuers discipline one another by weekly or more frequent settlements while a single issuer may go unchecked for long periods (Gregory 1929 i: 81). The Bank's critics were supported by the example of the banking system to the North. Scottish bank failures had been one-sixth the failure rate in England (White 1984: table 2.3).

The two systems differed primarily in the less official control in the North. Scotland had no central bank or monetary policy beyond those implied by the gold standard. Entry was free and the right of note issue universal. No bank enjoyed the legal advantages of the Bank of England in the South, and there were no limits on the size, structure, or location of banking businesses. Instead of hundreds of English banks limited to small communities, the Scottish system had a few large banks with branches over broad regions or throughout the country. The lower failure rate of Scottish banks suggests that their expansions were not ill-advised, that there were significant economies of scale in banking. Those economies were not unlimited, however, because unlike the Bank of England, no Scottish bank approached a dominant position. The largest note issue in 1845, by the British Linen Co., was 14 percent of the total Scottish issue and one-sixth greater than its closest competitor.

The Scottish system was stable. On the one hand, regular note exchanges meant that no bank could for long increase its notes beyond the willingness of the public to hold them. Membership in the Note Exchange System meant the bank had passed the scrutiny of members, and improved the demand for its notes. Trust was finite, however, and notes were redeemed on a regular basis. No such system developed in England because the dominant bank, the Bank of England, refused to accept the notes of other banks, and the other banks were too small, numerous, and geographically diverse to accept each others' notes (White 1984: ch. 2). The contrast between the stability of the Scottish system and the fluctuations experienced in England was explained by the founder and first editor of *The Economist*:

> we have only to look to Scotland to see what has been the effect of a long career of perfect freedom and competition upon the character and credit of the banking establishments of that country.
>
> (Wilson 1859: 30)

Nevertheless, not for the last time, a government chose monopoly and its apparent ease of regulation over what it saw as the chaos of competition. "A single issuer might be easy to deal with," a Bank director wrote to the Chancellor of the Exchequer, "but how are we to deal with five hundred?" (Feavearyear 1931: 245) A Chancellor of the Exchequer told the House of Commons (White 1984: 67):

> if you can contrive an adequate check upon the conduct of a single bank, it will be more advantageous that such a single bank should manage the circulation of the country, than that it should be left to the competition of different and rival institutions.

The Bank Charter Act of 1844 gave the Bank a monopoly of the currency and bound it to a rule that constrained the circulation. Its note issue was tied one-for-one with its gold, causing the money supply, defined as the public's gold coin and Bank notes, to vary as in a pure gold standard. The Bank would otherwise behave as an ordinary bank without public responsibilities, accepting deposits and making loans for profit. This rule became a model in the nineteenth century, especially for colonial currency boards, although not for the United States, where notes were issued by many banks on a variety of collateral (Giannini 2011: 72).

Problems with the new system soon appeared after the Bank joined the railway boom of the mid 1840s. When the bust came in 1847, and the Bank, as formerly, raised its interest rate to protect its deleted reserve, there was a panic demand for its notes. Poor harvests had caused gold to leave the country, and the Bank was unable to supply the demand for cash. Eventually, a letter from the government authorized it to break the law (promising an indemnifying act if needed) by issuing notes not backed by gold. News that notes were available ended the panic and they were not needed (Feavearyear 1931: 261–263). The Act was also suspended during the crises of 1857 and 1866.

Tying Bank notes to gold may have promoted the value of the currency in the long run, but it had caused currency shortages in the short run. There are more important things than convertibility, John Stuart Mill wrote for the 1857 edition of *Principles of Political Economy* (657): "I think myself justified in affirming that the mitigation of commercial revulsions [rather than the avowed objective of convertibility of the issue] is the real, and only serious, purpose of the Act of 1844. No Government would hesitate a moment" to stop convertibility in order to assure the continuity of the Bank of England's support of the financial system "if suspension of the Act of 1844 proved insufficient." No government until after World War I, that is, when convertibility and reserve ratios began to take precedence over stability in Great Britain and the United States. This throws light on Barrett Whale's (1944) centenary appraisal of the 1844 rule: It "worked satisfactorily because it did not work in the way designed," meaning that the Bank and government learned to relax it to relieve currency crises.

Attention to the short run did not interfere with long-run goals because the Bank's commitment to convertibility in the long run was understood. The principal central banks, including the Bank of England, did not play by "the rules of the gold standard game" before 1914. That is, they did not permit gold losses to starve liquidity, which did not cause flights from their currencies because of the credibilities of their commitments. This explains why the demand for the Bank's notes was fairly strong after the 1797 suspension, which was expected, correctly as it turned out, to be temporary (Bloomfield 1959; Bordo and White 1991).

Lender of last resort

Writing as editor of *The Economist* after the panic of 1866, Bagehot (1866) criticized the Bank's uncertain responses to crisis demands for cash. It aggravated panics by withholding credit to safeguard its own reserve before eventually reversing course, usually under government pressure. Announcements that cash was available had ended the panics. The lesson Bagehot drew from these experiences was that as keeper "of the banking reserve of the country" – no other bank kept cash "above what is wanted for its daily business" – the Bank should remove uncertainty by committing to its availability. "[I]n time of panic it must advance freely and vigorously to the public out of the reserve," subject to two qualifications: "That these loans should only be made at a very high rate of interest ... as a heavy fine on unreasonable timidity," and be limited to "good banking securities" (1873: 27, 187–188).

This was more than being lender of last resort. That had been understood at least since Baring in 1797. Henry Thornton described the Bank's role in maintaining payments in 1802 (113–116):

> in order to effect the vast and accustomed payments daily made in London, payments which are most of them promised beforehand, a circulating sum in bank notes nearly equal to whatever may have been its customary amount is necessary.... They serve ... both to sustain and regulate the whole paper credit of the country [and] any very great and sudden diminution of Bank of England notes would be attended with the most serious effects...

The idea which some persons have entertained of its being at all times a paramount duty of the Bank of England to diminish its notes in some sort of regular proportion to that diminution which it experiences in gold is, then, an idea which is merely theoretic.

This warning was ignored by the Act of 1844 (as written, though not as eventually applied) and other unqualified rules:

I would not like to see what would happen if under such a provision [Professor Friedman's proposal of a legal limit on the rate at which a monopolistic issuer of money was allowed to increase the quantity in circulation] it ever became known that the amount of cash in circulation was approaching the upper limit and that therefore a need for increased liquidity could not be met.

(Hayek 1990: 81)

Bagehot called the "system of entrusting all our reserve to a single" bank "anomalous" and "dangerous." A more natural system, which would exist "if government had let banking alone," would see the reserve distributed among banks. He did not propose an end to the single-reserve, however, because

an immense system of credit, founded on the Bank of England as its pivot and its basis, now exists [and] and rests on an instinctive confidence generated by use and years.... You must take what you ... find..., and work with it.... A theorist may easily map out a scheme, [but] generations must elapse before at all the same trust would be placed

as in the present system. We must be content with "a clear understanding between the Bank and the public" in the present system (1873: 65–70). The founders of the Fed reversed these recommendations in just about every way possible by shifting from reserves (and currency issues) in many banks to their concentration in a novel government agency whose goals were unclear to the public, the government, and itself.

Bagehot's advice was never publicly accepted by the Bank. In his 1867 text on *The Principles of Banking*, Bank director and former governor Thomson Hankey called it

the most mischievous doctrine ever broached in the monetary or banking world in this country; viz., that it is the proper function of the Bank of England to keep money available at all times to supply the demands of bankers who have rendered their own assets unavailable.

(25)

Hankey was not the only one who understood the future implications of current actions, rediscovered by economists a century later as the "inconsistency of optimal plans" (Kydland and Prescott 1977). Provision to suspend the Act had been suggested during the 1844 debate. Banker and member of Parliament Henry Bosanquet feared that "there will be moments when sudden voids will be created in the circulation ... which if not in some way provided for, may be the cause at times of a total suspension of business throughout the country." He presented a request by 30 London bankers that

> during the first five years of the new system, whenever the rate of interest at the Bank of England shall have risen to eight percent, it shall be lawful for the Issue Department to make advances at that rate of interest on the deposit of Exchequer Bills; the loans to be repaid and the bills sold whenever the rate of interest shall have fallen below eight percent.

Prime Minister Robert Peel rejected this and similar proposals (Parker 1899: 140–141):

> My confidence is unshaken that we are taking all the precautions which legislation can prudently take against the recurrence of a monetary crisis. It *may* occur in spite of our precautions, and if it does, and *if it be necessary* to assume a grave responsibility for the purpose of meeting it, I dare say men will be found willing to assume such a responsibility.
>   I would rather trust to this than impair the efficiency and probable success of those measures by which one hopes to control evil tendencies in their beginning, and to diminish the risk that extraordinary measures may be necessary.

Samuel Jones Loyd, the main author of the 1844 Act, had advised against a contingency plan for the rule's suspension. Unless it is "strictly adhered to," he wrote,

> it becomes a nullity.... Any special provision ... for suspending its application at critical periods must prove mischievous by weakening the conviction that the measure will be adhered to, and thus checking the growth of the feelings and habits which are intimately connected with its success.
>
> (1844: 439)

A formal request for emergency suspensions by a committee of the House of Lords after the 1847 suspension was dismissed on the same grounds by the Bank and the government (House of Lords 1848; Wood 2005: 101–105). Nor was the Bank eager to adopt Bagehot's advice to increase its emergency lending ability by holding a larger reserve. When in 1891 the Chancellor of the Exchequer pressed the Bank to keep more reserves, the governor replied that "the larger the Bank's own reserves, the less the bankers like to keep *their* reserves unused" (Clapham 1944 ii: 344).

Reserves grew with gold production beginning in the late 1890s, but "Anxiety about the national gold reserve was in no way abated" in the new century.

> For the four peace years, 1903–6, the [reserve] averaged only £33,000,000, at a time when countries with fewer liabilities and a less delicately balanced financial system carried far greater quantities, as indeed they long had; at a time too when almost the whole civilized world was on the gold basis, so that, through the international banks, claims might be made on London from any, or all, of half a dozen or more financial centres. A centre so new, remote and incalculable as Tokio now kept very large balances in London.
>
> (Clapham 1944 ii: 379)

The "ultimate answer to Bagehot's problem," another Bank historian wrote, was "a powerful Bank Rate weapon with a 'thin film of gold' " – powerful because of its credibility, that is, the public's confidence in convertibility in the long-run, giving the Bank leeway to address problems in the short run (Sayers 1951). The larger reserves of the US Treasury and then the Federal Reserve, as well as the Bank of England in the 1920s, reflected the opposite of confidence.

Broad economic changes may have contributed more than its central bank to British economic stability, particularly free trade that reduced the balance-of-trade effects of poor harvests, the end of the system of small, fragile banks by the consolidation of the banking system, and the end of wartime fiscal deficits. However, Frank Fetter believed that "the Bank, although officially silent, was taking to heart the advice of Bagehot, and the ever increasing importance of deposit banking made it less likely that the special note restriction [of the 1844 Bank Act] would present any problem" (Wood 2005: 107–110; Fetter 1965: 282).

The Bank's policy might be described as *constructive ambiguity*, that is, attempting to overcome the inconsistency of optimal plans by holding out the possibility that assistance might not be forthcoming, as suggested by Peel and more recent writers (Goodfriend and Lacker 1999).

The Bank's circumspect behavior in the Baring crisis of 1890 (or *non-crisis* as Ralph Hawtrey called it) was no exception. Barings merchant bank had underwritten a large quantity of Argentine securities when the market for them "suddenly dried up" because of investor doubts of that country's capacity to pay. The bank "found that they had undertaken more than they could perform," and after failing to obtain relief from other houses in the City, indicated to the Bank of England "that they were about to suspend payment.... Had Barings been merely an issuing house, concerned with the flotation of loans, the repercussions would have been limited." But they had a large accepting business, in which they accepted the bills of traders, enabling them to finance their purchases. Barings' failure would have disrupted the bill market (Hawtrey 1938: 105–107).

An investigation satisfied Bank governor William Lidderdale "that there was a reasonable expectation that [Barings], if given time to realize its assets without forced sales, would prove to be solvent." He asked Chancellor G.J. Goschen for a government guarantee.

That Goschen could not give. He promised in case of need to authorize the suspension of the fiduciary limit, but the prospect of asking the House of Commons to ... meet the losses of a private firm he would not face.

"Lidderdale was driven back on the resources of the City, [and] formed a syndicate of the principal banks and financial houses to share the burden of the guarantee." The Bank also increased its reserves by borrowing from foreign central banks, and raised the Bank rate. There was no panic or losses among the guarantors. The Bank's behavior during the Baring crisis is comparable with that of 1866, when it refused Overend Gurney's request for assistance because that firm's solvency was doubtful (Hawtrey 1938: 107–109; Feavearyear 1931: 285–286).

The bailout question is still with us, but often in twisted form. Moral hazard was understood by Liverpool, Loyd, Peel, and Hankey in the nineteenth century, but refused by Paulson and Bernanke in the twenty-first century, although possibly less on intellectual grounds than because of the Fed's incentives and unlimited powers that are the subject of this book. The distinction between illiquidity and insolvency was also understood before the Fed – and exercised by Hamilton (see below) and Lidderdale – although they have come to be confused as part of the official rationale for bailouts of the politically favored.

The first Bank of the United States, 1791–1811

Patterned after the Bank of England, the purposes of the Bank of the United States were credit and banking services for the government as well as the encouragement of finance, industry, the use of money, and a reliable payments system in a developing economy. Its performance received high marks but whether it filled a void is questionable. Congress' refusal to renew its charter after 20 years reflected a skeptical public and the growth of a private banking system that resented the competition of a government-favored bank.

The Bank was as much a tribute to Hamilton's powers of persuasion as to its prospects. Congress was jealous of its powers during its first 100 years. Few independent agencies were created and all were closely monitored. The Bank's caution was also encouraged by the hostile President Jefferson (1801–9) and sympathetic but attentive Treasury secretaries, including Hamilton (1789–95) and Albert Gallatin (1803–14).

Arguments over the Bank

The first Secretary of the Treasury, Alexander Hamilton, wanted an active central government, including a national bank, whose advantages would include the promotion of industry by enabling gold and silver to "become the basis of a paper circulation, ... greater facility to the Government in obtaining pecuniary aids, especially in sudden emergencies, ... and the facilitating of the payment of taxes." He wanted the bank privately owned to prevent the abuse of credit that might follow from government control. Congress pledged to establish no other bank during the life of the Bank of the United States. It was clearly patterned after the Bank of England (Hamilton 1790; Krooss 1969: 230–261).

John Marshall wrote that Hamilton's economic plans, especially for a national bank,

> made a deep impression on many members of the legislature; and contributed, not inconsiderably, to the complete organization of those distinct and visible parties, which, in their long and dubious conflict for power, have since shaken the United States to their centre.
>
> (1807 iv: 244; Beard 1915: 109–113)

Opposition to a national bank came from two overlapping groups: rural elements, especially in the South, who disliked banks in general because they were associated with trade and manufactures and threatened a way of life, and constitutionalists, also primarily Southern, who saw national banks as part of the central government's assault on states' rights and personal liberties.

James Madison opposed the Bank in the House of Representatives on the grounds that it would expose the public "to all the evils of a run on the bank," and also because its charter

> did not make so good a bargain for the public as was due to its interests. The charter to the Bank of England had been granted only for eleven years, and was paid for by a loan to the Government on terms better than could be elsewhere got. Every renewal of the charter had, in like manner, been purchased; in some instances at a very high price.
>
> (House of Representatives February 2, 1791: Krooss 1969: 262–263)

Madison also doubted the bank's legality. The US Constitution was a limiting document in which "particular powers" had been granted to the federal government, "leaving the general mass in other hands." It did not mention banks, nor did Congress' financial powers under the Constitution make a national bank "necessary and proper," he argued. Nevertheless, the bill passed. The House vote was 39 to 19, with 34 of 35 representatives from above the Mason–Dixon Line in favor compared with five of 23 Southerners (Table 2.2; Senate votes were not yet reported).

The President consulted Attorney-General Edmund Randolph and Secretary of State Thomas Jefferson, both Virginians and both of the opinion the bank was unconstitutional. Jefferson argued that

> existing banks will, without a doubt, enter into arrangements for lending their agency, and the more favorable, as there will be a competition among them for it; whereas the bill delivers us up bound to the national bank, who are free to refuse all arrangement, but on their own terms.

Table 2.2 Congressional votes for and against the national banks

	All	NE[1]	SE[1]	Other slave[2]	NWT[3]	W[4]	
1791[5]	39–19	33–1	6–18				House
1811	64–65	44–25	18–34	2–5	0–1		House
	17–17[6]	9–7	7–5	1–3	0–2		Senate
1816	80–71	35–43	34–21	3–2	8–5		House
	22–12	8–7	7–4	6–0	1–1		Senate
1832	107–82	65–28	20–34	12–15	10–5		House
	28–20	14–4	4–8	5–7	5–1		Senate
1841	127–98	61–43	28–31	18–16	20–8		House
	26–23	11–7	7–3	4–9	4–4		Senate
1913	287–85	59–35	39–1	74–11	75–9	40–29	House
	54–34	6–10	10–2	14–2	4–6	20–14	Senate
1927[7]	298–22 Yeas and nays not taken, January 24.						House
	Accepted with other amendments without separate vote.						Senate

Sources: Annals of Congress, Congressional Globe, Congressional Record.

Notes
1 Original 13 states and ME and VT, above and below the Mason–Dixon Line.
2 KY, TN, LA, MO, MS, AL, AK, FL, TX, WV.
3 Northwest Territory: OH, IN, IL, MI, WI.
4 Others (all west of the Mississippi River).
5 Senate proceedings not published.
6 Vice-president broke tie vote against the Bank.
7 FR charter for 20 years (FR Act, Sec. 4), extended indefinitely in 1927 by McFadden Banking Act, Sec. 18. (cont. next page)
Dates of votes. 1791: H 2/8 S 2/14. 1811: H 1/24 S 2/20; 1816 H 3/14 S 4/13; 1832: H 7/3 S 6/11. 1841: H 8/6 S 7/28. 1913: H 9/18 S 12/19.

The Treasury already employed the services of banks, "which alone suffices to prevent the existence of that *necessity* alleged to justify it." Jefferson accepted the Constitution as a balance between the necessary powers of government and the equally necessary protection against their excesses. "Can it be thought," he asked, "that the constitution intended that, for a shade or two of *convenience*, more or less, Congress should be authorized to break down the most ancient and fundamental laws of the several States, such as those against mortmain, … the laws of monopoly, etc." (Krooss 1969: 274; Meacham 2012: 250).

Nevertheless, the Secretary of the Treasury (from New York) got his way. It was sufficient, Hamilton argued, that the bank had a "natural relation" to such powers expressly granted by the Constitution as collecting taxes, regulating trade, and providing for the common defense. Setting aside the veto message that he had asked Madison to write, Washington approved the bill (Krooss 1969: 91–92, 295; Clarke and Hall 1832: ch. 2).

The structure of the Bank

The Act provided for 25 directors, all elected by the stockholders, and with rotation similar to the Bank of England's; not more than three-fourths were eligible for reelection each year. The Bank was not to lend more than $100,000 to the United States, nor more than $50,000 to any State, nor lend to a foreign prince or State unless authorized by act of Congress. A report of the Bank's condition was to be furnished on demand to the Secretary of the Treasury, but not more often than once a week, and that officer had the right to inspect the books, except private accounts.

Hamilton followed English rather than continental precedent in placing the Bank under private management with powers similar to the Bank of England's. He wanted the Bank as much to support the payments system as for the public credit. As early as 1779, still in the army, he had written to government financier Robert Morris favoring a bank of issue based on landed security (which he later dropped). In 1780, when the Revolutionary finances were at low ebb and the currency of the country was depreciating, Hamilton wrote: "The only plan that can preserve the currency is one that will make it the immediate interest of the moneyed men to cooperate with the Government in its support" (Holdsworth 1910: 9, 21). The first advantage that Hamilton claimed for the Bank in his *Report* (1790) was "the augmentation of the active or productive capital of a country," not meaning "the creation of additional capital," Holdsworth (1910: 14) wrote, "but more effective utilization of capital by which scattered and otherwise idle amounts are concentrated and made to serve the uses of business." Without notes coin must be remitted from place to place with "trouble, delay, expense, and risk." Bank notes and checks, however, enable large sums to be transferred safely by post or other convenient conveyance.

The Bank began operations with a professional staff, including its president, Thomas Willing, who moved from the presidency of the Bank of North America. The presidency had first been offered to the younger (30 years old instead of 60) Oliver Wolcott, Jr., Hamilton's assistant as comptroller of the Treasury, who declined it, "preferring the public service, and believing that such a station would be deemed unsuitable for a young man without property." The care taken with the first US Bank's management may help explain its less troubled record than the second US Bank's.

The record

The Bank's services were in demand from the beginning, and it had branches in Boston, New York, Baltimore, and Charleston within a few months of opening the main office in Philadelphia in December 1791 (Hammond 1957: 126; Wettereau 1942). It was a useful source of credit and an efficient fiscal agent for the government (Nettels 1962: 118–120, 300–301). It also financed state banks by holding their notes, occasionally acting like a modern central bank "by pressing the [state] banks for redemption of their notes and checks and thereby restraining their extension of credit" (Hammond 1957: 199).

Hamilton was surprised by and initially disapproved of the Bank's branches. Writing to the cashier of the Bank of New York, of which he had been a founder and retained an interest, Hamilton said: "Strange as it may appear to you, it is not more strange than true that the whole affair of branches was begun, continued, and ended, not only without my participation, but against my judgment." "Apparently he had hoped to make the Bank of New York the exclusive fiscal agent of the Government in that city" (Holdsworth 1910: 39). Nevertheless, Hamilton acceded to the dominance of the US Bank's branch in that regard, and before long acknowledged that branch banks could be safely managed.

The Treasury and eventually the Bank worked for financial stability, beginning with support of the market for the securities issued in connection with the federal government's assumption of State and Continental Congress debts. These securities were objects of speculation, financed by bank lending, with sharp price rises broken by declines and crises in 1791 and 1792. The crises were met by a sinking fund that was separate from the Treasury, although it had been proposed and was directed by Hamilton, and was entitled to buy government debt "while it continues below its true value." The fund alleviated the crises by buying securities with funds borrowed from existing banks against the security of future government revenues, "to keep the Stock from falling too low in case the embarrassments of the dealers should lead to sacrifices" (Sylla *et al.* 2009).

This assistance anticipated Bagehot's advice to the Bank of England, and was unlike the taxpayer-funded bailouts 200 years later. Hamilton did not intend that specific firms be bailed out, but rather addressed the market. To maintain payments and credit under stress, he recommended to the Bank of New York's cashier in March 1792 to lend on the security of stock (bonds) up to 10 shillings on the pound (50 cents on the dollar), with depositors entitled to "their Stock at any time, paying in specie the sums credited ... with a right to the Bank after six months to sell the bonds and pay them the overplus." In addition,

> Let the Bank engage at the end of six months to pay the amount of these Credits in Gold or Silver for ... a compensation in interest at the rate of 7 per centum per annum. I take it for granted in the prevailing disposition of your City, transfers of these Credits under the promise of the Bank to pay in Specie ["in kind," i.e., gold or silver coins] at the end of six months would operate as Cash in mutual payments between Individuals – while the Bank would be safe from the danger of a run & undoubtedly safe eventually. To render the operation more perfectly safe to the Bank, I will engage at the expiration of six months to take off your hands at the rate specified to the amount of 500,000 Dollars – in case the parties should not redeem & and there should be no adequate demand. Which however is not supposeable. I have thought a good deal of this plan & I really believe it is a good one & will tend to obviate the necessity of ruinous sacrifice of the Public Stock by parties indebted.

Hamilton's plan, which like Bagehot's used high interest and good collateral, was adopted and banks began to lend "pretty liberally." This included the "new U.S. central bank," which after "having initially contributed to the bubble, began to contribute to the alleviation of the bubble's collapse" (Sylla *et al.* 2009)).

"The panic of 1792 barely fazed the U.S. economy, [and] the financial system remained remarkably stable," Sylla *et al.* (2009) pointed out. The country "did not suffer a bank failure until 1809, nor did it undergo another systemic peacetime financial crisis until 1819," following the Treasury's efforts to resume convertibility after the inflation and suspension caused by its wartime money creation.

"From the outset the U.S. Bank entered into friendly cooperation with the State banks," John Holdsworth (1910: 40–41) wrote in his history for the National Monetary Commission. It conferred with other banks on a regular basis "for the purpose of communicating freely upon the business of both, as well as to prevent improper interference with each other, [including the adoption of] uniform rules regarding discounts and other matters of routine." Although it did not have the resources for bailouts, the US Bank understood that its fortunes were linked to those of other banks, unlike the next century's Federal Reserve, whose existence was guaranteed.

This was demonstrated again in 1796, when European stringency spread to the United States. The Bank of New York, which had lent liberally to the government and was in debt to the Bank of the United States, was pressed for cash. Hamilton, now a private citizen, advised Secretary Wolcott to come to the aid of the New York bank. "It would be wise," he wrote, "if possible, to anticipate a particular payment" (Holdsworth 1910: 42). He wanted to avoid the failure of a key bank as well as a useful lender to the Treasury.

"These institutions have all been mismanaged," Wolcott replied. "I look upon them with terror ... and I fear they will prove the ruin of the government. Immense operations depend on the trifling capital fluctuating between the coffers of the different banks." However, he did "not shed his central bank responsibility," Hammond wrote, nor "did his successor, Albert Gallatin, whom the Bank of Pennsylvania asked for relief in 1802 because 'they fall regularly $100,000 per week in debt to the Bank of the United States' in consequence of the Treasury's deposits in the latter" (Hammond 1957: 201; Gallatin 1879 i: June 18, 1802). The Treasury was thus called on to offset the shift in funds arising from the government's bank.

The government took advantage of the Bank's credit, bordering on abuse, in its early years. Spending exceeded revenue partly because of Congress' unwillingness to tax. Borrowing was necessary even for routine expenses, and rose with exigencies brought by Indian wars and threatened hostilities with England and France.

> [I]t appears that the Bank of the United States accommodated the Government whenever called upon and continued the loans to suit its convenience.... This indebtedness ... finally amounted to $6,200,000 at the close of ... 1795, ... nearly two-thirds of the entire capital of the bank. The bank naturally became restive and impatient; the loan of so large a proportion of its funds crippled its services to commerce and manufactures and made it difficult to "facilitate the financial operations of the Government by temporary loans."

It declined to continue the monopolization of its credit, and the government had to turn elsewhere, such as bond issues and even selling its Bank stock, which was "rendered necessary by the stupid failure of Congress to provide adequate revenues by resort to taxation, or its desire to embarrass the administration" (Holdsworth 1910: 44, 45, 49).

The use of Barings investment bank to finance the Louisiana Purchase of 1803, and current budget surpluses under Presidents Jefferson and Madison, combined with their continued disapproval of the Bank, meant little government resort to Bank credit during the second half of its life. Nevertheless, it had a friend in Treasury Secretary Gallatin (1809), who reported to Congress in support of the Bank's renewal that its

> affairs ... have been wisely and skillfully managed.... The numerous banks now established, under the authority of the several States, might, it is true, afford considerable assistance to Government in its fiscal operations. There is none, however, which could effect the transmission of public moneys with the same facility, and to the same extent, as the Bank of the United States is enabled to do, through its several branches.

Furthermore, it will, being dependent for its existence on the National Legislature "feel stronger inducements, both from interest and from a sense of duty, to afford to the Union every assistance within its power."

Nevertheless, the Bank's charter was not renewed even though hostilities with Britain suggested the need for more government finance in the near future (Walters 1957: 238). The line-ups for and against it had changed since its beginning. Some of the business interests that had found the Bank useful at the beginning now resented its competition and restraint. The Bank was a creditor of the state banks, and when it presented their notes for payment in coin it acted "as a brake on credit expansion [and] antagonized sanguine entrepreneurs who sought loans for their speculative ventures," in the opinion of sound-money historians (Nettels 1962: 301). Some agrarians had been reconciled to banking but resented federal interference. Kentucky Congressman Richard Johnson complained that the Bank "would contract very much the circulation of the state bank notes, and would in many other respects come in collision with state rights" (Clarke and Hall 1832: 232). On the other hand, Georgia Senator (and future Secretary of the Treasury, 1816–25) William Crawford thought the check exerted by one state bank against another's "excessive discounts and emissions" was not sufficient – they could both double their discounts without anyone being the wiser before the damage was done (Clarke and Hall 1832: 393; Krooss 1969: 302–315). Renewal failed by one vote in the House and in the Senate by the tie-breaking vote of the vice-president.

The second Bank of the United States, 1816–36

> I am humble Abe Lincoln.... My politics are short and sweet, like the old woman's dance. I am in favor of a national bank. I am in favor of the internal improvement system, and a high protective tariff.
> (Announcement of candidacy for the state legislature, March 1, 1832)

The second Bank's experience was mixed. It was proposed to help finance the War of 1812, but when too late for that, to assist resumption after the wartime suspension and inflation. It made matters worse, at first, and did not settle into a productive regimen until 1823. The Bank enjoyed half a dozen good years, and regrets over its passing stem from what might have been, although it is not clear how even a well-behaving US bank could have brought solvency and stability to the American system of hundreds then thousands of small banks in a volatile developing economy.

The argument continued

The War of 1812 was financed by debt, bought mostly with state bank notes. Federal revenues, mainly customs duties, fell, and the administration would not raise internal taxes. The national debt, which the Jeffersonians had reduced from $83 million to $45 million, reached its pre-Civil War peak of $127 million in 1815 (Dewey 1928: ch. 6). Between 1811 and 1816, the number of banks in the United States rose from 88 to 246, and their circulation from $23 million to $68 million, while their metallic reserve ratio fell from 42 percent to 28 percent (Dewey 1928: ch. 6; Gallatin 1830: 286–296).

The British raids on Washington and Baltimore in August 1814 induced runs on the specie of the weakened banks, which suspended payment in most of the country. Hammond (1957: 227) attributed banking conditions to the removal of the "regulator of bank credit," that is, the Bank of the United States, even though the Bank of England failed to prevent large increases in banks and the price level after the 1797 suspension in that country (Pressnell 1956: 11). In the United States, as in England, the unrestrained banks continued to operate, and even proliferate, and their notes circulated at discounts (Gallatin 1830: 283–284; Nettels 1962: 332–334).

These conditions continued with the return of peace, and a year later President Madison called it "essential … that the benefits of an uniform national currency should be restored to the community. The absence of the precious metals will, it is believed, be a temporary evil; but until they can again be rendered the general medium of exchange, it devolves on the wisdom of Congress to provide a substitute" (Clarke and Hall 1832: 609). If the state banks could not or would not provide a sound currency, a national bank deserved consideration. Debates over the monetary standard and the roles of central and local banks paralleled those across the Atlantic.

Notwithstanding his earlier opposition, as President, Madison was persuaded of the "expediency and almost necessity" of a national bank, and later defended its constitutionality on the basis of "deliberate and reiterated precedents." It had "throughout a period of twenty years with annual legislative recognitions" received "the entire acquiescence of all the local authorities as well as the nation at large" (Clarke and Hall 1832: 778–780).

Congress as well as the President wanted a bank, but had not agreed about its powers. In October 1814, Treasury Secretary A.J. Dallas proposed a national bank empowered to "loan to the United States $30,000,000 at an interest of six percent at such periods and in such sums as shall be convenient" (Krooss 1969: 396–400). This was rejected by Congress as not sufficiently limiting, and saw its own version vetoed by the President. "The objection of Congress to the original plan," Bray Hammond wrote, "had been that the Bank had too much of the Government in it. President Madison's objection was that in the Bank proposed by Congress the Government was left out" (Hammond 1957: 232).

In his veto message of January 15, 1815, Madison complained that the capital of Congress' bank was insufficient "to produce, in favor of the public credit, any considerable or lasting elevation of the market price" (Krooss 1969: 401–403). He also protested that "under the fetters imposed by the bill," particularly the "obligation to pay its notes in specie," the Bank "cannot be relied on during the war to provide a circulating medium nor to furnish loans on anticipations of the public revenue."

The peace treaty was signed in Ghent, Belgium, on December 24, 1814, but news did not reach America until February, when Congress suspended its consideration of a bank. Some still wanted a national bank for its contribution to government finance, but Pennsylvania Congressman William Findley probably spoke for the majority under the new conditions when he said "the erection of a Bank was not so desirable on account of the Government as for the general convenience of the country," meaning the resumption of convertibility (Clarke and Hall 1832: 475). Although hardly necessary to the purpose (except possibly as a political buffer; see below), the second Bank of the United States was adopted primarily as a means of forcing resumption on the state banks. Their profits were reputed to be large and their specie reserves adequate, but they were not inclined to resume payment and their state legislatures would not force them. Senator Daniel Webster contended that a national bank was unnecessary, that the situation simply required a compulsory redemption, and he obtained a resolution that the government would only accept payment in coin or redeemable bank notes, and would keep no deposits in "any bank which shall not pay its notes, when demanded, in the lawful money of the United States" (Hammond 1957: 232; US Congress April 30, 1816; Catterall 1902: 23).

Shepherding the Bank bill through the House, John Calhoun argued that the constitution required Congress to establish an agency for the regulation of the currency. "No one ... could doubt that" the power "to coin money [and] regulate the value thereof" meant "the money of the United States was intended to be placed entirely under the control of Congress." Not foreseen by the founders, money now consisted principally of paper currency which had been allowed to develop in a way that defied the Constitution. The states were prohibited from issuing money, but "In point of fact," added Speaker Henry Clay, "the regulation of the general currency is in the hands of the state Governments, or, which is the same thing, of the banks created by them." Calhoun argued that "By a sort of under-current" in the form of a "revolution in the currency ..., the power of Congress to regulate the money of the country had caved in, and upon its ruins had sprung up those institutions which now exercised the right of making money for and in the United States." It was "incumbent upon Congress to recover ... control," Clay said, and although direct regulation of the state banks was impracticable, the situation might be remedied, and a sound currency regained, by the restraining influence of a national bank. Votes for the Bank were 80–71 in the House and 22–12 in the Senate (US Congress February 26 and March 9, 1816; Clarke and Hall 1832: 630–634, 669–672, 681–682, 706). The geographical distribution of votes tended to be the reverse of 1791, with most of the opposition coming from the Northeast, where state banking was strongest.

A central bank?

The second Bank was more directly involved in politics from its beginning than its predecessor. Five of the 25 directors were government appointments. "It was the general expectation that the bank would be Republican, and ... accordingly President Madison named all the government directors from his own party." Those elected by the stockholders were split evenly between Republicans and Federalists, and the administration was successful in getting a party man, William Jones, recently secretary of the Navy and acting Secretary of the Treasury (1813–14), elected to the presidency.

The Bank got off to a rocky start. The resumption of 1817 was "neither universal nor genuine," and the Bank joined a credit boom as enthusiastically as the state banks it was supposed to restrain (Smith 1953: 104). It pursued an aggressive branching policy – 18 by the end of 1817, 25 by 1830 – and the head office failed to control them. The notes of any branch were redeemable at all, and several vied to see who would be largest. However, prices had increased, gold had left the country, and the Treasury's resumption was beginning to bite. The Treasury's postwar surplus meant the redemption of its currency, which served as bank reserves and had been the basis of much of the wartime credit expansion.

There was a scramble for liquidity, and the failures almost included the Bank of the United States. The "grim efforts" to collect its debts aroused a popular hatred of the Bank that "was never extinguished," Hammond (1957: 259) wrote. Andrew Jackson's bank-hating adviser, William Gouge (1833 ii: 110), wrote of the episode that "The Bank was saved and the people were ruined."

The second Bank had found its feet by 1823, when another government director, Nicholas Biddle, became president and managed a conservative but profitable enterprise for several years. In particular

> We have had enough, and more than enough of banking in the interior. We have been crippled and almost destroyed by it. It is time to concentrate our business – to bank where there is some use and some profit in it, [in] the large commercial cities.

The New York branch "was made the center of extensive operations, being instructed to secure all the good paper it possibly could," while its funds were managed "to protect it against inimical action by state banks, ... which opposed particularly the plan of weekly liquidation of balances" (Catterall 1902: 95–96). These actions benefited Bank profits more than its popularity.

In 1832, Jackson's opponents in Congress made the Bank a campaign issue by passing a bill to renew its charter four years before its expiration. It was during this period that Lincoln delivered the speech above. His principles corresponded with the Whig Party's anti-Jackson platform (Holt 1999: 17–27). The bill to renew the charter passed the House 107–85 and the Senate 28–20, but Old Hickory obliged them with a veto, and following the vindication of his reelection, withdrew government deposits from the Bank (Catterall 1902: 235–239, 293).

Appraisal of the Bank's performance under normal conditions might be limited to the period from 1823, after it had recovered from the vicissitudes of resumption, to 1832, although Hammond preferred 1823–30, before the Bank War, as the period of the Bank as a possible central bank (1957: 300). The new president, Biddle, was more committed to – at least more outspoken about – an active stabilizing role for the Bank than his predecessors, and was more strongly positioned to act on that belief.

From an old and influential American family, the classically trained Biddle served in foreign legations for the United States and later edited a magazine. He also took an interest in banking as a Pennsylvania legislator, and lobbied for the Bank's charter. President Monroe appointed him a government director in the Bank in 1819 (Govan 1959: 1–27, 59). "I think," Biddle wrote,

> that experience has demonstrated the vital importance of such an institution to the fiscal concerns of this country and that the Government, which is so jealous of the exclusive privilege of stamping its eagles on a few dollars, should be much more tenacious of its rights over the more universal currency, and never again abandon its finances to the mercy of four or five hundred banks, independent, irresponsible, and precarious.
>
> (Hammond 1957: 301)

The larger view seemed to be borne out by the Bank's maintenance of its credit in the face of the gold drain of 1831. "Not only did it expand loans, notes, and deposits while reserves fell," Richard Timberlake wrote, "but it practiced forbearance in presenting notes of other banks for redemption.... The bank clearly acted like a central bank in 1831" (1993: 38–39).

In the course of explaining the Bank's policies to a congressional committee in 1831, Biddle denied that it had ever "oppressed" the state banks. But he continued with what Hammond called "perhaps the most profound descent into indiscretion he ever made." "There are very few banks," Biddle told a congressional inquiry, "which might not have been destroyed by an exertion of the power of the Bank. None have ever been injured. Many have been saved. And more have been, and are, constantly relieved when it is found that they are solvent but are suffering under temporary difficulty" (US Congress 1832).

"This is enough! Proof enough!" cried Missouri Senator Thomas "Old Bullion" Benton, "for all who are unwilling to see a moneyed oligarchy established in this land and the entire Union subjected to its sovereign will. The power to destroy all other banks is admitted and declared; the inclination to do so is known to all rational beings to reside with the power! Policy may restrain the destroying faculties for the present; but they exist; and will come forth when interest prompts and policy permits" (Krooss 1969: 716–717).

The Bank's supporters, on the other hand, pointed to its contributions to sound money, and some historians have argued that it was the first conscious central bank (Catterall 1902: 453–477; Hammond 1957: 286–325). However, the record does not support the central banking hypothesis in the sense of a stabilizing *policy* (Meerman 1963; Temin 1969). As a counter-example to the 1831 episode, in the summer of 1825 the Bank (like the Bank of England a few months later) sought safety for itself by contracting credit while it was losing specie (Timberlake 1993: 38; Smith 1953: 140). On the other hand, Benton's hypothesis of a predatory Bank finds no support in the data. The Bank moved in line with the state banks, expanding in good times (reducing its reserve ratio) and contracting in hard times, although more conservatively than banks generally. It did not finance expansions at the expense of the state banks by returning their notes more quickly than usual (Highfield *et al.* 1991).

The Bank's behavior was more consistent with a third hypothesis, between the benevolent central bank and the predatory monopolist claimed by its supporters and detractors, namely that it was a large firm interested in survival as well as profits. Large firms typically behave conservatively.[5] There is no evidence that the Bank's decisions affected the stock prices of state banks or influenced macroeconomic variables such as the price level or exchange rates. Its record was that of a passive, accidental central bank guided by microeconomic rules of behavior rather than macroeconomic goals. Animosity toward the Bank is explained not so much by what the Bank did as by what it restrained others from doing. By acting as a check on general financial expansion, it provided an important central banking function, and to this extent justified the praise of its sound-money advocates.

The Bank War

The Bank's enemies feared its potential for damage, and in the charter-renewal debate of 1832, Benton proposed a revision along lines that in the next decade were rejected in England. If the government had need of its own privileged banking facilities (which Benton doubted), he "was convinced of the advantage of several banks over one." History had demonstrated "the advantage of checking powers in banking Governments as well as political Governments" (Krooss 1969: 806–812).

Benton's amendment was defeated, but more important, the reasons for the Bank's establishment had vanished, namely for special facilities to the government as its depository and collector and disburser of public moneys, and the regulation of the currency. However, with the public debt nearly paid off, there would soon be "no moneys to transfer." And the currency did not now need the Bank. It had been advocated as an aid to resumption following the depreciation made necessary by the war. Clay, who had opposed the renewal of the first Bank in 1811, was later persuaded that "War could not be carried on without the aid of banks" (*Congressional Globe* July 15, 1841). But "Times have changed," Benton said, "The war made the bank; peace will unmake it" (Krooss 1969: 736).

The government had less need of a special banker, and desires for currency regulation had to contend with popular dislike of the Bank. Its unimpressive performance as regulator and its competition for the business of the state banks were two more strikes against it. Furthermore, the era of democracy, opposition to privilege, and free incorporation had come. The criticisms of Jackson as economically unsophisticated are wide of the mark. Whether one is for or against the Bank, positions for which there are valid economic arguments, it must be admitted that Jackson's understanding of markets showed an intellectual grasp of economic principles greater than his authoritarian critics (Hummel 1978). The call for authority to supplant what is called the chaos of the market has always been popular. It justified the Bank of England's monopoly of the issue, and many critics of Jackson's opposition to the Bank of the United States, some who admired him in other respects, also favored government controls during the Progressive and New Deal periods of the next century: William Graham Sumner (1883: 397) wrote that in waging war on the Bank "Jackson's administration unjustly, passionately, ignorantly, and without regard to truth, assailed a great and valuable financial institution"; Catterall (1902: 476) wrote in his history of the Bank that "few greater enormities are chargeable to politicians than the destruction of the Bank of the United States"; Arthur Schlesinger, Jr. (1948: 218) charged that "In destroying the Bank, Jackson had removed a valuable brake on credit expansion"; and Richard Hofstadter (1948: 63) complained that Jackson "had left the nation committed to a currency and credit system even more inadequate than the one he had inherited." None of these critics even tried to explain how a competitive banking system must be inferior. In all their writings they never approached the understanding of market processes shown by Jackson and Jefferson.

The same arguments applied to the Bank of England, but in that case Parliament compromised by reining in the Bank's discretionary powers and relaxing restrictions on other banks. In neither nation was the choice of institutions inevitable. Congress voted for national banks in 1832 and 1841, and only the death of President William Henry Harrison prevented approval in the latter case, when the democrat John Tyler vetoed a Bank bill on Harrison's death. Nevertheless, it is difficult to refrain from the observation that much of the political strength of the Bank of England, even after the government's credit no longer depended on it, derived from its usefulness to the financial community. However much other bankers complained of its privileges, and of its occasional failures to justify them, they benefited from its willingness to bear the costs of the country's reserve. What the British thought prudent, Americans considered restrictive, and the fates of the latter's national banks suggest that the policies of the Bank of England would have been more resented in the credit-hungry New World than in the Old.

Notes

1 The link with gold was not formally cut until after World War I, the exchange rate being maintained by controls and the high cost of shipping gold (Feavearyear 1931: 299–314).
2 Petty (1682), in answer to Question 26: "What remedy is there if we have too little money?" Other proposals of the time are in Horsefield (1960).
3 The Bubble Act, which made corporate charters more difficult to obtain, came before and may have contributed to the collapse (Harris 1994); the Securities Acts of the 1930s aimed to reduce dishonesty by more transparency even though the losses of the Great Depression had been caused by the economic decline (Wood 2014: ch. 2); the Banking Act of 1935 centralized Federal Reserve control even though its failures had been mainly at the center; and Dodd–Frank increased the interferences with free markets that had contributed to the Great Recession.
4 Morgan (1797), discussed by Sraffa in Ricardo's *Works* (iv), and Klein (1997: ch. 4).
5 Scherer and Ross (1990: ch. 10). However, whereas dominant firms typically lose market share over time, the Bank's grew slightly between 1823 and 1832 (Fenstermaker 1965: 66–67).

3   Central banking in the United States, 1847–1913

Be it enacted..., Sec. 6. That the treasurer of the United States ... and all public officers of whatsoever character are hereby required to keep safely, without loaning, using, depositing in banks, or exchanging for other funds than as allowed by this act, all the public money collected by them ... till the same is ordered by the proper department or officer of the Government to be transferred or paid out....

Sec. 18. That on January 1, 1847, and thereafter, all duties, taxes, sales of public lands, debts, and sums of money accruing or becoming due to the United States ... shall be paid in gold and silver coin only, or in treasury notes...

That on April 1, 1847, and thereafter, every officer or agent engaged in making disbursements on account of the United States ... shall make all payments in gold and silver coin, or in treasury notes if the creditor agree to receive said notes.
Independent Treasury Act, August 6, 1846

The United States possessed all the elements of a productive and stable banking system, including the services normally associated with a central bank, in the decades before the creation of the Federal Reserve. The gold standard, with its competitively determined money and limits on government intervention, provided relatively stable prices over long periods, and the private sector was developing institutions and practices conducive to financial stability in the face of official restrictions and a growing economy hungry for credit. These institutions included Congress and the US Treasury, which were constrained but sensitive to the money markets and the electorate. This partnership, in combination with the growing bank clearing houses, was on the way to supporting the payments system as efficiently as a formal central bank.

The Independent Treasury, 1847–1913

It is not easy to defend the Independent Treasury Act, which if administered literally would have exposed the monetary base to shocks from the federal budget. Made responsible for the currency, however, Congress and the Treasury took their job seriously and responded to shocks with more flexibility and more sensitivity to the electorate than American monetary authorities before or since.

Origins and the development of monetary policy

The withdrawal of government deposits from the US Bank required new depositories.[1] The 1836 Act to Regulate the Deposits of Public Money required their distribution among the states "in proportion to their respective representation in the Senate and House of Representatives" (Krooss 1969: 972). However, political controversy connected with government deposits in "pet banks" and losses due to bank failures arising from the panic of 1837 and the ensuing depression induced Congress to require that the government's money be kept in its own vaults at the Treasury or subtreasuries under the care of public officials. Webster was appalled:

> The use of money is in the exchange. It is designed to circulate, not to be hoarded. All the Government should have to do with it is to receive it today, that it may pay it away tomorrow. It should not receive it before it needs it, and it should part with it as soon as it owes it. To keep it – that is, to detain it, to hold it back from general use, to hoard it, is a conception belonging to barbarous times and barbarous Governments.
>
> (US Senate, March 12, 1838)

Lincoln evaluated the alternatives during a debate in Illinois. "[T]he subtreasury will reduce the quantity of money in circulation," especially since "the revenue is to be collected in specie," which is the basis of the paper circulation. On the other hand, a bank will pay for the opportunity to keep the public money, which "will be more secure in a national bank than in the hands of individuals, as proposed in the subtreasury" – not because bank officers are necessarily more honest than other men but because, unlike subtreasurers, the interest of the bank is on the side of its duty.

> Take instances: A subtreasurer has in his hands one hundred thousand dollars of public money; his duty says, "You ought to pay this money over," but his interest says, "You ought to run away with this sum, and be a nabob the balance of your life." And who knows anything of human nature doubts that in many instances, interest will prevail over duty, and that the subtreasurer will prefer opulent knavery in a foreign land to honest poverty at home. But how different is it with a bank. Besides the government money deposited with it, it is doing business upon a large capital of its own. If it proves faithful to the government it continues its business; if unfaithful, it forfeits its charter, breaks up its business, and thereby loses more than all it can make by seizing upon the government funds in its possession. Its interest, therefore, is on the side of its duty.
>
> (Springfield, IL, December 20, 1839 (Lincoln 1907 i))

This was less an argument for a national bank than against the subtreasury system because any privately owned bank satisfies Lincoln's criteria. Although his fame does not rest on his economic sophistication, Lincoln recognized the role of incentives as well as the value of bank charters that is an important part of modern bank analysis (Furlong and Kwan 2006).

An independent treasury bill was adopted in 1840, but repealed the next year by the Whig Congress in preparation for a third United States Bank that was vetoed by former vice-president John Tyler after the death of President William Henry Harrison. The reestablishment of the Independent Treasury System in 1847 linked the monetary base to the federal budget. Seasonal movements in net Treasury receipts reduced bank reserves at inconvenient times, and the fiscal surpluses of the nineteenth century, seen in Figure 5.2, threatened longer-term deflationary effects. During the two decades of falling prices before the mid 1890s (Figure 3.1), Treasury cash rose from $51 million to $258 million, significant amounts compared with the average monetary base of $1 billion (Taus 1943: 268–269; Friedman and Schwartz 1963: 799).

The Treasury often countered these effects by supplying funds through debt redemptions and early interest payments, which were effectively open-market purchases. In 1853, Secretary James Guthrie reported:

> the amount still continuing to accumulate in the Treasury, apprehensions were entertained that a contraction of discounts by the city banks of New York would result, ... and ... might have an injurious influence on financial and commercial operations. With a view, therefore, to give public assurance that money would not be permitted to accumulate in the Treasury, a public offer was made on the 30th of July to redeem ... the sum of $5 million of the loans of 1847 and 1848.
>
> (*Congressional Globe*, 33rd Congress, 2nd sess., appendix, p. 250)

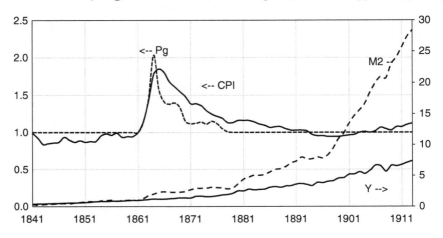

Figure 3.1 Real GNP (Y), money (M2), price level (CPI), and gold price (Pg), 1841–1913 (1860 = 1).

The *Treasury Report* of 1856 (31–32) called attention to the uncertainties that destroy

> confidence, and with it credit, inducing the hoarding of the precious metals, the withdrawal of deposits, the return of bank notes for redemption, the consequent stagnation of commerce in all its channels and operations, the reduction of prices and wages with inability to purchase and pay, bank suspensions and general insolvency.... The independent treasury, when overtrading takes place, gradually fills its vaults, withdraws the deposits, and, pressing the banks, the merchants and the dealers, exercises that temperate and timely control which serves to secure the fortunes of individuals and preserve the general prosperity.
>
> The independent treasury, however, may exercise a fatal control over the currency, the banks and the trade of the country ... whenever the revenue shall greatly exceed the expenditure.... [Without the debt purchases since March 1853, the accumulated surplus] would have acted fatally on the banks and on trade.

Secretary Howell Cobb carried this approach into the panic of 1857, until the Treasury's balance, depleted by the federal budget's turn to deficit, approached the $6,000,000 regarded as a minimum. Cobb defended his halt to debt purchases in the 1857 Treasury *Annual Report* (11–12):

> There are many persons who seem to think that it is the duty of the Government to provide relief in all cases of trouble and distress ... and their necessities, not their judgments, force them to the conclusion that the Government not only can, but ought to relieve them.

The Treasury, monitored by Congress, was the monetary authority, and took seriously a responsibility for stability even if it meant a liberal interpretation of the law. Its sensitivity to the economy and the electorate was particularly clear during the politically charged resumption that followed the Civil War.

War, suspension, and resumption

The rapid increase in military spending after the fall of Fort Sumter in April 1861 induced runs on gold and suspensions of convertibility by banks and the Treasury at the end of the year. The fears of those demanding gold were justified. Most war spending was financed by debt, much of it inconvertible currency – "greenbacks" – and the dollar price of gold doubled between 1861 and 1864 (Figure 3.1). The prices of goods in general rose 75 percent. The postwar resumption of the dollar's convertibility at the pre-war par called for a corresponding deflation.

Three approaches were considered. The first, favored by the Greenback Party, among others, opposed deflation. The Treasury and the majority in Congress took the opposite – "sound money" – view, and in December 1865, a House resolution stating "the necessity for a contraction of the currency with a view to as early a resumption of specie payment as the business interests of the country would permit" passed by a vote of 144–6. This suited Treasury Secretary Hugh McCulloch, whose "chief aim," he told his staff on taking office, was to use the postwar surplus "to discharge the claims upon the Treasury at the earliest date practicable, and to institute measures to bring the country gradually back to the specie basis, a departure from which ... is no less damaging and demoralizing to the people than expensive to the Government" (Unger 1964: 41).

The "resolution soon proved not to reflect the real sentiment of the people," and the secretary was denounced – from a sample of letters to Congress – as an impractical and dangerous theorist who expected to achieve specie payments by a " 'few legislative *whereases* and *be it enacteds*', while American industry was paralyzed by the deflation and uncertainty resulting from his 'species of experiment' " (Dewey 1928: 335; Unger 1959). Congress quickly responded, limiting redemptions of the currency to $10,000,000 a month for the next six months and $4,000,000 a month thereafter.

McCulloch proceeded as rapidly as he was allowed, and had cut greenbacks almost by half when Congress halted the process in February 1868, at the amount then in circulation – $347 million. House Republican leader James G. Blaine (1886: 328) described the pressures on Congress:

> Mr. McCulloch, in trying to enforce the policy of contraction represented an apparently consistent theory in finance; but the great host of debtors who did not wish their obligations to be made more onerous and the great host of creditors who did not desire that their debtors should be embarrassed and possibly rendered unable to liquidate united on the practical side of the question and aroused public opinion against the course of the Treasury Department. In the end, outside of banking and financial centers, there was a strong and persistent demand for repeal of the Contraction Act. [A]lthough it might be admitted that the entire nation would be benefited by the ultimate result, the people knew that the process would bring embarrassment to vast numbers and would reduce not a few to bankruptcy and ruin.

Southern and western sentiment was voiced by Georgia Senator John Gordon.

> The people of the South and West are debtors; ... their obligations were formed ... when gold was at 110 to 150; and now to force them to pay in a currency equal to gold would be simply to increase their debts by the amount of 10 to 50 percent.

Furthermore, resumption would restore the former inflexibility, when what was needed, as Thornton had written, was the means to prevent money and prices from falling (Timberlake 1993: 109).

The middle way advocated by John Sherman of Ohio, chairman of the Senate Finance Committee – that resumption should occur naturally by letting the country grow into the stock of currency (it might have been called "benign neglect") – became the effective policy. After losing control of Congress in the 1874 elections because, they thought, of their lack of a firm policy, the lame-duck Republican Congress came together in the Specie Payment Resumption Act of January 1875, which mandated the convertibility of the dollar at the pre-war rate "on and after January 1, 1879" (Friedman and Schwartz 1963: 47–48).

The next Congress, with a Democratic House and a narrowed Republican majority in the Senate, formed a joint commission that repeated the arguments against the resumption of a monometallic currency at the pre-war rate that had been used in England after 1815, and would be used again after 1918, along with the case for silver and bimetallism. Republicans kept the White House, however, and its opponents were unable to repeal the Resumption Act (US Congress 1877; Grant 1869–77, Hayes 1877–81).

Sherman was appointed Secretary of the Treasury to administer his Act. The method was an $80 reduction in greenbacks for every $100 increase in national bank notes, with a $300 million floor on greenbacks. This was not inflationary because greenbacks were high-powered money. Figure 3.1 shows steady money and output growth, and declines in the price level and the gold premium. Resumption on schedule was assisted by an inflow of gold brought by the coincidence of poor harvests in Europe and their opposite in the United States, but was nevertheless "a remarkable political and economic achievement" (Timberlake 1978: 117).

The post-Civil War resumption was the least painful of those pursued in the United States (1816–23, 1864–79) and the United Kingdom (1813–21, 1918–25) in the nineteenth and twentieth centuries, perhaps because it was the longest. Nature was generally allowed to take its course. The economy grew into the money stock. Histories – including those of the National Bureau of Economic Research in Mitchell's *Business Cycles* (1913) and Thorp's *Annals* (1926) mis-labeled 1873–9 a depression probably because that explanation accorded with the traditional association of deflation with depression as well as the better documentation of prices. In fact, annual aggregate output fell only in 1874, and rose 4 percent per annum during the period (Balke and Gordon 1989).

The Act's administrators were ready to be lenient. Sherman's ideal monetary system, described in the 1877 Treasury *Annual Report*, included (1) mainly paper currency issued by the government and national banks, backed respectively by gold and government bonds, plus (2) limited coinage of silver as a minor currency. He thought the Treasury was "a safer custodian of reserves than a multitude of scattered banks," but banks were better for handling "the ebb and flow of currency caused by varying crops, productions and seasons." His system allowed the suspension of specie payments under stress, which was actually carried out on several occasions (Timberlake 1993: 114). Would that Sherman and his colleagues, with their institutions, had been in place in the 1930s!

The attitudes and institutions described above help explain why the resumption took so long. The electorate, acting through Congress, was involved in the decision, and while feelings often ran high, important groups were characterized by moderation. Furthermore, there was no third party whom politicians could assign to administer the medicine. This was the era of what the young Woodrow Wilson called *Congressional Government*. "The checks and balances which once obtained," he wrote, "are no longer effective." The federal courts were under the appointive power of Congress, and the Supreme Court had declared its reluctance "to interfere with the *political discretion* of either Congress or the President." "There is no distincter tendency in congressional history than the tendency to subject even the details of administration to the constant supervision, and all policy to the watchful intervention of, the Standing Committees." The President's cabinet had been made "humble servants" of Congress, which in the course of exercising its power of the purse expected the Secretary of the Treasury to be its agent (Wilson 1885: 43–50).

Speaking for the Morrison resolution that would prescribe the Treasury's cash management (see below), Senator James Beck reminded his colleagues that whereas the laws creating the other executive departments enjoined their secretaries to advise and act under the direction of the President, the Secretary of the Treasury was required

> to make report and give information to either branch of the Legislature ... and generally to perform all such services relative to the finances as he shall be directed to perform.... We with the Secretary of the Treasury manage the purse; the president and the other secretaries control the sword.
>
> (*Congressional Record*, July 29, 1886)

Monetary policy benefited from the partnership of Congress and the Treasury that was cemented by similar ideas and experiences. Treasury secretaries had been senators or congressmen three-fourths of the time during the nineteenth century, compared with two years after 1946.[2] Congress' sophistication in the nineteenth century, before it gave way to the Executive in the twentieth, has often been remarked upon, and it certainly applies to economics. Crawford, Calhoun, Clay, Webster, Benton, Sherman, and their colleagues regularly quoted Thornton, Loyd, and other economists, and knew past and present monetary affairs at home and abroad. The political costs of imposing pain is given as a reason for divorcing politics from money. There is clearly another side to the story. It is noteworthy that the House of Representatives was the part of government most anxious to prevent the fall in money during the Great Depression, and the slowest to approve Main Street's bailout of Wall Street in 2008.

Conservative historians – and admirers of authority – censured the politically sensitive, the slow and erratic, resumption

> which revealed remarkable weaknesses in economic thought and moral standards.... It was the decade of the Tweed Ring ... of Black Friday ... the gold conspiracy and railway financing of Jay Gould, James Fisk, and their kind. In sum, it was a time when men preferred to revel in the gambling

uncertainties of paper money rather than to face the sacrifice which recuperation from a monetary debauch required.

Nevertheless, Don Barrett (1931: 172–173) admitted, "In spite of these adverse conditions ... the country experienced ... great forward movements in industry and trade" (see also Noyes 1909: 17–18).

Woodrow Wilson got his way in 1913, in a new institution remote from the electorate, whose fluctuating relations with Congress are considered in the following chapters.

Discretionary monetary management

President Grant's first Secretary of the Treasury, George Boutwell, looked out for the money market. He engaged in open-market purchases, especially in the autumn, and in October 1872 reissued $5,000,000 of retired greenbacks by interpreting the prescription of 1868 as a minimum rather than as a fixed figure. Sherman and the majority of his committee protested, but the minority sympathized with Boutwell's response that relief from panics had never been achieved even in England "without the personal intervention of men possessing power." Furthermore, deflation ought to be avoided because "we have no right morally" to alter debtor–creditor relations. Employment of the greenback "reserve" was

> in its effect ... substantially what is done by the Government of Great Britain through the Bank of England. The Secretary furnished temporary relief ... by adding to the circulation of the country, diminishing its value ... and changing the relations of debtor and creditor.... Clothed with authority by law, ... the Secretary of the Treasury could not sit silent and inactive while ruin was blasting the prospects of many and creating the most serious apprehensions in all parts of the country. It was a great responsibility; but it is a responsibility which must be taken by men who are clothed with the authority.[3]

The Treasury also used a legal loophole left over from the war which allowed it to deposit "the moneys obtained on any of the loans now authorized by law ... in such solvent specie-paying banks as he may select" (Krooss 1969: 1174). Secretary Charles Fairchild (1887–9), who "always considered the needs of banks," raised the Treasury's bank deposits from $13 million to $54 million. These increases, as well as Treasury debt purchases, were timed for the autumn and other periods of financial stringency, and the banks came to depend on the Treasury instead of making adequate preparations, *The Commercial and Financial Chronicle* complained. Unfortunately for the banks, Fairchild was succeeded by William Windom (1889–91), "a strict observer of the letter of the Law of 1846 [who] believed that the policy of depositing public money in banks was wholly unjustifiable," and cut Treasury bank deposits to $21 million (Taus 1943: 80–82, 88).

Congressmen complained of the large sums in Treasury vaults that might be applied to the debt to save interest expenses, and the Appropriation Act of 1881 gave the Treasury discretion to that end. Deposits remained high, however, and rose under the sound-money Cleveland administrations (1885–9, 1893–7) which desired a "prudent" reserve (Timberlake 1993: 154). In 1886, those wanting easier money secured House and Senate agreement to the Morrison resolution calling on the Treasury to apply its "surplus or balance ... over ... $100,000,000 ... to the payment of the interest-bearing indebtedness of the United States" at a maximum rate of $10,000,000 a month. A.J. Warner of Ohio quoted Lord Overstone (Samuel Jones Loyd) – "In adopting a paper circulation we must unavoidably depend for a maintenance of its due value upon the adoption of a strict and judicious rule for the regulation of its amount" – and asked why it was necessary to "hoard $228,000,000 in the Treasury of the United States? Is it to purchase the favor of Wall street and the banks? If so it is altogether too dear a price" (*Congressional Record*, July 13, 1886).

The argument over rules versus discretion was ongoing. Senator Beck contended that it was Congress' responsibility to direct the secretary in order to relieve him of temptation and political embarrassment. Nelson Dingley of Maine, on the other hand, objected to Congress' interference

> with a question which exclusively pertains to administration. This is the first attempt, I think, in the history of this Government to determine by a legislative resolution what should be the working balance of the Treasury.... No cast-iron rule can be laid down on a matter of this kind.

Conservatives were able to insert a contingency balance of $20,000,000 in the resolution, as well as authority for the secretary to suspend debt purchases in emergencies. Benjamin Butterworth of Ohio believed discretion on the part of the secretary was "indispensable to the maintenance of the national credit," and called the Treasury reserve "the ballast which keeps our monetary ship steady as she moves through the sea of financial troubles which constantly threaten" (*Congressional Record*, July 14, 29, August 4, 1886).

The silver question

The foremost monetary debate during the last decades of the nineteenth century concerned the coinage of silver. Deflation, the falling price of silver, the silver interests of the new States (six between 1886 and 1890), and recession led to the Sherman Silver Purchase Act of 1890, which raised the rate of silver purchases (at an above-market price) with Treasury notes issued for the purpose and redeemable in gold or silver coin (Krooss 1969: 1917–18, 1952–60). This action coincided with falls in exports and government receipts that contributed to gold losses. The overpricing of silver opened arbitrage profits which threatened the Treasury's ability to redeem its notes in gold, President Grover Cleveland told the special session of Congress that he called to repeal the 1890 Act after panic struck in early 1893.

Repeal did not come easily. Cleveland was at odds with much of his Democratic Party, whose 1892 platform was pro-silver. His Treasury Secretary, John Carlisle, was a champion of free silver as a congressman (1877–92), but had changed his views. His "eloquent tongue is silenced by a Cabinet office" (or responsibility?), South Carolina Congressman John McLaurin observed. Showing an understanding of the workings of a commodity standard beyond that of many economists, the 1893 *Treasury Report* pointed out that

> the amount of money in the country is greater than is required for the transaction of the business of the people at this time [presumably meaning at the current price level].... Money does not create business, but business creates a demand for money, and unless there is such a revival of industry and trade as to require the use of the circulating medium now outstanding, it would be hazardous to arbitrarily increase the volume by law.
>
> (Timberlake 1993: 172–175)

Despite the strong Democratic majorities (218–127 and 44–38 in the House and Senate [Democrats did not control both Houses again for 20 years]), silver interests were on the defensive. Proposals for free coinage at 16-, 17-, 18-, 19-, and 20-to-1 failed on successive votes. The relative gold–silver market price averaged 26 in 1893, compared with 15 in 1859 (the year of the Comstock Lode, the first major silver strike in the United States), 18 in 1879, 22 in 1889, and 35 in 1899. A century later, in 2013, it was 60. The long-term stability of prices under the gold standard was due to the physical coincidence of the approximate long-term constancy of the relative availabilities/costs of gold and other goods. That was not true of silver after the middle of the nineteenth century. The approximate equality of price levels in 1790 and 1914 under the gold standard would have been replaced by more than a doubling under a silver standard. This still would have meant inflation less than 1 percent per annum over the entire period, although about 2 percent for the last 30 years (US Bureau of Census 1975).

Congress repealed the Silver Purchase Act by "astonishing" margins, given the Democratic majorities and the depressed economy. Their reluctant response to the crisis demonstrated "the importance legislators attached to a viable gold standard" (Timberlake 1993: 174–175).

The gold drain nevertheless continued. The Treasury went to the markets for gold, selling securities and borrowing from banks, but "finally recognized the futility of selling bonds for gold, most of which was shortly drawn out of the Treasury by the presentation of legal-tender notes for redemption." In February 1895, the government turned to a syndicate of investment bankers led by J.P. Morgan, which arranged an issue of 30-year bonds for 3,500,000 ounces of gold, at least half of which was to be procured abroad. Nevertheless, "the reserve remained near the traditional danger line" until after William Jennings Bryan and silver were defeated in the presidential election of 1896, and was not generally thought sufficient until world gold production increased later in the decade (Dewey 1928: 441, 454).

The United States formally adopted a single-metallic standard in 1900. The Gold Standard Act declared

> That the dollar consisting of twenty-five and eight-tenths grains of gold nine-tenths fine ... shall be the standard unit of value, and all forms of money issued or coined by the United States shall be maintained at a parity of value with this standard, and it shall be the duty of the Secretary of the Treasury to maintain such parity.

The Treasury issued and redeemed notes for gold, a task that elsewhere was performed by central banks, and the Act required a reserve fund of $150,000,000 in gold coin and bullion to be "set apart in the Treasury." If the "fund shall at any time fall below $100,000,000, then it shall be [the secretary's] duty to restore the same to the maximum sum of $150,000,000 by borrowing money on the credit of the United States," specifically by issuing bonds "to be payable, principal and interest, in gold coin of the present standard value."

Monetary policy as defense of the currency

It is instructive that Cleveland's call for monetary restraint came during severe depression. The decline in business that began in 1892 turned to financial panic the following summer, and the President issued his call to Congress in June. His message to the legislators blamed the nation's economic problems on a lack of confidence in the gold convertibility of the dollar. The proposed solution, as we saw above, was to secure stability by ending the monetization of silver. Cleveland's approach was similar to President Herbert Hoover's in a later crisis. Both believed an essential condition of economic recovery to be confidence in the currency – meaning its convertibility with gold at a fixed rate of exchange. They considered credit expansions based on the monetization of silver to be counterproductive by raising doubts of the government's commitment to gold, leading to its disappearance abroad and into domestic hoards.

Sherman's reaction to the repeal of his act casts light on contemporary attitudes towards the stabilization possibilities of monetary policy, as well as the flexibility of politicians who saw themselves as managers instead of the disjointed observers of post-1913:

> Sir, "give the devil his due." The law of 1890 may have many faults, but I stand by it yet, and I will defend it, not as a permanent public policy, not as a measure that I take any pride in, because I yielded to the necessity of granting relief.... Without it, in 1891 and 1892 we would have met difficulties that would have staggered us much more than the passing breeze of the hour.... The immediate result of the measure was to increase our currency, and thus relieve our people from the panic then imminent, similar to that which we now suffer. The very men who now denounce from Wall

Street this compromise were shouting "Hallelujah!" for their escape by it from free coinage.

(Miller 1913 xiv: 398)

However, conditions had changed. The Act had begun to injure money and trade. Now the right approach was to restore confidence in the currency.

A central bank?

The first decade of the twentieth century, at the same time calls for fundamental change were growing, has been called the heyday of the Treasury's monetary policy, in which its "central-banking activities ... were being converted from emergency measures to a fairly regular and predictable operating function" (Friedman and Schwartz 1963: 149).

The secretaries were active. The party in power was committed to the gold standard, and understood that it functioned neither perfectly nor automatically. In his 1899 *Report*, Secretary Lyman Gage (1897–1902) said the "Stability [of the] currency should be safely guarded, [although] *flexibility* – the power of needful expansion – must also be provided," and referred to the outflow of funds from New York to the country banks the previous autumn, wreaking "havoc ... in the regular ongoing of our commercial life."

They were also innovative. Faced with the constraint that customs receipts had to be kept in the Treasury, Secretary Leslie Shaw (1902–7) declared depository banks to be offices of the Treasury. When the popular press and academic economists condemned his actions as autocratic and primarily for the relief of "a ring of powerful Wall Street speculators," he replied: "It has been the fixed policy of the Treasury Department for more than half a century to anticipate monetary stringencies, and so far as possible prevent panics" (Timberlake 1993: 192).

The Treasury's effectiveness as a central bank is difficult to gauge. Its shifts of funds to banks under pressure, especially in 1907, were large. On the other hand, although the first decade of the new century was more prosperous than the depressed 1890s, there is little evidence of improved financial stability. There were as many "major panics," and more "minor panics," in the later decade as the earlier, and notwithstanding the secretaries' pride in assisting crop movements, there was no lessening of seasonal fluctuations in interest rates (Kemmerer 1910: 222–223; Miron 1986; Federal Reserve Board 1943: 448).

Institutional changes were debated. Secretary George Cortelyou (1907–9) thought a monetary framework that would "adapt the movement of currency more nearly automatically to the requirements of business" would be superior to the Treasury's discretion, and Secretary Gage anticipated the Federal Reserve when he asked: "Can not the principle of federation be applied, under which the banks as individual units, preserving their independence of action in local relationships, may yet be united in a great central institution?" Secretary Shaw claimed in his 1906 *Report* that if the secretary were given powers over bank reserves and reserve ratios (later given to the Federal Reserve), "no panic as distinguished from industrial stagnation could threaten either the United States or Europe that he could not avert" (US Treasury *Annual Reports* 1901: 77 and 1906: 49; US Congress 1908: 32; Timberlake 1993: 195).

Several changes were made along the lines suggested. The Republican Party controlled both houses of Congress from 1895 to 1911, and the presidency from 1897 to 1913. Led by Nelson Aldrich, chairman of the Senate Finance Committee from 1898 to 1911, friend of banks and sound money, and father-in-law of John D. Rockefeller, Jr., the 60th Congress (1907–8) adopted several measures

> which expressly sanctioned certain actions of Mr. Shaw.... The collateral required of depository banks was to be left to the discretion of the Secretary of the Treasury. No longer was the Treasury forbidden to deposit customs receipts in national depositories.
>
> Government funds could now be placed in properly qualified national banks [and] no reserve need be held against deposits of public money.

In addition, the Aldrich–Vreeland Act reacted to the 1907 panic by authorizing the formation of groups of banks with the power to issue "emergency currency" under the administration of the Secretary of the Treasury. These powers were applied by Wilson's Treasury Secretary William McAdoo during the crisis of August–October 1914 (Taus 1943: 119–142).

These and other amendments "which permit the use of the banks for practically all the business of the Government, have ... virtually abolished the [Independent Treasury] system," David Kinley (1910: 206–207) wrote in a study for the National Monetary Commission that was created by the Aldrich–Vreeland Act. The Treasury's powers were no longer limited by its depositories.

Money centers and clearing houses, 1853–1913

> Shortly after the panic or currency famine of 1893 ... there was issued fully $100,000,000 of clearing-house certificates used in settlement between banks, of certified checks, certificates of deposit, cashier's checks in round amounts (as $1, $5, $10, $20, and $50), due bills from manufacturers and other employers of labor, and clearing-house certificates ... all designed to take the place of currency in the hands of the public. Clearing-house certificates, issued and used in settling debit balances between banks, were in no wise prohibited, but all of the other above-described evidences of debt which were issued to circulate among the public as money, were clearly subject to the ten per cent tax enacted for the purpose of getting rid of state bank circulation. This temporary currency, however, performed so valuable a service in such a crucial period, in moving the crops and keeping business machinery in motion, that the Government, after due deliberation, wisely forbore to prosecute. In other words, the want of elasticity in our currency system was thus partially supplied. It is worthy of note that no loss resulted from the use of this makeshift currency.
>
> (Hepburn 1903: 374)

New York rivaled London in its money markets and as keeper of the nation's reserve. Its importance to trade and finance were preserved and even increased by the canals, railroads, and telegraph as the population moved west. As soon as the developing regions had banks they had accounts in New York. Many of these funds were sent on to banks outside New York. Like London, New York was an intermediary between surplus and deficit areas, between the savings of the low-interest East and the investment opportunities of the West. Large amounts were also lent on call to stock buyers, much of it through the "money desk" of the New York Stock Exchange. The call loan market "gradually became the final reservoir for the banking reserves of the nation," Margaret Myers wrote in her history of *The New York Money Market* (1931: 135), "and upon it, in emergency, fell the final responsibility for providing banks with funds." When the country banks withdrew their balances from the cities to finance crop movements in the autumn, the city banks called in their loans to the stock exchange. Autumn was frequently a period of financial stringency and high interest rates. This was expected, but if an additional strain occurred, the money market was hard-pressed to deal with it.

Clearing houses and clearinghouse money

The New York Clearing House Association was formed in 1853, and had "a stabilizing effect in forcing banks to make daily, rather than weekly, settlements, and in preventing the accumulation of large adverse balances, with the consequent dangerous lowering of reserves and scramble for funds in the call market" (Myers 1931: 95). The check-clearing arrangement was developed for micro-efficiency purposes, but also had positive macro effects. It was soon asked to do more.

"The panic of 1857 was so severe and so prolonged that the Clearing House was practically forced into action, and it began timidly to feel its way towards an emergency technique" (Myers 1931: 97). Reserves were leaving New York in August, when the stoppage of payment by the New York branch of the Ohio Life Insurance and Trust Company caused country banks to accelerate their withdrawals. The collapse of Ohio Life, in which western banks had deposited half-a-million dollars, followed the default of many of its call loans after a fall in stock prices.

On September 2, the Mechanics' Bank was suspended from the Clearing House because it failed to meet the daily settlements, and other banks looked to their positions.

> The instinct of each one was to curtail its loans in order to protect its reserves, yet nothing was more certain to intensify the panic. The banks, therefore, on September 20, agreed that all would increase their loans so that the Clearing House balances of all of them would be increased proportionately and would cancel each other without reducing their slender stock of specie.
>
> (Myers 1931: 97)

The drain continued, however, and Clearing House certificates used in the daily settlements as evidences of claims on specie declined along with the specie. Something more was needed, and

> the Clearing House committee decided to issue certificates also against notes of New York state banks. This group of banks agreed to pay 6 per cent interest on the notes..., and the city banks were willing to hold them on those terms.
>
> (Myers 1931: 98)

These steps – private responses to need with regulatory forbearance – anticipated *Lombard Street*. They did not prevent the suspension of specie payments between October 13 and December 13, but they enabled the country and city banks to continue lending, and they were employed again.

"In every instance, though, some new wrinkles were added." In 1860, collateral was extended to New York State and US Treasury bonds. In 1873, irredeemable certified checks were issued without collateral. Any member of the Clearing House might put them into circulation, stamped or written "Payable through the Clearing House." Other "banks accepted them as settlement media by common consent through their clearinghouse association, but did not have to redeem them with legal tender." When the Treasury stopped issuing gold certificates in 1893 because of a decline in its gold reserve, "the Clearing House filled the gap with an issue of its own gold certificates" (Myers 1931: 257; Timberlake 1993: 200–201; Sprague 1910: 54; Cannon 1910: 75–116).

The system extended beyond New York, and the risk-sharing agreement of the Boston clearinghouse became the model:

> The Associated Banks of the Clearinghouse severally agree with the others that the Bills received instead of specie at the Clearinghouse from the Debtor Banks ... shall ... be and remain at the joint risk of all the Associated Banks in proportion to the amount of their Capitals respectively.
>
> (Redlich 1951: 159)

Clearinghouse loan certificates allowed banks to maintain their loans and deposits despite gold losses – a violation of legal reserve requirements. They were effectively additions to bank reserves. "The banking industry simply reinstituted itself as an ad hoc central bank" (Timberlake 1984). The credibility of clearinghouse money is illustrated in Figure 3.2 by the currency premium during the Panic of 1907. Clearinghouse money issued at the height of the panic traded at 3- to 4-percent discounts to gold and government currency but gradually achieved par in the panics of 1873 and 1893 as well as 1907 (Gorton 1984).

The certificates included denominations small enough to serve as currency. This did not go unnoticed by the authorities, such as Comptroller A. Barton Hepburn, who as we saw above, only winked, and became a bank executive.[4] His successor, James Eckels, also praised the clearinghouse issues, and issued an

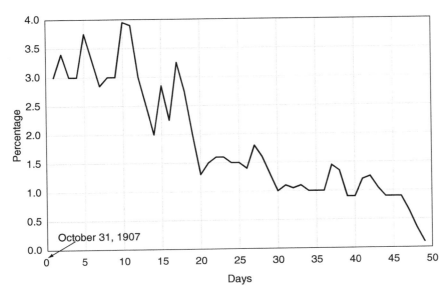

Figure 3.2 The currency premium during the Panic of 1907 (source: Gorton 1984).

official denial that they were currency. If they had been used as currency, he reasoned, the offending banks would have been fined. Eckels became president of the Commerce Bank of Chicago on leaving the Comptroller's office (1907 *Annual Report*: 64; Timberlake 1993: 207).

Make them official?

O.M.W Sprague (1910: 90) suggested that by means of their loan certificates, the clearinghouse banks

> were converted, to all intents and purposes, into a central bank, which, although without power to issue notes, was in other respects more powerful than a European central bank because it included virtually all the banking power of the city.

Official support, or even acceptance, of their emergency issues would have been a logical step in the development of their central banking functions. This was done temporarily in the Aldrich–Vreeland Act, but was allowed to elapse in favor of the Federal Reserve.

Businessman Theodore Gilman (1898: 44–45, 71, 157) argued along these lines when he advocated a "grade of banks higher than our ordinary commercial banks" which could support the latter. He suggested the legalization of existing practices by the federal incorporation of a clearing house in each state. Their notes would be guaranteed first by security collateral, second by the banks issuing them, and third by the clearinghouse associations. This would be better than a separate reserve held outside the banking system because it might never be needed. "[I]t should not be provided by capital withdrawn from productive use. It will cost nothing and will be just as serviceable if it is provided by law as a power which may be used in case of need." Clearinghouse committees would be "conservative" in their issues because of their "pecuniary interest as stock-holders in banks." Furthermore, the 6-percent interest charge to banks issuing clearinghouse currency, as recommended by Bagehot, "would act as a check upon their issue, and they would not be taken so much for profit as for protection and necessity."

New York City lawyer and Republican Congressman Benjamin Fairchild introduced a bill embodying Gilman's plan in 1896. It was referred to the House Committee on Banking and Currency, but never appeared again nor was advocated by a popular movement (Timberlake 1993: 205–206). The probable benefits were politically insufficient. Much better for banks was a government institution that held reserves and would supply liquidity on demand.

Charles Goodhart took the opposite tack in his discussion of the necessity and indeed inevitability of official unconstrained central banks such as the Federal Reserve and the post-1914 Bank of England. Goodhart argued that imperfections prevented clearing houses from being an effective means of ameliorating panics. They suffered from limited means, inadequate information of bank positions, and conflicts of interest. An effective central bank, Goodhart argued, must be "above the competitive battle." It must be "a noncompetitive, non-profit-maximizing body" with supernormal reserves and a government-sanctioned monopoly of the currency (1988: 45).

These arguments smack of the (theoretical and untried) "grass is always greener" (than the known and imperfect) attitude against which Burke warned, and in this case disregards the experience of the Great Depression (and subsequently the Great Recession). Nothing is said about incentives and the common goals even of competing banks, nor of the costs of information. In fact, profit-seeking financial institutions have incentives to know each others' risks. The incentives of regulators to acquire information beyond the routine, on the other hand, are known to be weak, and are often unused for political reasons (discussed below in the chapter on regulation). The Great Recession revealed again that institutions respond to one another's conditions before officials even know there are problems. Nevertheless, the encouragement of clearing houses was bypassed in favor of an innovative organization with characteristics taken from the public banks of Europe.

Timberlake (1993: 212) anticipated the bailouts of the future – not too difficult because they continued the past – when he pointed out that "Goodhart's government central bank, rather than being an answer to the potential problems he raises, becomes an aggravation." The dispensing of government central bank largess is "governed by political favoritism and political pressures in support of special interests" which aggravate liquidity problems that were provoked by government interventions in the first place.

The National Banking System, 1863–

It will be seen at a glance that the amount to be derived from taxation forms but a small portion of the sums required for the expenses of the war. For the rest, the reliance must be placed on loans.... [Interest rates above 6 percent are] higher than the United States, with their vast and accumulating resources, ought to pay. To enable the government to obtain the necessary means for prosecuting the war to a successful issue, without unnecessary cost, is a problem which must engage the most careful attention of the legislature.

The circulation of the banks of the United States on January 1, 1861 was ... $150,000,000 ... in States now loyal.... The whole of this circulation constitutes a loan without interest from the people to the banks...; and it deserves consideration whether sound policy does not require that the advantages of the loan be transferred, in part at least, from the banks, representing only the interests of the stockholders, to the government, representing the aggregate interests of the whole people.

It has been well questioned by the most eminent statesmen whether a currency of bank notes, issued by local institutions under State laws, is not, in fact, prohibited by the national Constitution.

(*Annual Treasury Report*, 1861)

Purposes

The National Bank Act of 1863 was first a measure of war finance. It established the Office of the Comptroller of the Currency to charter and supervise "national" banks whose primary purpose was investment in government debt: currency as cash reserves and government bonds as backing for a "uniform currency," that is, national bank notes secured by US bonds deposited with the treasurer of the United States. The notes were engraved by the treasurer in a standard design but with the name of the issuing bank (Krooss 1969: 1381–1411; Robertson 1968: 51). They peaked at 32 percent of the currency in 1915, the remainder being gold and silver certificates and greenbacks (Munn and Garcia 1983: 636).

The chartering of banks for state financial assistance was not new. We have seen that the charters of the Bank of England and the first and second Banks of the United States required investments in national debt. State bank charters similarly required investments in state bonds, resulting in interest rate risk that was a significant cause of bank failure (Rolnick and Weber 1984).

The National Banking System got underway too late for the war effort, but it was also a reform measure. Secretary Salmon Chase said the time had come for Congress to exercise its responsibility "to regulate the value of coin" by controlling

the credit circulation.... The value of the existing bank note circulation depends on the laws of thirty-four states and the character of some sixteen hundred private corporations. It is usually furnished in the greatest proportions by institutions of least actual capital.

(US Treasury *Annual Report*, 1861: 16–17)

Response to the national system was disappointing. Few charters were issued the first year, most to small organizations, and few of those were conversions of state banks. Among the comptroller's reasons for the reluctance of state banks to convert to national status was fear that government credit would be inadequate support for their notes in a crisis, the threat of "Congressional interference with their business for partisan purposes," and Chase's insistence that they relinquish their names for numbers. "Do you expect that the Bank of Commerce," its president asked, "will relinquish its honored name and be known as the Tenth or Twentieth National Bank of New York?" (McCulloch 1888: 169). Chase gave way on this point, but more important was Congress' imposition in March 1865 of a prohibitive 10-percent annual tax on state bank notes. Most state banks changed their charters, and between June 1865 and June 1866, the ratio of national to state banks turned from 467/1,089 to 1,294/349. In succeeding years, however, with the growth of deposit banking, stimulated by the tax, most small banks reverted to state charters and their easier regulations. City national banks, on the other hand, were attracted by their role as bank reserve depositories. By 1914, 70 percent of commercial banks had state charters while national banks had half the deposits (Federal Reserve Board 1943: 16–17).

The dual, national and state, system of charters and regulations still exists, with membership of the Federal Reserve System still required of the former but not the latter, although differences in reserve requirements were removed by the Depository Institutions and Deregulation Act of 1980. The number of banks fell by half the next three decades, mainly by mergers, but most, especially the small ones, still have state charters (Figure 7.1).

An inelastic currency

The National Banking System enters monetary histories primarily as a regime from which bankers and reformers sought to escape. They wanted an "elastic" money supply unrestrained by the cash reserve requirements of national banks or the US bond collateralization of the currency. Laurence Laughlin of the University of Chicago and the National Citizens League for the Promotion of Sound Banking wrote: "an elastic banknote circulation, slowly rising, but expanding and contracting sharply with seasonal demand is imperative. Our present national bank circulation does not provide for this elasticity" (1912: 61).

Congressman Carter Glass' introduction of the Federal Reserve bill in September 1913 referred to the "intense dissatisfaction with the prevailing national banking and currency system" (Krooss 1969: 2343–2346):

Financial textbook writers of Europe have characterized our American system as "barbarous," and eminent bankers of this country who, from time to time, have appeared before the Banking and Currency Committee of the House have not hesitated to confess that this bitter criticism is merited.... Five times within the last 30 years financial catastrophe has overtaken the country under this system;... The System literally has no reserve force. The currency based upon the Nation's debt is absolutely unresponsive to the Nation's business needs. The lack of cooperation and coordination among the more than 7,300 national banks produces a curtailment of facilities at all periods of exceptional demand for credit.

Glass hoped to shift the country's reserve to a new institution separate from the "stock gambling operations" of New York – a reference to the provincial bank practice of keeping their liquidity in the form of stock exchange call loans through the intermediation of New York banks. Unaware of the role of financial intermediation in the economy, he believed that money belonged at home. It is ironic that the first emergency use of the Fed's reserves was assistance to New York banks affected by the 1929 stock crash.

Referring to the alleged unresponsiveness of credit, a belief in which Glass was not alone, US bonds did not in fact limit national bank notes, which were never more than 30 percent of the amount permitted. John James (1976) attributed this to the greater profitability of loans than of bond investments. The replacement of national bank currency by Federal Reserve notes made this so-called problem irrelevant, but did not terminate the now irrelevant national bank charters. The comptroller was retained as an extra, competing, chartering agency and regulator that Congress is still trying to reconcile with other agencies.

Notes

1 The US Bank continued to operate with a Pennsylvania charter until its failure in 1844 (Hammond 1957: ch. 16).
2 The two years were 12/68–1/69 (Joseph Barr) and 1/93–12/94 (Lloyd Bentsen).
3 In the Senate, to which he had been elected in 1872. *Cong. Record*, 43d Cong., 1st sess., app., January 22, 1874.
4 Vice-president and president of the Third National Bank of New York, vice-president of the National City Bank of New York, and president and chairman of the Chase National Bank.

4   The Federal Reserve System, 1913–51

An Act to provide for the establishment of Federal reserve banks, to furnish an elastic currency, to afford means of rediscounting commercial paper, to establish a more effective supervision of banking in the United States, and for other purposes.

Title of Federal Reserve Act, December 23, 1913

The Federal Reserve was unlike any previous American institution. It was not adapted from the Independent Treasury or private clearing houses. Nor was it a bank. Unlike the Bank of England and the Banks of the United States, it did not lend to or keep the deposits of private citizens. Existing banks did not want competition from a national bank that enjoyed a special relationship with the government, although they saw the benefits of a public institution that was ready to lend to them and bear the costs of the nation's reserve. The Fed was endowed with unprecedented powers of the printing press, free of market or electoral constraints (although gold reserves were a loose restraint at the beginning), which would be used in the interests of its patron banks and enable Congress to escape accountability for its spending. Those powers would prove to have enormous costs in economic volatility and the destruction of the monetary system the Fed was created to assist.

Founding[1]

Three forces combined to make an American central bank in 1913: an emergency mentality produced by the panic of 1907; a reform administration which delivered the Democratic Party that had traditionally opposed a national bank; and money center banks' desire for an institution that would support but not compete with them.

The 1907 crisis drew the usual market and official responses: clearinghouse loan certificates, increased Treasury bank deposits, an emergency pool arranged by J.P. Morgan, and a suspension of payments in New York that spread to the interior (Friedman and Schwartz 1963: 156–168; Krooss 1969: 2083–2085; Sprague 1910: ch. 5; Andrew 1908). In addition, 1907 differed from previous crises in the response of Congress.

The Aldrich–Vreeland Act provided for temporary currency during emergencies, as well as, looking toward more fundamental solutions, a National Monetary Commission of legislators "to inquire into and report to Congress at the earliest date practicable what changes are necessary or desirable in the monetary system of the United States or in the laws relating to banking and currency" (Sec. 17–18). Several interesting studies resulted, but the ideas behind the Federal Reserve Act preceded the work of the Commission.[2]

Senator Aldrich had proposed that banks form voluntary National Currency Associations empowered – "if, in the judgment of the Secretary of the Treasury, business conditions in the locality demand additional circulation, and if he be satisfied with the character and value of the securities proposed" – to issue currency secured by government and railroad bonds. This was attacked by western bankers as a scheme to make a market for the securities held by New York banks and the "money trust." An alternative version, with commercial paper as security, was proposed in the House. The Aldrich–Vreeland Act was a compromise in which bonds (but not railroad bonds) and short-term "notes representing actual commercial transactions [bearing] the names of at least two responsible parties" became bases for emergency currency. The Act was applied once before its expiration in 1915 – to counteract foreign currency withdrawals at the outbreak of war in 1914. Its issues, amounting to a quarter of the public's currency, "probably prevented a monetary panic and the restriction of payments by the banking system," and "would have been equally effective" in the next "crisis which arose in late 1930" (Friedman and Schwartz 1963: 170–172). The Act would probably have been implemented by Secretary Ogden Mills (1932–3), who was critical of the Fed's inaction, although perhaps not by the liquidationist Andrew Mellon (1921–32) (discussed below).

The more ambitious bill that Aldrich submitted in 1912 possessed a European flavor and had been outlined by investment banker Paul Warburg. Of the Hamburg family firm, Warburg settled in New York in 1902, joined Kuhn, Loeb & Co., became interested in American monetary reform, and took part with Aldrich in the famous 1910 meeting on Jekyll Island (Warburg 1907, 1910; Griffin 1995). He was appointed to a four-year term on the first Federal Reserve Board.

The Aldrich/Warburg bill resembled the Federal Reserve Act as finally adopted, but its timing was unfortunate as Republicans lost control of the House in the 1910 election, and would also lose the Senate and the presidency in 1912 (Warburg 1930 i: 178–365). Democrats associated Aldrich with the "money trust" and opposed his bill in the 1912 campaign.

The big banks continued to push for reform, however, and found an ally in Carter Glass of the House Banking and Currency Committee. Festus Wade, St. Louis banker and member of the Currency Committee of the American Bankers Association (ABA), promised Glass the ABA's cooperation "in devising a financial system for this country." He personally favored the Aldrich bill, but "any bill you submit will be a vast improvement on our present system." Even if it were called "central supervisory control" rather than "central bank,"

Plate 1 Signing of the Federal Reserve Act, December 23, 1913 (courtesy of Woodrow Wilson Presidential Library; Painting by Wilbur G. Kurtz).

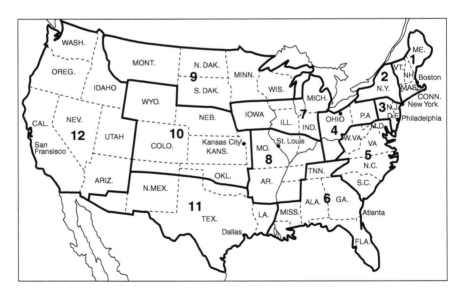

Plate 2 New US banking system announced (*The Sun*, [New York] April 1914).

it would "be a central bank in its final analysis." Chicago banker and ABA president, George Reynolds, said he was opposed to a true central bank (that is, a bankers' bank with branches competing with existing banks), although Glass could "count on at least good treatment and a reasonable measure of cooperation by the ABA [for an] organization with branches located in various sections of the country dealing only with banks and the Government" (Kolko 1963: 226; Glass 1927: 80).

Glass objected to Aldrich's central board as interfering with his hope to break Wall Street's dominance (Willis 1915: 142–143). However, although President Wilson accepted the bill as the first major legislation of the New Freedom, he wanted a "capstone" – a central board – to control and coordinate the system. Glass was privately aghast at this backward step towards Aldrich's centralization, but accommodated Wilson with a Federal Reserve Board of six public members appointed by the president and three bankers chosen by the regional banks, although the bankers were dropped to placate William Jennings Bryan and his populist following (Link 1956: 212). Bryan also prevailed over the protestations of Wilson and Glass to make Federal Reserve currency a liability of the United States instead of the regional Fed banks. Biographer Arthur Link noted the weak resistance of Wilson, who was evidently swayed by advisor Louis Brandeis' (1913) argument that

> The power to issue currency should be vested exclusively in Government officials, even when the currency is issued against commercial paper. The American people will not be content to have the discretion necessarily involved vested in a Board composed wholly or in part of bankers; for their judgment may be biased by private interest or affiliation.... The conflict between the policies of the Administration and the desires of the financiers and of big business is an irreconcilable one.

This was pretense or illusion. Bankers would dominate the regional Federal Reserve Banks where most of the business was done, especially in the early days, and monetary policy would be carried out in the course of the Fed's support of bank markets. These were only the first of bank subsidies that would culminate, we hope, in the massive bailouts of the Great Recession.

The Federal Reserve Act had something for all the politically powerful interests, especially the banks. The burden of the nation's reserve was shifted to a public institution that did not compete with privately owned banks, the market for commercial paper was supported by the discount window, legal impediments to bank participation in international finance were reduced – Aldrich's (1909) promise of a plan "to make the United States the financial center of the world" was kept – and although national banks were required to join the Federal Reserve System, the pain was lessened by reduced reserve requirements. Membership was not even required because national banks could switch to state charters, and opposition from state banks was circumvented by making Fed membership voluntary. Few joined, although they would be disappointed if they hoped to escape the consequences of the new institution. No one would survive the Fed's control of money unscathed. Progressive feelings were assuaged by government currency and the central "capstone."

Outlook for the new institution

The novelty of the Fed meant that it lacked the knowledge of an evolving institution. Its creation preempted the traditional crisis responses of clearing houses and investment bankers without itself stepping into the breach, leaving a gap that was revealed in the Great Depression (Friedman and Schwartz 1963: 267–268, 311–312; Timberlake 1993: 198–213). The large banks did not foresee the contradictions in their support of the Fed, including the threat to their interest in economic stability implicit in its powers. Congressmen of both parties warned that good intentions were not enough. California Republican Everis Hayes complained that many of the Fed's advocates had only a superficial book knowledge of the subject, "not supplemented by any practical business or banking experience. These men generally became enamored of some foreign system … which would if adopted here be wholly revolutionary in character and … not at all adapted to our conditions."

> Any person studying this most important and complex subject should bear constantly in mind one fundamental and controlling fact, namely, every banking and currency system worthy of the name is an evolution brought about by the efforts of the bankers, legislators, and businessmen of the different countries to meet the commercial needs of the people. Unlike Minerva, who sprang miraculously and instantly perfect from the brain of Jove, no one of these systems came complete from the brain of any one man or set of men. All these systems … have gradually grown up from more imperfect beginnings to their present state of perfection and usefulness.... Each … is adapted to the conditions, habits, traditions, sentiments, and business needs of the people whom it serves.
>
> (*Congressional Record*, September 10, 1913)

Hayes preferred to "legalize and enlarge the present clearing-house associations under proper governmental regulation," although it must be admitted that the unprecedented natures of many future problems proved beyond intelligent responses even of the seasoned central banks. Before the final vote, Glass responded to accusations of big-bank control:

> no sense of acquisitiveness prompts [the Federal Reserve Board's] operations; no banking interest is behind, and no financial interest can pervert or control it. It is an altruistic institution, a part of Government itself, representing the American people, with powers such as no man would dare misuse.
>
> (*Congressional Record*, December 10, 1913)

The President called the system "a democracy of credit" directed by "a public board of disinterested officers of the Government" (Wilson 1914). The trusting natures of Wilson and Glass differed from the precautions of earlier generations, although not everyone in Congress was thoughtless of interests and incentives. Republican Frank Mondell of Wyoming warned that Congress was being asked to consider a radical departure, "the most powerful banking institution in all the world," with "the control and management of the banking and the credits of this country," with little thought about how those powers would be exercised. The framers of the bill are "flamboyantly eloquent in their declarations ... that the people, through their Government, alone have the right to control the issue of currency and supervise the business of banking. The gentlemen may as well save themselves that kind of effort, for they will fool nobody whose opinion is worthwhile." Supervision "so far as is necessary for the benefit and protection of all the people" is generally accepted. However, "The people pretty clearly understand nowadays that control through a Government bureau, by political appointees, is not synonymous with control by the people and for the people. Neither do people of ordinary intelligence confuse regulation and management. We regulate the railroads, we do not manage them. We regulate the packing of meats, we do not appoint the men who run the business" (*Congressional Record*, September 10, 1913).

Speaker Champ Clark assured the House that presidents would "appoint men only of ability, character, and patriotism on the Federal reserve board, and then keep close watch on them to the end that all the people may be treated impartially and that our prosperity may increase." Mondell replied for the minority and the nineteenth century when he pleaded for a self-regulating system under the law. The

> Speaker unwittingly suggests the strongest argument against the proposed plan when he [takes] the view that it is wise or necessary to add to the present tremendous power of the presidential office a further "stupendous trust" which he can only hope to properly fulfill by keeping a "close watch" on his appointees.
>
> (*Congressional Record*, September 10, 1913)

House Majority Leader Oscar Underwood declared that the issue "resolved itself into faith in the President's Board, the whole question being whether the board was angel or devil." So the President controlled the Board, Texas Democrat Oscar Callaway ridiculed, and the board and banks controlled the currency. But "Where," he asked, "will the people come in? We are told to ask no questions; have faith, simple faith.... Faith, faith, faith; faith in man, fallible man, swept by all the passions, prejudices, and ambitions, mental misgivings, shortsightedness, and misconceptions of man." The country had experienced discretionary government, and "Who usually gets a hearing, the man on the ground or the trusting man?" (*Congressional Record*, September 16, 1913) These fears were soon realized by the government's seizure of the Fed for war finance.

Early years, 1913–22

The Fed's powers resided in its control of the monetary base (currency and bank reserves) by means of open-market operations in government securities and the rediscounting of banks' commercial paper. That power was supposed to be limited by the gold standard, which was affirmed by the Federal Reserve Act (Sec. 13, 14, 26). However, the gold reserve ratio on Federal Reserve notes was insufficient for stability when gold inflows in payment for war materials and safekeeping enabled a vast increase in Fed credit. The Fed sowed the seeds of the Great Depression by doubling money and prices between 1914 and 1920, which under the gold standard had to be reversed. Figure 2.1 shows that the rise and fall in price levels between 1914 and 1932 duplicated other war and postwar experiences (Mazumder and Wood 2013).

The "discount window" was part of Warburg's plan to recast American credit markets in the European mold, although he was behind developments even in Europe. Borrowers increasingly preferred direct credit relations with their banks, and observers wondered at the Federal Reserve Act's attempt to "change the commercial credit practices of this country in directions thought to be an improvement" (Harr and Harris 1936: 433). The lack of eligible paper was cited by Fed officials as an obstacle to credit expansion during the Great Depression (although this was disputed by Friedman and Schwartz 1963: 399–406), and was supplemented by ordinary Fed lending to banks by a Congress eager for more money (in the Glass–Steagall Act of 1932), although the process continued to be referred to as the discount window.

The Fed's finance was principally decided and executed by the 12 Reserve Banks under the supervision of the Board in Washington, although lines of authority were unclear (Wood 2005: 189–191). Reserve Bank governors (called presidents after the Banking Act of 1935) were (and are) chosen by their directors. There were (and are) nine directors divided into three classes: *A* chosen by stock-holding banks; *B* representing commerce, agriculture, and industry; and *C* chosen by the Board to represent the public. In addition to making discount rate recommendations subject to the approval of the Board, the directors choose representatives to a Federal Advisory Council that advises the Board (Havrilesky 1993: 251–284).

The original Board (Table 4.1) had seven members: the Secretary of the Treasury and comptroller of the currency, ex officio, and five (increased to six in 1922) appointed by the President, subject to the approval of the Senate, for rotating ten-year terms. They took their elasticity assignment seriously. Pressures on bank reserves came during seasons of high loan and currency demands, when interest rates tended to be higher, and panics more frequent. The Board's first *Annual Report* (1914) addressed "the proper place and function of the Federal Reserve Banks in our banking and credit system," and concluded that

> Its duty is not to await emergencies but by anticipation, to do what it can to prevent them. So also if, at any time, commerce, industry or agriculture are,

in the opinion of the Federal Reserve Board, burdened unduly with excessive interest charges, it will be the clear and imperative duty of the Reserve Board acting through the discount rate and open market powers, to secure a wider diffusion of credit facilities at reasonable rate.... The more complete adaptation of the credit mechanism and facilities of the country to the needs of industry, commerce, and agriculture – with all their seasonal fluctuations and contingencies – should be the constant aim of a Reserve Bank's management.

The seasonal in interest rates was replaced by one in Fed credit (Miron 1986).

The Fed also supported price cartels. New York City banks had long tried to suppress rate competition for deposits from the interior, and in February 1918, the Federal Reserve Board asked members of the New York Clearing House to tie their deposit rates to the Fed's discount rate (Sprague 1910: 385–386). The March *Federal Reserve Bulletin* expressed regret over the aggressive competition for deposits that threatened to "put the banking system upon an unprofitable basis, thereby weakening our entire banking structure." The Board wished "it understood that it does not favor any movement to increase these rates and that it will do all in its powers to discourage it." It is notable that at the same time the Fed was producing double-digit inflation.

Rate competition continued and legal support of collusion came in the Banking Act of 1933, which prohibited interest on demand deposits and empowered the

Table 4.1 The first Federal Reserve Board

Years of initial appointment	Member and years of service	Background
	William Gibbs McAdoo	Secretary of Treasury, 1913–18
	John Skelton Williams	Comptroller of Currency, 1914–21
10	Adolph Miller, 1914–36	Professor of economics; assisstant to Secretary of the Interior
8	W.P.G. Harding, 1914–22	Commercial banker
6	Frederic Delano, 1914–18	Railroad executive
4	Paul Warburg, 1914–18	Investment banker
2	Charles Hamlin, 1914–36	Lawyer; assisstant Secretary of Treasury

Source: *Who's Who in America; Federal Reserve Bulletin*, September 1988.

Notes
FR Act, Sec. 10: In selecting the five appointive members, not more than one shall be from any FR district, and the president shall have due regard to a fair representation of the commercial, industrial, and geographical divisions of the country.

Members shall be ineligible during the time they are in office and for two years thereafter to be employed by any member bank.

Of the five appointed, at least two shall be experienced in banking or finance; and one shall be designated by the president as governor (and executive officer) and one as vice governor.

A 1922 amendment added a sixth member and "financial and agricultural" to the "divisions" represented.

Hamlin reappointed 1916 and 1926, Miller 1924 and 1934, term ended by Banking Act of 1935.

Fed to set ceilings on rates on time deposits. Those ceilings were often evaded and eventually eliminated as rates rose after World War II (Wood and Wood 1985: 31–41).

Monetary policy during the Great Depression of 1929–33 tends to be characterized as the Fed's "great mistake," as if that period saw a deviation from normally constructive Fed behavior. In fact, it was just the greatest of several destabilizing performances during its first quarter century, sometimes under government pressure. Monetary policy during the war was described by the Federal Reserve Board's director of research:

> [T]he Federal reserve banks were guided in their rate policy chiefly by the necessity for supporting the Treasury. The level of discount rates was kept low and preferential rates were granted on loans secured by Government obligations ... and the discount rate was thus not used as a means of credit control – but as a method of helping the Government to raise the funds necessary for the prosecution of the war.
>
> (Goldenweiser 1925: 40)

Any doubt of support was removed by the Overman Act of 1918, which authorized the President, "for the national security and defense, for the successful prosecution of the war ... to make such a redistribution of function among executive agencies as he may deem necessary."

Less clear was when monetization of the deficit would no longer be the chief end of monetary policy. The war ended in November 1918, but the Treasury's desire for cheap borrowing continued. Although the Board considered rate increases in January 1919, the Treasury was in the midst of a conversion of short-term to long-term debt, and "There was considerable sympathy within the Board for the problems facing the Treasury" (Wicker 1966: 30). Board Chairman W.P.G. Harding (1925: 148) wrote in reply to Reserve Bank requests for rate increases in April that the Secretary of the Treasury (now Carter Glass, who presumably would have denied the Fed's powers were being "misused") had communicated to him that the "failure" of the government's loans "would be disastrous for the country. The Board, therefore, did not approve any advance in rates." Requests were denied again in July. Assistant Secretary of the Treasury Russell Leffingwell (1921) said the Treasury was "honor bound" to avoid inflicting capital losses on the patriotic citizens who had financed the war effort.

Fed officials apparently felt they had to take account of the "strong outcry in Congress for the protection of the interests of holders of ... Liberty loans," although the New York Fed's Benjamin Strong had "a feeling – possibly because I do not live in the atmosphere of Washington – that it could have been resisted" (US Congress 1922: 503–504; Wicker 1966: 34; Strong 1930: 87). The Board sided with the Treasury in 1919 despite Strong's threat of a public protest unless a discount-rate increase was approved. Strong believed that attempts to ration credit by non-price means were futile, whereas Leffingwell urged that it be checked by "a firm discrimination in making loans." He was "weary of the copybook texts" which claimed that credit was reduced by making it more expensive (Wicker 1966: 37–38). Glass asserted the Board's complete power over discount rates, and threatened to ask the President to remove Strong (Chandler 1958: 163).

Glass came to regret his actions, and as US senator, in the interests of Fed independence, was able through the Banking Act of 1935 to drop the Secretary of the Treasury (and the comptroller of the currency) from the Federal Reserve Board. Leffingwell, as a partner in J.P. Morgan & Co., urged President Truman to end the cap on interest rates after World War II (Chernow 1990: 491).

Increases in the discount rate – from 4 to 6 percent between November 1919 and January 1920 – came after the Treasury informed the Fed that its support of the government bond market was no longer required. The Fed was also concerned for its gold reserve. The law provided for taxes on the Reserve banks if their reserves fell below 40 percent of Federal Reserve notes. The January rate increase coincided with the peak in business activity, but it was raised again in June (Chandler 1958: 162; Goldenweiser 1925: 90).

The 60-percent fall in Fed credit in 1920–1 was matched by that in prices, and the contraction of output was one of the sharpest in history. Chairman Harding later defended the Fed against "the contention that ... rates should have been substantially lowered in April or May, 1920." The drastic falls abroad required a "corresponding fall of prices in this country," he said. Furthermore:

> The United States was a free gold market, and had it remained at the same time the cheapest money market in the world, our financial structure would have been subject to the severest strain. The Board in that event would have been forced to suspend the reserve requirements, which would probably have resulted in the presentation of large amounts of Federal Reserve notes for redemption in gold for hoarding, which would have reduced reserves still further. In such circumstances prices would have been sustained only in terms of irredeemable paper money.
>
> (Harding 1925: 165–166)

The Fed gave precedence to its gold reserve over economic stability rather than following the Bank of England's historic strategy of short-term stability enabled by its long-term credibility. It might be claimed as an excuse that the new institution had not had the time to build a reputation. On the other hand, matters did not improve the next decade, when payments and prosperity continued to take a back seat to financial ratios.

The Fed's first peacetime actions were heavily criticized. The Joint (congressional) Commission of Agricultural Inquiry reported (US Congress 1922, Pt. 2: 7, 12, 44):

> The debacle of prices in 1920 and 1921 reduced the farmer to a condition worse than he has suffered under for 30 years.... Farm indebtedness has doubled in the last 10 years, and the drop in prices has the effect of again

doubling this indebtedness. Farmers are having the greatest difficulty in paying the debts incurred in producing the crops of 1920 and in securing credit necessary for new production.

The committee believed that these difficulties were due "to the credit restrictions and limitations of the past 18 months," which followed from the earlier subordination of Federal Reserve discount policy "to the Treasury policy in securing its credit requirements."

It is the opinion of the commission that a policy of restriction of loans and discounts by advances in the discount rates of the Federal Reserve banks could and should have been adopted in the early part of 1919, notwithstanding the difficulties which the Treasury Department anticipated in floating the Victory loan if such a policy were adopted.

The lesson of this experience, the report concluded, was that "the discount policy of the Federal Reserve should not have yielded to the apprehension of the Treasury Department." Congress' support of the Fed – after the fact, it should be noted – may have contributed to the reluctance of the President and Congress to interfere with monetary policy during the coming emergency (Wood 2005: 172–174).

This was the first of several times that Congress asserted its authority or supported the Fed's independence after a period of Executive dominance. The Treasury took control of monetary policy during the economic emergency of 1933, and kept it until 1951, when Congress again helped the Fed regain control, and Congress reacted to the Fed's submission to the President in the early 1970s with new forms of monitoring later in that decade (Havrilesky 1993: ch. 3). It remains to be seen whether, and if so, how, the present (2014) subservience will be addressed.

The "high tide" of the Fed, 1923–8

The US economy (except agriculture) boomed between 1921 and 1929, although it was surrounded by a world of deflationary pressures. Inflation abroad had made a strong dollar, reinforced by the growth in American gold reserves from 27 to 44 percent of the world's total. When the United Kingdom "returned to gold" in 1925, by restoring the pre-war dollar parity of the pound ($4.86), it expected (or hoped) their tight monetary policy would be relieved by easy money in America on the basis of its increased gold. International cooperation was much discussed, but American inflation did not materialize (Moggridge 1972: 27; Clarke 1967).

Benjamin Strong spoke for Federal Reserve policy when he said:

I believe that it should be the policy of the Federal Reserve System, by the employment of the various means at its command, to maintain the volume of credit and currency in this country at such a level so that, to the extent that the volume has any influence upon prices, it cannot possibly become the means for either promoting speculative advances in prices, or of a depression of prices.

(Benjamin Strong, speech to the Farm Bureau Convention, December 13, 1922 (Chandler 1958: 200))

The price level was about the same in 1929 as 1921–2, and its variance was among the lowest in American history, before or after the 1920s. The method was a monetary base rule. In June 1923, Strong wrote to Professor Charles Bullock:

If I were Czar of the Federal Reserve System I'd see that the total of our earning assets did not go much above or below their past year's average, after deducting an amount equaling from time to time our total new gold imports.

(Chandler 1958: 191)

Figure 4.1 shows the Fed's sterilization of gold, which continued into the 1930s, when the world changed so that what was consistent with price stability until 1929 was disastrous in succeeding years.[3]

Some economists and legislators wanted to make price stability an explicit goal of monetary policy, notably Keynes (1923) and Irving Fisher (1920). In 1922, Maryland Congressman Alan Goldsborough introduced a bill based on Fisher's proposal for a "compensated dollar" – derided by critics as the "rubber dollar" – in which the price of gold would be linked to a commodity price index. If the index rose, the price of gold would be reduced in the same proportion, and

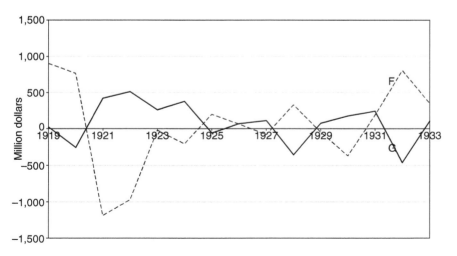

Figure 4.1 Changes in Federal Reserve credit (F) and gold (G), 1919–33.

the lower value of gold reserves would force an anti-inflationary monetary contraction. The bill did not attract much support at the time, but another effort passed the House in 1932 by a vote of 289–60 before its suppression in the Senate.

A 1926 bill would have required the discount rate to be set "with a view to accommodating commerce and promoting a stable price level for commodities in general. All of the powers of the Federal reserve system shall be used for promoting stability in the price level" (Krooss 1969: 2667). Strong and his colleagues desired stable prices and admitted the Fed's considerable influence, but resisted full responsibility. Such an unqualified objective interfered with other goals, financial stability in particular. Strong wrote to his economics research staff in 1923:

> Now I don't like to talk about stabilizing gold, the purchasing power of money, or prices being stabilized by the Federal Reserve System, at all. It is bound to lead to confusion, heartburn and headache....
>
> *Our job is credit.* It makes no difference if it's a deposit or a bank note. If we regulate and keep fairly constant the volume of this credit, – always with due regard to gold imports and exports, which is a part of the credit problem – we are doing our whole duty. Other price influences may then be dealt with by [Secretary of Commerce] Hoover, *et al.* They are not our job. Of course we should watch prices – and production and consumption and speculation, and lots of things – to insure that our "play" is correct in regulating volume. To come boldly forward, and volunteer to take the price problem onto our backs, and then *fail*, as we would surely do – is just criminal suicide.
>
> (Chandler 1958: 202–203)

Even if it is assumed, Strong said, possibly thinking of the "quantity theory extremists" of whom he complained, that the Fed

> has the power to raise or lower the price level by some automatic method, by some magic mathematical formula, what safeguards are we going to introduce in regard to ignorance, stupidity, and bad judgment in the exercise of this power? How are we to deal with the problem of divided counsels in the system, where no action is possible because of differences of opinion?

He also feared that such power would be the object of irresistible political pressures. What is the appropriate price index? The obligation to fix prices will be interpreted by each group as an obligation to "fix their prices" (Chandler 1958: 203; US Congress 1926: April 8).

Under "such a mandate," he had written to Professor Bullock in 1923,

> Within the past six months or so we would first have gone to jail for high sugar prices, and as soon as out on bail, been rearrested for low wheat prices

(not to mention gasoline, building costs, wages, freight rates, professors'
salaries and such like).

(Chandler 1958: 203)

His fears were realized in the proposer of the 1926 stable-price bill, Kansas Congressman James Strong, who wished to validate the wartime commodity price
inflation for his indebted constituents. "Our yardstick has a stable number of
inches and our money should be stabilized in its purchasing power," he told the
House. "The price level now stands at 160, a drop from 251," referring to
the wholesale price index at its peak in 1920 rather than the 160 of mid 1916 or the
100 of 1913 (US Congress 1926: January 18).

Sixty years later, during another agricultural depression, another Kansan
urged that monetary policy be directed at the stabilization of a basket of commodity prices. At his "confirmation hearing before the Senate Banking Committee," Wayne Angell's "voice rose in indignation – nearly cracking at one
point – when he described how sagging farm prices were affecting agricultural lenders. (He was part owner of a farm and two banks before joining the
Fed.)" Angell had been a state legislator, and after failing in a bid for the
Republican nomination to the US Senate, Senate Majority Leader Robert
Dole, also of Kansas, "vigorously lobbied the White House" for him as "a
perfect candidate to represent agriculture on the Board" (*Wall Street Journal*
April 24, 1986).[4]

Although farm and oil prices fell, the Consumer Price Index continued its
rise, and the new Fed Chairman Alan Greenspan followed in Benjamin Strong's
footsteps when he told a congressional committee:

We must ... be wary of special factors that may affect the prices of individual commodity price averages significantly in the short run. Especially
when the causes are of a transitory character – for example, a temporary
supply disruption – the proper macroeconomic policy responses may well
be different from those appropriate to major cyclical booms in commodity
markets. For this reason the coverage of any index used in the international
context should be broad.

(*Federal Reserve Bulletin* February 1988: 104).

It should be noted that the prices of farm products and fuel fell 12 and 30
percent, respectively, between 1981 and 1986, while the Producer Price Index
rose 2 percent, and the CPI and the GNP deflator rose 23 percent (US Department of Commerce, *Business Statistics, 1963–91*). Nevertheless, Angell joined
with another new Board member and two oddly named "supply-siders" in a 4–3
vote for a reduction in the discount rate – "much to [Chairmen Volcker's
(Volcker and Gyohten 1992: 274)] surprise and for motives I still do not fully
understand." Although shortly reversed, this palace revolt while Volcker was
negotiating a joint policy with other central banks illustrates the vulnerability of
even the semi-independent Fed of the 1980s.

The Great Depression, 1929–33

> To imagine that at the centre of the intricate web of man's economic activities stand a few constructive and controlling intelligences is to entertain a romantic illusion. There are no such Olympians. The intricate system of finance has been built and is operated by thousands of men, of keen but limited vision, each working within the limits of his own special sphere. For the most part the system has constructed itself from the separate work of specialists who built into the environment they found about them. Those who have made and worked this system have normally not understood it as a whole, those who have come nearest to understanding it, the academic economists [he gave us too much credit], have not made it and do not direct it. The economic and financial structure under which we have grown up is indeed more like one of the marvelously intricate structures built by the instincts of beavers or ants than the deliberately designed and rational works of man.
>
> (Salter 1932: 13)

The Great Depression is memorable for several reasons, not least as the occasion of the Fed's greatest failure as well as a much-cited source of lessons for modern policies. We need to look closely at the period to determine whether the Fed, and the rest of us, have learned the right lessons.

The end of the boom

The Dow Jones Industrial Average tripled between August 1921 and February 1928, and doubled the next year and a half to its peak in September 1929. When in February 1929 the New York Reserve Bank requested approval to raise its discount rate, the Board refused and advised direct pressure. Washington continued to rely less on market forces and more on nonmarket interventions than the Reserve Banks, a tendency that still prevails. The Board advised that "a member bank is not within its reasonable claims for rediscount facilities at its Federal reserve bank when it borrows ... for the purpose of making speculative loans," and asked the Reserve Banks for reports

> (a) as to how they keep themselves fully informed of the use made of borrowings by their member banks, (b) what methods they employ to protect their institution against the improper use of its credit facilities by member banks, and (c) how effective these methods have been.
>
> (Federal Reserve Board *Annual Report* 1929: 3;
> Friedman and Schwartz 1963: 257)

It can't be done, the Banks replied (Chandler 1958: 156–157).

> *Roy Young (Minneapolis)*: I think that they can be controlled to a certain extent, but when it comes to the final analysis, there really is no control.

You can ask the banks what they want to use the money for, and they can camouflage their reply more or less and, in making their reply, they do not mind making any statement, because, in their own minds, they are making a right statement.

E.F. Fancher (Cleveland): I think that close inquiry of the borrowing banks as to what the funds are used for ... will have some effect but it will not right the situation we now face. Any curtailment of credit is bound to bring higher interest rates.

Richard L. Van Zandt (Dallas): We have tried it out for a year and a half. We have admonished the banks, and have withheld credit at times from those that cannot explain satisfactorily uses of the funds which they want to borrow, and while that has some effect, it is not what you would call effective in any way.

In April, the Board suggested that the "desire to see money rates at a lower general level" arose not only from the "bad effects [of high rates] on domestic business," but also from an "unwillingness to draw gold from abroad" (*Federal Reserve Bulletin* April 1929).[5]

At ten subsequent meetings, the last on May 23, 1929, the New York Bank directors voted to raise discount rates.... Each time, the Board disapproved, though by a steadily narrowing margin – on February 14, the final vote by the Board was unanimously adverse; on May 23, the adverse vote was 5 to 3.

(Friedman and Schwartz 1963: 259)

Before the Board could be moved, signs of an economic slowdown caused the Reserve Banks to back away from their requests for higher rates. The stock market was still advancing, but on May 31 the New York Bank wrote to the Board: "In view of recent changes in the business and credit situation ... it may soon be necessary: To establish a less restrictive discount policy [and] be prepared to increase the Federal Reserve bank portfolios." On August 9, the Board approved New York's compromise plan to raise its discount rate to 6 percent "as a warning against the excessive use of credit" and to encourage member banks to reduce their indebtedness to the Fed, but also to increase Fed credit by open market purchases (Wicker 1966: 139–140; Friedman and Schwartz 1963: 264).

The jump in US interest rates reversed international capital flows. US net lending fell from over $1,000 million in 1927 to under $700 million in 1928, and became negative in 1929. Service of the massive dollar loans forced monetary contractions abroad (Eichengreen 1992: 224–226).

What was the Fed's model during the Great Depression, and did it learn from its mistakes?

It is widely agreed that the Fed failed in the Great Depression, although whether because of sins of omission or commission, for causing the money stock to fall by one-third between 1929 and 1933, or for failing to contest a fall due to other causes, is not settled (Friedman and Schwartz 1963: 362–419; Temin 1976). Nor is there consensus about the reasons for its behavior. We hear of "lessons of the Great Depression," followed by a pitch for preferred policy, usually Keynesian or monetarist, but there can be no lessons until we understand why the Fed behaved as it did. Better monetary policy requires an understanding of what needs to be improved, and – this is my point – whether that is possible without changing policymakers' incentives. It is less a question of monetary rules than of incentives to be guided by one rule or another. We will see that the answers to the questions at the top of this paragraph are, respectively, "much like today's" and "no."

In discussions of monetary policy during the Great Depression, the Fed's policy guide, depending on the writer, was the fallacious real bills doctrine, a confusion of market and natural rates of interest, the liquidation of speculative excesses, an obsession with the stock boom, misperceived constraints of the gold standard, or a narrow focus on financial stability. The following survey confronts these six policy models with the data in order to determine which, if any, explained monetary policy. It ends with an argument that the importance of the gold standard to the Great Depression, although increasingly appreciated in recent years, remains understated. The period of analysis is from 1922, when the Fed became a free agent, that is, after the Treasury released it from the obligation to support bond prices and the economy went through the postwar boom and bust, through 1932, after which the New Deal took control.

1 The real bills doctrine

> if only "real" bills are discounted, the expansion of bank money will be in proportion to any extension in trade that may take place, or to the "needs of trade," and ... when trade contracts, bank loans will be correspondingly paid off.... I shall designate these ideas as "the real-bills doctrine."
>
> (Mints 1945: 9)

The real bills doctrine asserts that changes in the quantity of money leave prices unchanged if money is created in the process of bank extensions of credit for the purchase of goods, i.e., in the context of nineteenth-century institutions, when bank credit consists of real bills of exchange. Self-liquidating paper money (M) thus rises with goods (output, y), and falls as they are consumed and the loans paid. Capital goods are assumed to be financed in the capital markets, that is, by the exchange of existing money balances.

An early application of the real bills doctrine was John Law's eighteenth-century land bank in France. The classic criticism is Thornton's (1802: 342), who said there was no unique relation between money and goods. "Mr. Law ... forgot ... that the increasing quantity [of paper] would contribute to the rise of commodities; and the rise of commodities require, and seem to justify, a still further increase."[6] The equation of exchange when money is created by loans proportionally to the expected value of goods is

$$MV = Py \text{ or } (aP^ey)V = Py \text{ or } P = aVP^e$$

The price level is undetermined. It is proportional to its expectation.

The Fed's commitment to the real bills doctrine in its early years is often alleged, as is the claim that the doctrine was written into the Federal Reserve Act.[7] Superficial support exists for both claims, but closer examination reveals that the Act and Fed practice deviated substantially from the doctrine. Beginning with the former, Section 13 ("Powers of Federal Reserve Banks") of the Act stated:

> Upon the indorsement of any of its member banks ..., any Federal reserve bank may discount notes, drafts, and bills of exchange arising out of actual commercial transactions; that is, notes, drafts, and bills of exchange issued or drawn for agricultural, industrial, or commercial purposes.

The gold standard still held. "Nothing in this Act ... shall be construed to repeal the parity provision" (a dollar consisting of 25.8 grains of gold, 9/10 fine) of the Gold Standard Act of 1900. Federal Reserve notes were redeemable in gold, and gold reserves were required against Fed notes and deposits. Bank credit and the price level were constrained by gold.

The Fed could have pursued the real bills doctrine for a while in spite of the Act. But here, too, the evidence indicates otherwise. Arguments over qualitative (real bills) and quantitative (interest rate) means of credit control existed at the Fed, but the latter, led by Benjamin Strong, prevailed. Timberlake argued that Fed behavior changed after Strong's death in 1928, and that the Board, led by Adolph Miller, assumed control and followed the real bills doctrine. However, in discussing "The real bills central bank in operation, 1929–33," Timberlake (2007) admitted that the Fed – "ironically" – refused loans even on "eligible paper." Other references to the real bills doctrine in the Federal Reserve Act and Fed policy are also accompanied by complaints of confusions and inconsistencies.[8] Monetarists identify the Fed's interest in credit rather than money as evidence of the real bills doctrine – without defining the doctrine – and find no consistency in consequence.

None of the claims that the Fed was guided by the real bills doctrine refers to the data. The first thing we would have to see, of course, is a constant discount rate, or at least invariant to bank credit. Figure 4.2 indicates that the Fed's discount rate varied with bank credit demands throughout the period, including 1929–32. In fact, as indicated in Table 4.2, the fall in short-term interest rates in 1929–32 exceeded those in previous twentieth-century recessions – nominally

Table 4.2 Inflation (*p*) in NBER expansions and contractions, and prime commercial paper rate (R_{CP}) and NY Fed discount rate (R_D) at peaks and troughs

Phase of business cycle		p	R_{CP}	R_d	Δp	ΔR_{CP}	ΔR_d	$\Delta R_{CP}/\Delta p$
E	12/00–9/02	3.68	6.17					
C	9/02–8/04	0.44	4.75		−3.24	−1.42		0.44
E	8/04–5/07	3.80	5.71					
C	5/07–6/08	−4.23	4.64		−8.03	−1.07		0.13
E	6/08–1/10	8.66	6.21					
C	1/10–1/12	−3.86	4.63		−12.52	−1.58		0.13
E	1/12–1/13	6.52	5.50					
C	1/13–12/14	−2.05	4.85		−8.57	−0.65		0.08
E	7/21–5/23	4.81	5.00	4.50				
C	5/23–7/24	−5.26	3.50	3.50	−10.07	−1.50	−1.00	0.15
E	7/24–10/26	1.77	4.38	4.00				
C	10/26–11/27	−2.89	4.00	3.50	−4.66	−0.38	−0.50	0.08
E	11/27–8/29	0.00	6.13	6.00				
C	8/29–3/33	−12.32	3.00	3.55	−12.32	−3.13	−2.50	0.25

Sources: *Standard Statistical Bulletin*, January 1932; Bureau of Labor Statistics release; Federal Reserve Board (1943).

Notes
E, expansion; C, contraction.

Table 4.3 Federal Reserve credit and the monetary gold stock, 1918–33 (annual averages, $ million)

	Federal Reserve credit					Gold stock[4]
	Bills discounted[1]	Bills bought[2]	US government securities	Other[3]	Total	
1918	1,134	287	134	168	1,723	2,871
1919	1,906	324	254	141	2,625	2,842
1920	2,523	385	324	158	3,390	2,582
1921	1,797	91	264	46	2,198	3,004
1922	571	159	455	41	1,226	3,515
1923	736	227	186	56	1,205	3,774
1924	373	172	402	49	996	4,152
1925	490	287	359	59	1,195	4,094
1926	572	281	350	55	1,258	4,165
1927	442	263	417	53	1,175	4,277
1928	840	328	297	40	1,505	3,919
1929	952	241	208	59	1,459	3,996
1930	272	213	564	38	1,087	4,173
1931	327	245	669	33	1,274	4,417
1932	521	71	1,461	24	2,077	3,952
1933	283	83	2,052	11	2,429	4,059

Source: Federal Reserve Board (1943).

Notes
1 Secured bank borrowing from the Fed.
2 Fed purchases of bills.
3 Mostly Fed float.
4 Held by the Treasury, the Fed, and as coin in circulation.

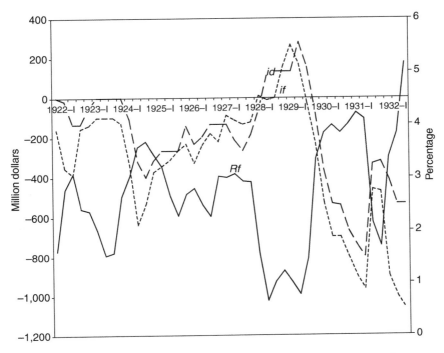

Figure 4.2 Fed discount rate (*id*), money market rate (*if*), and free reserves (*Rf*).

and, with one exception, as proportions of the rate of deflation.[9] Furthermore, Table 4.3 shows that US securities overtook discounts as a source of Federal Reserve credit in the Great Depression. The Fed might have been guilty of too much attention to credit as opposed to money; perhaps it should have injected more credit into the economy, and it is true that some officials expressed real-bills-doctrine-like sentiments, but policy was far removed from the real bills doctrine.

Allegiance to the doctrine has been exaggerated, Keith Horsefield (1946) observed in his review of Mints, who had admitted as much when he wrote that "it is not entirely clear why [real bills adherents] should have insisted upon the necessity of [paper/gold] convertibility."

2 Nominal and real rates of interest

It has been argued that the Fed misunderstood the historically low rates of interest during the Depression, believing they signified easy money while the deflation actually meant high real rates (Friedman and Schwartz 1963: 514; Brunner and Meltzer 1968; Meltzer 2003: 730). There may be considerable truth in this statement without its helping us understand the Great Depression. The main problem with treating interest rates as indicators of the monetary policies that caused the Great Depression is that their behavior, although unsatisfactory, was normal. Hawtrey's (1938: 208–222) theory of the business cycle was based on the Bank of England's tardy adjustments of Bank Rate to variations in its reserve, exacerbating excess demands in expansions and deficient demands in downturns. Irving Fisher (1922: 59–60, 271–273) saw the same relation, or lack thereof, between interest and prices in the United States, which in his pre-1911 sample had no central bank (also Wicksell 1898: 189). Table 4.2 shows that the Great Depression was no exception to the record.

3 Liquidation

The Fed has been accused of leaning towards the liquidationist approach to contractions which it believed were reactions to the excesses of previous booms (Meltzer 2003: 400). Lionel Robbins wrote: "Both in the sphere of finance and in the sphere of production, when the boom breaks, ... bad commitments are revealed. Now in order that revival may commence again, it is essential that these positions should be liquidated." Eichengreen wrote:

> Treasury Secretary Andrew Mellon's notorious advice to President Hoover to "Liquidate labor, liquidate stocks, liquidate the farmers, liquidate real estate ... purge the rottenness out of the system" neatly encapsulated the dominant view not only within the Treasury but on the Federal Reserve Board as well.
>
> (Robbins 1934: 118; Eichengreen 1992: 251; Hoover 1952: 30)

Liquidation overlaps the real bills doctrine when new bills fail to replace the expiration and default of existing bills. Hence the data that refuted the latter do the same to the former. Falling interest rates and increases in Fed credit (Tables 4.2 and 4.3; Figure 4.2), while not enough to suit monetarists, suggest that even if some officials sometimes inclined towards liquidation, monetary policy aimed at moderation. The Board's Adolph Miller complained to a Senate committee that the Fed's easy-money response to the 1927 recession was

> one of the most costly errors committed by it or any banking system in the last 75 years. I am inclined to think that a different policy at that time would have left us with a different condition at this time.... That was a time of business recession. Business could not use and was not asking for increased money at that time.
>
> (US Congress 1931: 134)

The Great Depression found the Fed's moderating tendencies still in effect. In June 1930, George Norris of the Philadelphia Reserve Bank objected to the Fed Open Market Policy Conference's policy of "abnormally low rates of interest" as an interference with the operation of the natural law of supply and demand in the money market.... We have been putting out credit in a period of depression, when it was not wanted and could not be used, and will have to withdraw credit when it is wanted and can be used.

(Friedman and Schwartz 1963: 372–373).

Hayek (1932) observed:

It is a fact that the present crisis is marked by the first attempt on a large scale to revive the economy ... by a systematic policy of lowering the interest rate accompanied by all other possible measures for preventing the normal process of liquidation, and that as a result the depression has assumed more devastating forms and lasted longer than ever before.

4 The Strong rule

Elmus Wicker (1969a) agreed with Karl Brunner and Allan Meltzer (1968) "that the period between 1922 and 1933 reveals a record of fundamental consistency and harmony with no sharp breaks in either the logic or interpretation of monetary policy."[10] This stability followed the guide outlined by Benjamin Strong in 1926.

As guide to the timing and extent of any purchases which might appear desirable, one of the best guides would be the amount of borrowing by member banks in principal centers, and particularly in New York and Chicago. Our experience has shown that when New York City banks are borrowing in the neighborhood of $100 million or more, there is then some real pressure for reducing loans, and money rates tend to be markedly higher than the discount rate. On the other hand, when borrowings of these banks are negligible, [and] member banks are owing us about 50 million dollars or less the situation appears to be comfortable.... In the event of business liquidation now appearing it would seem advisable to keep the New York City banks out of debt beyond something in the neighborhood of $50 million. It would probably be well if some similar rule could be applied to the Chicago banks, although the amount would, of course, be smaller and the difficulties greater because of the influence of the New York market.

(Chandler 1958: 240)[11]

The Strong rule became known as the free-reserves guide (excess reserves less bank borrowing from the Fed), and is presented as R_f in Figure 4.2, although it was dominated by borrowing until mid 1932.[12] The rule's/guide's importance through the 1920s and into the Great Depression is also evident in Table 4.4, where the regressions indicate that short-term rates varied inversely with free reserves. The rate on bankers' acceptances (i) is used as an indicator of short-term rates. The Fed's discount rate gives similar results. Lagged i is included to

Table 4.4 Estimates of the Strong rule, 1922.I–1932.IV (dependent variable: change in rate on bankers acceptances, i)

Const.	dR_f	dS	dG	di_{-1}	R^2/h
−0.03(0.44)	−2.27(6.42)			0.02(0.16)	0.52/0.49
−0.03(0.46)	−2.18(4.57)	−0.0002(0.19)	−0.20(0.27)	0.03(0.24)	0.49/0.69

Source: Federal Reserve Board (1943).

Definitions
d = change between quarters; R_f = average free reserves, billions of dollars; annual percentages of i, S (rate of change of S&P industrial common stock index), and G (ratio of excess to required gold reserve ratio on Fed liabilities; see Wood 2005: 175); absolute values of t statistics in parentheses; R^2 = coefficient of determination adjusted for degrees of freedom; h = Durbin's statistic for serial correlation with a lagged dependent variable (the hypothesis of no serial correlation is not rejected).

capture interest smoothing, although it was not statistically significant in this period.

The Fed's inactivity during the Great Depression has been attributed to Strong's death, but successors continued his policy. The Fed assisted the money market in the wake of the October 1929 crash, and when assistance was no longer required, that is, when the New York and Chicago banks were out of debt to the Fed, it was ended.

> It was [George] Harrison's [who succeeded Strong in 1928] opinion that so long as the New York member banks remained practically out of debt, there was no justification for forcing further funds upon the market. To this position he adhered unswervingly throughout 1930 and 1931.
>
> (Wicker 1966: 153; Wheelock 1991)

The Fed's disregard of the waves of regional bank failures during the Great Depression was not a failure to assist the money markets. This and the Fed's attention to those markets during and after the stock crash mean that complaints (Friedman and Schwartz 1963: 395; Meltzer 2003: 20) that the Federal Reserve neglected Bagehot's lender of last resort advice are unfounded.

The decline in bank borrowing (increase in free reserves, see Table 4.3 and Figure 4.3) from the Fed after 1929 was greater than in previous downturns, as, consistent with the Strong rule, was the Fed's interest-rate response. Harrison's reason for recommending the end of open-market purchases in July 1930 (even though M had fallen 10 percent and industrial production had fallen 20 percent since the previous October), was that the "principal New York City banks have paid off all their discounts here and at present have a surplus of reserves" (Meltzer 2003: 312). This time, the decline in borrowing was associated with a deeper fall in output than previously. "Unfortunately, as commonly used," James Meigs (1962: 87) wrote about another time, the free-reserves "doctrine has had a serious defect: There has been a tendency to interpret equal volumes of free reserves as having approximately equal influence on bank behavior at all times."

The Fed failed to consider the relations between bank borrowing and economic activity (Wheelock 1990).

5 The stock boom

Notwithstanding the attention it received, the evidence suggests that stock prices did not affect Fed policy directly. The rate of change in stock prices does not improve the explanation of the discount rate in Table 4.4.

6 Golden fetters

The effects of the gold standard on monetary policy were much discussed at the time and since, and we have seen the Fed's concern with its gold reserves while under pressure from the Treasury after World War I. However, evidence of a systematic direct effect between 1922 and 1932 is lacking (Figure 4.4). Although Fed spokesmen gave gold as a reason for the lack of monetary expansion (Eichengreen 1992: 293–298), policy continued to be described by the Strong rule. Like the stock market, any effect of gold on monetary policy was indirect through bank borrowing from the Fed to recover their reserves. As far as the direct effect of gold goes, Table 4.3 and Figure 4.2 indicate that Fed credit reinforced the gold inflow in 1931, and more than offset gold losses in 1932. Some suggest that the Fed need not have been constrained by the gold standard during the Great Depression – and it wasn't, at least any more than previously (Bordo *et al.* 2002; Hsieh and Romer 2006).

Central bank failures to understand the gold standard led to great mistakes in the United States and elsewhere. Under the gold standard, that is, a fixed gold content of the dollar, and an unchanged relative cost of production of gold, the dollar had to resume its pre-war level sometime. European countries seeking postwar resumption hoped to avoid deflation by economizing/sharing gold reserves. That failed, however, as reserve demands rose in the uncertain interwar environment. Furthermore, the necessary deflations were underestimated because they aimed at pre-war values relative to the US dollar – not taking into account the necessary increase in the value of that currency.[13]

The former deputy-governor of the Bank of France recalled the circumstances:

> The idea that such an enormous loss of the buying power of gold as resulted in the War and after the War, could be maintained, has always seemed to me chimerical.... Benjamin Strong ... was of quite another opinion. He thought that, with the big banks and the possibility of enormous credits, one would be able to maintain prices much better than one could do it before the war. I remember, however, his words during his last visit in Paris in 1928, [when, observing the European deflations and deflationary monetary policies] he admitted frankly: "Well, till now the facts have proved you right."
> (Rist 1931)

That a choice had to be made between the abandonment of gold, devaluation, or deflation was understood in 1813, 1864, and in a few countries outside the United States in the 1920s. However, even if the problem and its economic solution had been understood, a sensitive political structure and perhaps a little courage would have been required for action. "Does the board maintain that there is no emergency?" Chicago Congressman A.J. Sabath had to ask the remote and unresponsive Fed Chairman Eugene Meyer in 1931 (US Congress 1931: January 19).

These problems, political and economic, should have surprised no one, British civil servant Sir Arthur Salter wrote (see above) after several years of working with governments and central banks. "We have involved ourselves in a colossal muddle," Keynes (1930) wrote, "having blundered in the control of a delicate machine, the working of which we do not understand," and could have added, "or possess the incentives or will to try to escape from."

The Fed's model

The Fed's inactivity can be traced to the structure of the system as it was created in 1913. The agency to which Congress delivered its responsibility for money was true to its interests and perceptions. The New York Fed was sensitive to its immediate surroundings, the money market, and so was the Board, and they felt little political pressure, especially after Congress affirmed its independence in 1921.

The Fed's attitude toward the general economic distress bordered on the cavalier. We can appreciate its lack of understanding of the gold standard, whose operations were complicated by unprecedented conditions. However, we must be less sympathetic to the absence of a sense of urgency. Certainly anything that might have brought relief from the depression, even the suspension of convertibility in an economy reduced to barter, should have been considered. In April 1932, Congressman Thomas Jefferson Busby of Mississippi urged the Fed "to cooperate with Congress, and launch out and shake off some of its fears about what might happen" if it tried to stop the deflation.

> I do not know whether you know it or not, but about one-fourth of the homes in my state have been sold for taxes during the present month.... Sixty thousand homes, 7,000,000 acres of land, one-fourth of all the property, because the people can not pay taxes; and when people get in that kind of condition, they can not ... listen to fine-spun theories of fears that might arise in the event you took some step forward.

> *Gov. Harrison* – Of course, you know Mr. Congressman, that up until the end of February we did not have capacity to do what you wanted us to do. Now, then, if you have any criticism of us, I think it is only since the 1st of March –

Mr. Goldsborough – I do not think that is hardly fair, Governor, for this reason: That the Federal Reserve Board were urged to help Congress pass such legislation long before last February.

Perhaps further legislation was needed?

Mr. Harrison – I do not think there is any necessity for further legislation at the present time, if we could assume that the provisions of the Glass-Steagall bill are permanent, rather than limited to one year. That is unavoidably a restraining influence, certainly, on some of the managers of the system –

Mr. Busby – If you drive right up to the time when you need it, when you need any extension, Congress will be in session next year....

Considering the large gold reserve, Busby said, "I can not understand ... the Federal Reserve Board taking such hesitant uncertain or undeclared attitudes toward tackling the economic depression with which we are overwhelmed." Harrison replied that such action ran the risk "of flooding the market or the banks with excess reserves faster than they can use them, or faster than is wise for them to use them ...", and could disrupt the "orderly operation of the open market."

Under the pressures of a Senate resolution asking the Board to state its program and public complaints of its inaction by Treasury Secretary Ogden Mills, the Fed bought government securities while Congress was in session from April 6, 1932, until shortly after its adjournment on July 16 (US Congress 1932: 492–493; Friedman and Schwartz 1963: 385; Federal Reserve Board 1943: 386).

Lessons not learned

Direct lessons from the Great Depression for modern monetary policy have to be limited because of the different monetary structure in the earlier period (Mazumder and Wood 2013). The World War I inflation required deflation (or cheaper gold, which did not occur), which the Fed could not have held back forever short of suspension or devaluation. Only with the latter did the payments system and the economy recover. Credit programs such as the Reconstruction Finance Program were futile. The lesson for the Fed would seem to be concentration on supporting the economy by maintaining the payments system. Its failure to learn was recently demonstrated during the Great Recession by its attention, as in the Great Depression, to bailouts and credit allocation (Chapter 6).

Another important lesson not learned concerned the Fed's existence. Its presence was a large part of the reason why other institutions and branches of government did not intervene. Clearinghouse certificates and other bank actions and forbearances, including emergency suspensions and the organized interventions of private financial leaders such as J.P. Morgan, were missing, and even discouraged by officials. Banks wanting to ration deposit payouts were denied Fed assistance and threatened with closure (Friedman and Schwartz 1963: 357–359; Wicker 1996: 122–123).

The 71st and 72nd Congresses (1929–33) were probably no more divided on monetary matters than the 43rd (1873–5) and 53rd (1893–5). Nevertheless, the nineteenth-century bodies adopted strong monetary measures, the former by committing to a date for resumption and the latter by reversing its Democratic predilections when earlier silver legislation threatened the monetary standard. These were sound-money actions. On the other hand, the Republican 39th and 40th Congresses, which favored sound money *in principle*, yielded, as we saw, to "the great hosts" of debtors and creditors "outside of banking and financial centers," to slow Secretary McCulloch's application of the Contraction Act. These responses were a far cry from what can only be called the Fed's indifference during the Great Depression.

Significant minorities cried out. Over 50 bills to increase money and prices were introduced in the 72nd Congress, all unsuccessful as the majority continued to rely on what the President later called "a weak reed for a nation to lean on in time of trouble" (Krooss 1969: 2661–2662; Hoover 1952: 210, 212).

Another lesson, contained in the distribution of opinions within the Fed and too clear to miss, one might have thought, was turned on its head. Most of those in the Fed who favored a more aggressive monetary policy during the depression were Reserve Bank presidents, who were opposed by the Board. The greater responsiveness of the Reserve Banks to economic conditions is not difficult to understand, and has continued. However, the administration's 1935 bill that purported to make the Fed more sensitive to economic conditions increased the relative strength of the Board (Chappell and McGregor 2000; Wood 2005: 347–349).

In conclusion, the price shock of 1929–33 was caused by the World War I inflation without an appreciation of the necessity of either a price reversal or a change in the monetary standard. The Federal Reserve did not understand the system with which it had been entrusted. More fundamentally, it was unwilling (nor was Congress willing to direct it) to suspend the system. Unlike the Bank of England in the nineteenth century and American commercial banks during crises, it failed to put economic conditions ahead of adherence to accounting ratios. There was no incentive to do so. The Fed's separation from the interests of the public and their representatives prevented them from doing what anyone under genuine stress would have jumped at.

Treasury control, 1933–51

The end of the gold standard

Upon assuming the presidency on March 4, 1933, Franklin Roosevelt issued proclamations that closed and reopened banks and ended the internal circulation of gold. The first orders used emergency powers from World War I, and to remove doubt of their legality, the Emergency Banking Act of March 9, 1933, provided:

During time of war or during any other period of national emergency declared by the President, the President may, through any agency that he may designate, ... investigate, regulate, or prohibit ... any transactions in foreign exchange, transfers of credit between or payments by banking institutions as defined by the President, and export, hoarding, melting, or earmarking of gold or silver coin or bullion or currency, by any person within the United States or any place subject to the jurisdiction thereof.

On April 5, the President declared private gold to be "hoarding," and ordered it delivered to the Federal Reserve by May 1. The conservation of reserves by forbidding their internal use followed Ricardo's Ingot Plan that was adopted temporarily by Britain in the Resumption Act of 1819, and permanently in the Gold Standard Act of 1925.

The Thomas Amendment to the Agricultural Adjustment Act of May 12, 1933, further empowered the President to direct the Secretary of the Treasury to (a) enter into agreements with the Federal Reserve for the latter's purchase of US securities up to $3 billion, (b) issue US notes ("greenbacks") under the Act of February 25, 1862, (c) fix the weights of gold and silver dollars at such amounts as he finds necessary to stabilize domestic prices or to protect the foreign commerce against the adverse effect of depreciated foreign currencies, but not to reduce the weight of the gold dollar more than 50 percent, and (d) (as a sop to the silver interests) accept silver in payment of foreign government debts to the United States for a period of six months up to an aggregate of $200 million.

In a Fireside Chat on October 22, 1933, the President said the government's gold operations were part of a policy "to restore" commodity price levels. "The object," he continued

has been the attainment of such a level as will enable agriculture and industry once more to give work to the unemployed.... This is a policy and not an expedient. It is not to be used merely to offset a temporary fall in prices. We are thus continuing to move toward a managed currency.

A permanent revaluation of the dollar would wait until "we have restored the price level," after which "we shall seek to establish and maintain a dollar which will not change its purchasing and debt-paying power during the succeeding generation."

The permanent revaluation came in the President's proclamation of January 31, 1934, which fixed the value of gold at $35 an ounce, compared with the $20.67 an ounce that, except for 1862–78, had prevailed since 1834. Ninety-four percent of the three-fold increase in the monetary base between 1932 and 1941 came from gold as its production responded to its price.

The gold standard was not formally ended until President Richard Nixon "closed the gold window" in 1971, but it was irrelevant to policy after 1933. A constraint that has been relaxed, and is expected to be relaxed when it threatens to bind, is not a constraint. The legal gold requirements on Federal Reserve deposits and notes were terminated in the 1960s.[14]

These changes required that something be done about gold contracts, which were eliminated accordingly. Investors who thought they had protected their wealth by indexing discovered otherwise. Instead of protector, government was predator, and there is no defense against those who make the laws. Since the silver scares of the late nineteenth century, most corporate and government bonds had been indexed to gold. For example, Norman C. Norman owned a $1,000 bond of the Baltimore and Ohio Railroad (B&O) with interest of 4.5 percent payable semi-annually "in gold coin of the United States of America of or equal to the standard weight and fineness existing on February 1, 1930." This and other gold clauses were abrogated on June 5, 1933, when Congress resolved

> That every provision contained in … any obligation which purports to give the obligee a right to require payment in gold or a particular kind of coin or currency, or in an amount in money of the United States measured thereby, is declared to be against public policy.… Every obligation, heretofore or hereafter incurred, whether or not any such provision is contained therein … shall be discharged upon payment, dollar for dollar, in any coin or currency which at the time of payment is legal tender for public and private debts.

When, following the dollar's devaluation, the B&O sent Mr. Norman $22.50 for his coupon, he sued for the contracted value of the gold, now $38.10. The Supreme Court upheld the congressional resolution by a 5–4 vote in spite of the fact that, as Justice James McReynolds pointed out in his dissent:

> Over and over again [the United States] have enjoyed the added value which [the gold clause] gave to their obligations. So late as May 2, 1933, they issued to the public more than $550,000,000 of their notes each of which carried a solemn promise to pay in standard coin.

All the better for the purpose of the policy, Oklahoma Senator Elmer Thomas had said:

> the amendment, in my judgment, is the most important proposition that has ever come before the American Congress.… It may transfer from one class to another class in these United States value to the extent of almost $200,000,000,000. This value will be transferred, first, from those who own the bank deposits. Secondly, this value will be transferred from those who own bonds and fixed investments.… Two hundred billion dollars now of wealth and buying power rests in the hands of those who own the bank deposits and fixed investments bonds and mortgages. That $200,000,000,000 these owners did not earn, they did not buy it, but they have it, and because they have it the masses of the people of this Republic are on the verge of starvation – 17,000,000 on charity, in the bread line.

If the amendment carries and the powers are exercised in a reasonable degree, it must transfer that $200,000,000,000 in the hands of persons who now have it, who did not buy it, who did not earn it, who do not deserve it, who must not retain it, back to the other side – the debtor class of the Republic.

(73rd Cong., 1st sess., April 24, 1933)

Chief Justice Charles Evans Hughes' majority opinion acknowledged that the abrogation of the gold clauses was part of a government policy of redistribution through inflation. However, the Court was bound by "the constitutional power of the Congress over the monetary system" – specifically the power "to coin money and regulate the value thereof" under Article I, Section 8. Congress was entitled in the exercise of that power to do just about anything it wanted, including nullify contracts, Hughes said.

The contention that these gold clauses are valid contracts and cannot be struck down proceeds upon the assumption that private parties, and States and municipalities, may make and enforce contracts which may limit that authority. Dismissing that untenable assumption, the facts must be faced. We think that it is clearly shown that these clauses interfere with the exertion of the power granted to the Congress and certainly it is not established that the Congress arbitrarily or capriciously decided that such an interference existed

(*Norman* v. *B&O RR Co.* 294 U.S. 240 (1935))

Justice McReynolds dissented.

Just men regard repudiation and spoliation of citizens by their sovereign with abhorrence; but we are asked to affirm that the Constitution has granted power to accomplish both.... By the so-called gold clause ... the creditor agrees to accept and the debtor undertakes to return the thing loaned or its equivalent. Thereby each secures protection, one against decrease in value of the currency, the other against an increase.

He pointed out that the contracts had long been in use, had no sinister purpose, were well understood, had been found enforceable by the courts, and the government itself had "enjoyed the added value which it gave to their obligations." The "gold clauses in no substantial way interfered with the power of coining money or regulating its value or providing an uniform currency." The real purpose of Congress, under the guise of exercising its constitutional powers to regulate the currency, was to inaugurate "a plan primarily designed to destroy private obligations, repudiate national debts, and drive into the treasury all the gold in the country in exchange for inconvertible promises to pay, of much less value."

The majority may have been swayed more by the political climate than the Constitution. The atmosphere was one of crisis, and there was widespread feeling in government and the press that the enforcement of the estimated $100 billion of outstanding gold contracts would cause serious economic dislocations (Lippman 1933). Even the chief justice felt obliged to defend the Court's opinion on these grounds:

> It requires no acute analysis or profound economic inquiry to disclose the dislocation of the domestic economy which would be caused by such a disparity of conditions in which … those debtors under gold clauses would be required to pay one dollar and sixty-nine cents in currency while respectively receiving their taxes, rates, charges and prices on the basis of one dollar of that currency.

These fears were misguided. The payments would be distributed over several years, with most principal payments many years in the future. Consumer prices rose 69 percent between 1933 and 1946, and more than doubled by 1953. Bondholders would have suffered even if gold clauses had been enforced. The retention of those clauses would have reduced rather than raised unanticipated wealth transfers.

On the other hand, investors may have been unrealistic in expecting honesty from the government. Gold clauses were a common form of inflation protection under the gold standard, but had always been invalidated when they were most needed, including England in 1429, Venice in 1517, and scores of countries during the inflations of World War I and its aftermath. The United States was merely added to the list in 1933 (Nussbaum 1939: 586–591).

The Banking Act of 1935[15]

> One would have to go back to the days of the Aldrich bill and the original Federal Reserve act to encounter as much controversy over a piece of banking legislation as attended the proposed Banking act of 1935 in its journey through the House and Senate committees.
>
> (Bradford 1935)

Authored by the new Board chairman, Marriner Eccles, the administration's bill to centralize the Fed's power in a Board subordinate to the President easily passed the House. The bill gave the Board control of bank cash reserve requirements, subject to the approval of the President, and broadened the securities – "any sound assets" – eligible as backing for Fed loans. The latter step continued Congress' effort to liberalize Fed lending. The Glass–Steagall Act of 1932 had provided that banks with inadequate eligible paper could still borrow from the Fed. Commercial banks' power to lend on real estate was also broadened. The governor and vice-governor of the Board were to be appointed by the President to serve at his pleasure, and when dismissed, to be deemed to have served their full terms. The open-market committee that had been formed by the Reserve Banks in the 1920s, and recognized in the Banking Act of 1933, was reorganized to consist of the governor and two other members of the Federal Reserve Board and two from the Reserve Banks. It would be the Board's duty "to promote conditions conducive to business stability and to mitigate by its influence unstabilizing fluctuations in ... production, trade, prices, and employment" (Bradford 1935; Friedman and Schwartz 1963: 404–406).

However, the Senate, led by Carter Glass, "defender of the Fed," resisted significant change. Glass disapproved of the House bill because it proposed

> that the Federal Reserve banks be stripped of every particle of local self-government and that we should establish here in Washington practically a central bank, to be operated by people who are not bankers, and have no technical knowledge of the banking business. That suggestion was so repugnant to the original purpose of the Federal Reserve Banking System that those who propounded the suggestion soon found it convenient to abandon their indefensible attitude. If anything was deliberately and decisively determined in 1913, ... it was that this country did not want a central bank....
>
> Instead of a central banking system, the Congress decided to create a regional reserve banking system, upon the theory that the respective regions established would know better how to manage their own credits and to respond to the requirements of their own people than any central bank established either in New York or at Washington.
>
> (*Congressional Record*, 74th Cong., 1st sess., July 2, 1935)

Neither Glass's naivety regarding the purposes of the Fed nor his lack of disapproval of the Fed's behavior during the depression, probably because of his sense of proprietorship, prevented him from getting a conservative bill that largely preserved the Fed's structure. The Federal Open Market Committee entered the law and the Board was empowered to raise member bank reserve requirements up to double those existing. On the other hand, the House's macroeconomic objectives were erased, and not adopted until the Employment Act of 1946. However, Eccles got his way in the current membership of the Board. "It would do little good to change the structure of the Federal Reserve," he wrote, "unless new blood was brought in to run it." He compared Roosevelt's problems with the Supreme Court to the "four old men" of the Federal Reserve Board:

> throughout 1935 Roosevelt became progressively more irritated by the decisions of the Supreme Court, the character of which he attributed to the fact that so many of the justices were in their seventies. His general mood of annoyance with the "Nine Old Men" communicated itself to other quarters of the Government, and for similar reasons. The new currents in the land created by the depression seemed not to have touched many of the aged men who held key posts in various administrative bodies where long tenure was the rule.
>
> This was as true of the Federal Reserve Board as of other administrative agencies. Four out of the six [appointed] members of the Board were

approaching seventy or were in their seventies. The Vice Governor, John Jacob Thomas, was sixty-six; George Roosa James, who had been appointed by Harding, was seventy; Adolph C. Miller, who had been appointed by Wilson, was seventy; and Charles S. Hamlin, another Wilson appointee, was seventy-four.

(Eccles 1951: 235–236)

The Act ended the terms of existing members on February 1, 1936, enabling the President to appoint a Board entirely of his own choosing. FDR renamed Eccles and M.S. Szymczak, whom he had appointed earlier, and five new members. This is a convenient place to consider the policy implications of the distribution of power between the Reserve Banks and the Board.

The decision structure of the Federal Reserve

The federal structure of the American central bank is unusual, and although designed to give voice to all sections of the country and politically necessary to the Federal Reserve Act in 1913, has been called undemocratic. Bills have been introduced in Congress to eliminate the policy role of Reserve Bank presidents because they are not elected or appointed by the President (Wood 2005: 347). It is appropriate to look at the Banks' record in light of these complaints. Fed Chairman Greenspan said while defending the Fed's structure that more important than whether the Bank presidents "are viewed as more public than private or more private than public, the real question remains: Does their participation on the FOMC make for better monetary policy?" Answering in the affirmative, he said:

> The input of Reserve Bank presidents who reside in and represent the various regions of the country has been an extremely useful element in the deliberations of the FOMC. By virtue of their day-to-day location and their ongoing ties to regions and communities outside of the nation's capital, the presidents see and understand developments that we in Washington can overlook. They consult routinely with a wide variety of sources within their districts, drawing information from manufacturing concerns, retail establishments, agricultural interests, financial institutions, consumer groups, labor and community leaders, and others.
>
> (Statement to House Committee on Banking, Finance, and Urban Affairs, October 13, 1993, *Federal Reserve Bulletin*, December 1993)

Although not mentioned by Greenspan, the presidents might also be judged by their preferences. They have been more inclined than the Board, first, to work for price stability, and second, to do it through market forces, that is, through interest rates rather than by direct controls. They provided most of the support in the Fed for action during the Great Depression, resistance to the Treasury's pegs after both world wars, resistance to the Viet Nam inflation, Chairman Paul

Table 4.5 Average preferred interest rates estimated from FOMC votes, and net dissents for ease, 1966–96; Board governors and Bank presidents including those with experience as academic economists

	Governors	*Presidents*
Desired interest rate (all)	6.35%	7.05%
(Economists)	6.38%	7.27%
Net dissents for ease (all)	1	–8
(Economists)	–3	–20

Source: Chappell and McGregor (2000).

Volcker's (who had just come from the New York Fed) policy of letting interest rates be market-determined in 1979, and opposition to the inflation and massive interventions of the new millennium.

These differences are indicated by the estimates of Bank president and Board members' preferences in Table 4.5, which shows that the former were more willing to extinguish inflationary demands by interest rates, and to dissent on the side of tightness during inflations. The second and fourth rows of the table indicate that the greater proximity to markets and the public than the pressures of Washington affects economists as much as others.

Bank presidents have also been "democratically responsive" to conditions in their regions. High regional unemployment has been associated with votes for ease (Gildea 1992). The most democratic part of the Federal Reserve Act might be the Reserve Banks.

The Federal Reserve Board uses its new powers

In mid-1937, the economy had climbed a long way from the bottom of the depression. Production had grown 60 percent, nearly regaining its 1929 level. In other respects, recovery was far from complete. Unemployment exceeded seven million, compared with 13 million in 1933 and less than two million in 1929. Fixed investment was a third less than in 1929. The banking system's contribution to recovery was disappointing. After falling from $42 billion to $22 billion between June 1929 and June 1933, bank loans had stuck at the lower level. Annual bank failures counted in the dozens instead of the thousands as in 1930–3 or the hundreds as in the 1920s, but bankers remained cautious.

Another reflection of caution was banks' huge excess reserves (Figure 4.3), remembering that "excess" is a legal rather than an economic modifier. A bank's cash is a choice, based on its considerations of profit and prudence. So-called excess reserves are cash desired in excess of legal requirements. In June 1929, member-bank excess reserves were one-tenth of 1 percent of deposits and 2 percent of total reserves. In October 1935, they were 8 percent of deposits and 53 percent of reserves.

Bank reserves rose rapidly after 1933, with the "golden avalanche" of world gold production. They had little effect on bank credit, however, as most went

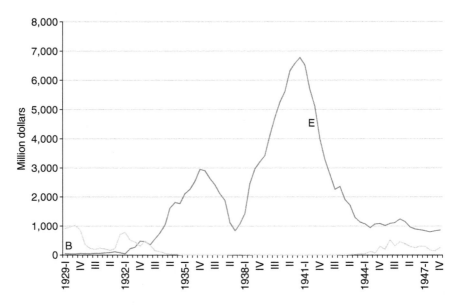

Figure 4.3 Member bank excess reserves and borrowings from the Fed, 1929–47.

into "excess." Depressed industry made loans unattractive, low bond yields raised the problem of capital losses if they returned to normal, and would be inadequate as "secondary reserves" if the unpredictable Fed tightened or gold flows were reversed. In any case, these securities were in short supply, and banks already held most of them (Cloos 1966; Cagan 1969).

The large excess reserves posed a "dilemma" – the word is a Fed official's – for monetary policy (Anderson 1968: 77). The Fed did not wish to hinder the recovery, but worried about the potential for inflation if banks decided to lend their excess reserves. They needed to be "mopped up." Raising discount rates would be ineffective because banks had no reason to borrow from the Fed. Nor would open-market operations do the job because excess reserves exceeded the Fed's portfolio of securities. The only feasible option seemed to be to exercise the Board's new power over reserve requirements. In October 1935, the FOMC announced:

> It was the unanimous opinion of the Committee that the primary objective of the System at the present time is still to lend its efforts towards the furtherance of recovery. While much progress has been made, it cannot be said that business activity on the whole is yet normal, or that the effects of the depression are yet overcome....
>
> But the Committee cannot fail to recognize that the rapid growth of bank deposits and bank reserves in the past year and a half is building up a credit base which may be very difficult to control if undue credit expansion should

become evident. [T]he Committee is of the opinion that steps should be taken by the Reserve System as promptly as may be possible to absorb at least some of these excess reserves, not with a view to checking some further expansion of credit, but rather to put the System in a better position to act effectively in the event that credit expansion should go too far.

(Anderson 1968: 79)

The Board waited several months – during which excess reserves remained large and a study group reported that even a doubling of reserve requirements, the maximum allowed by law, would leave substantial sums – before announcing a 50-percent increase in requirements, effective August 15, 1936 (*Federal Reserve Bulletin* August 1936). More increases came March 1 and May 1, 1937, bringing requirements to twice the levels of the previous summer. The first increase cut excess reserves (in billions) from $3.2 to $1.8. They recovered to $2.1 before being cut to $1.3 by the March action, and to $1.6 before the May action reduced them to $0.9. Just over a year later, they were $2.4 and in October 1938 had regained their August 1936 level (Figure 4.3). Bank loans fell 10 percent during the severe economic decline lasting from May 1937 to June 1938.

Fed officials failed to foresee, or even recognize, the connections between the increase in reserve requirements and the ensuing contraction. This was another potentially damaging failure to learn. The Fed's confident predictions of a smooth exit from the massive excess reserves accumulated by banks since 2008 reveal no institutional memory of 1936–8, or knowledge of the economics of finance, according to which portfolios anticipate and respond very rapidly – too rapidly for would-be regulators – to expectations of change (FOMC June 21–22, 2011).

The Fed did not accept that the excess reserves were bank choices, and indicated no feeling of responsibility for the recession (Meltzer 2003: 495–515). Of course a significant part of the cause must be attributed to fiscal policy. Social security "contributions" – an employment tax – began in January 1937, and "improved economic conditions through the first part of 1937 seemed to offer an opportunity at last to bring the budget into balance." Relief programs were cut and a tax was levied on undistributed profits (Myers 1970: 326). The Treasury saw retained earnings as evasion of taxes on dividends, and Eccles, more interested in fiscal than monetary policy, pushed for the tax because he thought it would stimulate demand by inducing firms to invest their earnings or pay dividends (Eccles 1951: 257–265; Lent 1948).

Money, prices, and output began to fall in the summer of 1937. The Federal Reserve Board's Index of Industrial Production fell from 118 in May to 79 in January 1938, and showed no signs of recovery in February or March. Unemployment climbed from seven to ten million, halfway back to the peak of 1933. The President had had enough. On April 14, he announced a recovery plan in which federal spending was to be increased, and

the Administration proposes immediately to make additional bank resources available for the credit needs of the country. This can be done without legislation. It will be done through the de-sterilization of approximately one billion four hundred millions of Treasury gold, accompanied by action on the part of the Federal Reserve Board to reduce reserve requirements by about three-quarters of a billion dollars.

(*Federal Reserve Bulletin*, May 1938[16])

World War II

The Fed monetized wartime deficits by undertaking to buy unlimited quantities of Treasury securities at 3/8 of 1 percent for three-month bills and between 2 and 2.5 percent for long-term bonds. The rise in federal debt from $48 billion to $235 billion between June 1941 and June 1945 was assisted by increases in Federal Reserve credit from $2 billion to $22 billion and in the money stock from $63 billion to $127 billion. The reported rise in prices was only 20 percent because of rationing and price controls. Most reported increases came after controls were lifted.

The Fed's differential peg was, of course, impossible. Investors could not be sure of the duration of the war or the peg, but their expectation that they would continue for some time is indicated by their overwhelming choice of the higher-yielding long-terms (seen in Table 4.6), leaving the preponderance of T bills in the hands of the Fed (Wicker 1969b).

Struggle for independence, 1945–51

In July 1945, a month before the end of the war, the Fed wrote to the Treasury that it was considering the elimination of the preferential discount rate on loans secured by short-term government securities. "The instance involved was a trivial one," Eccles recalled. "For that reason alone the sharp response it brought from Treasury circles speaks all the more of the frame of mind that prevailed there." Secretary Fred Vinson objected to the Fed's proposal because it "might be interpreted by the market as an indication that the Government had abandoned its low-interest rate policy and was veering in the direction of higher rates" (Eccles 1951: 422–423).

The preferential rate remained. Eccles raised the issue again in December, with the same result. He was told by Vinson "that the proposed action would

Table 4.6 Yields and ownership of US bills and bonds, June 1942 and 1947

Ownership ($ billion)	T bills		Bonds	
	6/42	**6/47**	**6/42**	**6/47**
Private	2.3	1.3	12.1	54.7
Federal Res.	0.2	14.5	0.4	0.1
% held by Fed	8.0	91.8	3.2	0.2
Yields	0.38	0.38	2.43	2.22

Source: Federal Reserve Board (1943).

increase the already large interest charge on the public debt. This was the dead-end position we were to reach in many other discussions," Eccles (1951: 423–424) recalled. In a tense meeting on January 31, 1946, the secretary "implied that we were proposing to stage a sit-down strike in refusing to carry out Treasury policy." However, "it was clear that if we carried out Treasury policy, we would default on the obligations Congress imposed on the Reserve System in the field of money and credit."

This particular skirmish in the six-year (1945–51) war between the Fed and the Treasury ended in April 1946, with the Board's approval of a unanimous recommendation by the Reserve Banks that the preferential discount rate be discontinued. "Though we were aware of the Treasury's opposition, we could not honestly veto a proposal that we fully believed was in the public interest" (Eccles 1951: 424). The following statement was issued at the time of the Board's action:

> The Board does not favor a higher level of interest rates on U.S. Securities than the Government is now paying. Discontinuance of the special rate will not involve any increase in the cost to the Government of carrying the public debt.
>
> (*Federal Reserve Bulletin* May 1946)

"Such statements were to accompany each step in the move to higher rates," Herb Stein (1969: 251) noted in his account of the politics of American monetary and fiscal policies.

> The process by which the Federal Reserve achieved its freedom consisted of a number of small steps from 1946 through 1949, each step resisted by the Treasury but none big enough to provoke a showdown, and one dramatic showdown in 1950–51 when the Treasury was not strong enough to brave an open fight in Congress.
>
> (Stein 1969: 250)

The most active fighter for an independent monetary policy, with fewer inhibitions about pressing for higher interest rates, was New York Reserve Bank President Allan Sproul. He had pushed for a higher peg – 3 percent on long terms – at the beginning of the war, and flexible interest rates after the war, higher if necessary, was called the New York position. The Board was willing to accept compromise legislation on reserve requirements, but got little support from the Reserve Banks. Sproul did not want to be lured into inaction while waiting for legislation that might not (and did not) come. He did not want to give the impression that the Fed did not already have sufficient powers to fight inflation. He told a congressional committee that the best course was simply to let interest rates rise (Stein 1969: 245, 426–433; Eccles 1951: 432).

Tensions between the Fed and the Treasury after World War II repeated those after World War I. The same trade-off (price stability vs. the interest cost of government debt) and ideas (the Treasury and some Board members believing that credit could be managed by direction) were involved. But why did the second episode last so long and end so acrimoniously, with the Federal Reserve finally forcing the issue, instead of, as in the earlier case, waiting (for much less time as it turned out) for the green light?

An important reason for the extended duration of the low-interest program – for the strength of the Treasury's determination, its support in Congress, and the weakness of the Federal Reserve's opposition – was the fear in all groups of the return of depression. Eccles admitted that "the basic long-range problem was to avoid deflation by providing a flow of necessary purchasing power.... For both political and economic reasons we could never go back to the 1939 levels of production" (Eccles 1951: 399–400).

The fear was lessened first by booming consumption and investment, and then relief that the inevitable downturn, when it came in 1948–9, was so mild (Friedman and Schwartz 1963: 597). The 1950's generation was underway with hardly a thought of the Great Depression. And the Treasury could no longer count on Congress. The Fed got a boost from the hearings and report of the *Subcommittee on Monetary Credit and Fiscal Policies* chaired by Illinois Senator Paul Douglas, a political Liberal but also a University of Chicago economist with classical views of money, interest, and prices. The subcommittee concluded:

> As a long run matter, we favor interest rates as low as they can be without inducing inflation, for low interest rates stimulate capital investment. But we believe that the advantages of avoiding inflation are so great and that a restrictive monetary policy can contribute so much to this end that the freedom of the Federal Reserve to restrict credit and raise interest rates for general stabilization purposes should be restored even if the cost should be a significant increase in service charges on the Federal debt.
>
> (Joint Committee on the Economic Report, Subcommittee on Monetary, Credit and Fiscal Policies, *Report*, 81st Cong., 2nd sess., 1950)

In presenting the subcommittee's report to the Senate, Douglas noted that "the Federal Reserve has done this guilty thing [caused inflation] protestingly and unwillingly" under pressure from the Treasury (*Congressional Record* December 1949: 1518). His comments were similar to the Chancellor of the Exchequer's in the House of Commons (*Parliamentary Debates* August 9, 1833):

> he thought that the blame which was often attributed to the Bank was often attributable to the action of the Government upon the Bank. He likewise was of the opinion that the Bank ought not to change its operations to accommodate the Government.

The Douglas committee brought no legislation, but it showed congressional sympathies on which the Fed soon drew. The outbreak of the Korean War in

June 1950 intensified the contest by reviving the Treasury's expectation of the Fed's wartime subservience, but also by increasing the Fed's fear of inflation. The president's unpopularity due to the distant war strengthened the Fed's position. The New York Reserve Bank renewed its request for an increase in the discount rate in July, and in the FOMC meeting of August 18, Sproul said he had tired of the Treasury's directions:

> We have marched up the hill several times and then marched down again. This time I think we should act on the basis of our unwillingness to continue to supply reserves to the market by supporting the existing rate structure and should advise the Treasury that this is what we intend to do – not seek instructions.

The Committee agreed, and later that day the Board announced an increase in the discount rate. Sniping between the Fed and the Treasury continued, with short rates inching upward. Early the next year, the Fed repulsed direct intervention by the president, and negotiated the following Accord with the Treasury on March 4, 1951:

> The Treasury and the Federal Reserve System have reached full accord with respect to debt-management and monetary policies to be pursued in furthering their common purpose to assure the successful financing of the Government's requirements and, at the same time, to minimize monetization of the public debt.

On March 8, for the first time in ten years, the Fed let the securities market stand on its own.

An earlier Fed effort to obtain policy freedom had included a voluntary 90-percent tax on its interest earnings. The original Federal Reserve Act's "franchise tax" on earnings was eliminated by the Banking Act of 1933. The Fed pays no interest on its liabilities, and its expenses are small relative to the earnings on its holdings of government debt. In 1951, for example, earnings, expenses, and member-bank dividends were $395, $98, and $14 million, respectively. Of the surplus of $283 million, $255 million was paid to the Treasury. The Fed's action was taken unilaterally after conferring with members of Congress rather than risking the vagaries of legislation (Anderson 1968: 102, 149).[17] The Fed's self-financing – returning to the Treasury what it doesn't need – is important because it is freed from the budgetary control to which other agencies are subject.

The Accord was followed by the resignation of Chairman Thomas McCabe as part of the price paid by the Fed (Stein 1968: 496). He was succeeded by William McChesney Martin, Jr., assistant Secretary of the Treasury and Missouri Democrat, who had led the Treasury side of negotiations for the Accord.

Notes

1 For discussions of the political, economic, and social forces leading to the Federal Reserve Act, see Kolko (1963), Livingston (1986), West (1977).

2 The National Monetary Commission's publications included Aldrich, Dewey, Holdsworth, Kinley, Sprague, and Warburg, cited below and reviewed in Mitchell (1911).

3 For a similar chart for 1922–6, see Burgess (1936: 247); also Wood (2005: 186).

4 An editorial in *Forbes* February 24, (1986) agreed with Angell's contention that commodity prices were good predictors of inflation, but researchers were unable to find statistical corroboration; e.g., Fullerton *et al.* (1991) and Furlong and Ingenito (1996).

5 For Fed explanations of its concern for the gold standard in the 1920s, see Young (1929: ch. 7).

6 Thornton (1802: 86) pointed out further fallacies in the real bills doctrine: the same bundle of goods can give rise to several bills, and it is often difficult in practice to distinguish real from fictitious bills. Also Mints (1945: 33–34), Girton (1974), and Humphrey (1982).

7 Friedman and Schwartz (1963: 193), Timberlake (2007), Humphrey (2001), Meltzer (2003: 58, 729), and Mishkin (2006: 420), although Friedman and Schwartz found the commitment erratic and Timberlake thought it fully developed only after 1928.

8 Friedman and Schwartz (1963: 193) and Meltzer (2003: 245–246, 398). Meltzer wrote: "the real bills or Riefler-Burgess doctrine is the main reason for the Federal Reserve's response, or lack of response, to the depression." In fact, these are different guides, the former have nothing in common with the interest-rate responses to bank borrowing in the latter.

9 Those of 1919 and 1921 are excluded because of the Treasury's influence on interest rates.

10 Where Wicker parted company with Brunner and Meltzer was over the latters' claim that the Strong rule was the sole policy guide. Wicker believed that gold also played a part.

11 The model underlying the Strong rule may be found in the Board's *Annual Report* for 1923 (Friedman and Schwartz 1963: 251–254; Wood 2005: 181–184).

12 See Brunner and Meltzer (1964). The Strong rule was similar to the Burgess (1936) and Riefler (1930) doctrine by which bank borrowing from the Fed was an indicator of monetary pressure and a guide to open-market operations (Meigs 1962: 8–9; Wheelock 1990).

13 Cassel (e.g., 1928) was one of the few who understood the situation, discussed by Mazumder and Wood (2013); also Ahamed (2009: 503). See Moggridge (1969) for the British focus on the dollar.

14 Act to eliminate gold reserves against Federal Reserve deposits, March 3, 1965; Act to eliminate the gold reserve against Federal Reserve notes, March 18, 1968 (Krooss 1969: 3070–3071, 3081).

15 Concerned with Title II, which deals with the Fed, to the exclusion of Title I (deposit insurance) and Title III (technical amendments to banking laws).

16 The arguments and maneuvering in the administration leading up to this program are discussed by Stein (1969: 109–112).

17 For Fed earnings and expenses, see the Board's *Annual Reports*; for payments to the Treasury, see its *Banking and Monetary Statistics* (1943: 465).

5 The Federal Reserve System, 1951–99

The Congress hereby declares that it is the continuing policy and responsibility of the Federal Government to use all practicable means consistent with its needs and obligations and other considerations of national policy ... to coordinate and utilize all its plans, functions, and resources ... to promote maximum employment, production, and purchasing power.

Employment Act of 1946, Sec. 2

Our purpose is to lean against the winds of deflation or inflation, whichever way they are blowing.

William McChesney Martin, Jr., US Senate Committee on Banking and Currency, *Nomination Hearings*, 1956

From the Accord to Operation Twist, 1951–64

The 1951 Accord was a historic occasion in the history of monetary policy. For the first time, a technically unconstrained central bank determined money and prices. The constraints of the gold standard had been terminated in the 1930s, succeeded by fiat money. Earlier fiat systems – such as the Civil War greenbacks – had been temporary. Constraints on money and prices had become entirely political in the relations between the Fed, Congress, and the Executive.

Whether the new monetary system could have been an improvement is unclear. Remembering the Great Depression, the loss of the anchor of the gold standard might have been offset by an attentive Congress more inclined to press the Fed to be sensitive to economic conditions. In fact, as our ancestors feared, the new freedom permitted irresponsibility in government and interminable inflation.

At the outset the President hoped to have a friend at the Fed, but in Martin got a chairman who wanted stable prices and resisted the monetary accommodation of fiscal deficits. These wishes had to be tempered by concerns for the Fed's survival – since the Fed was a creation and agent of Congress – so that monetary policy was a tug of war between the classical economics of Martin's Fed, for most of whose members inflation was an unqualified evil, and a substantial part of Congress (supported by most economists) that wanted easy money for

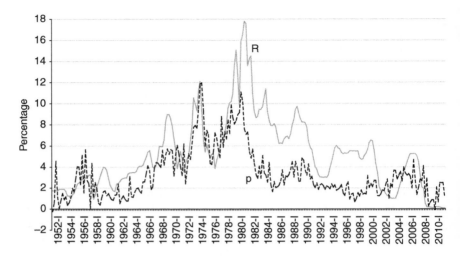

Figure 5.1 Money-market (Fed funds) interest rate (*R*) and inflation (*p*), 1952–2011.

government finance and economic stimulation. The balance was pulled increasingly toward the latter for nearly three decades after the Accord.

Figure 5.1 shows inflation and a short-term interest rate from 1952 to 2011. What needs to be explained are the continuous inflation and its increase from about 2 percent between mid 1950 and mid 1960 to double digits in the 1970s and its return to the earlier figure in the 1980s and thereafter. The explanation offered below relies more on the federal government's fiscal needs, modified by the public's reactions to inflation, than on changes in economic theory. After all, except for those in self-denial or for their own reasons, it has long been known that inflation is caused by money (Locke 1691; Viner 1937: ch. 3–5; Blaug 1995).

Bills only

The Fed controls the monetary base by buying and selling securities, and is therefore concerned with the workings of those markets. Adjustments had to be made after the Accord from when the Fed last enjoyed substantial operational freedom, that is, before the coming of the New Deal in 1933. The discounting of private securities had been replaced as its chief policy instrument by open market operations in government securities. In 1929, the Fed held an average of US securities worth $449 million, compared with its total credit of $1,459 million; most of the difference was discounted private bills. In 1950, after the Fed's monetization of the wartime deficit, US securities were $18,410 million of total Fed credit of $19,062 million (Federal Reserve Board 1943: table 100; 1970: table 10.1).

The Fed wanted healthy (profitable) financial markets and institutions for monetary policy and an efficient credit system. Looking for ways in which it might govern reserves – buying and selling large and variable quantities of securities –

without interfering with market liquidity or efficiency, the Committee decided on *bills only*, as the policy was called, although *bills preferably* would have been more appropriate. An ad hoc subcommittee of the Federal Open Market Committee (FOMC 1952), initiated and led by the new chairman, concluded that operations in Treasury bills (90-day promises) would be as effective as in long terms, with less market disruption. Although long-term rates might be primary objects of policy, fluctuations in long-term prices increased risk and might impede market efficiency. Direct operations in long terms should therefore be avoided, but arbitrage made operations in short terms as effective as in long terms, with less market disturbance. (Arbitrage is illustrated in connection with Operation Twist below.) Bills-only was expected to promote *breadth*, *depth*, and *resilience* of the government securities market, which were also desired characteristics of the New York Stock Exchange. That was more than coincidence. Martin had been a member and president of the Exchange in the 1930s (Bremner 2004: ch. 2–3; Wood 2006).

Although he agreed with its objectives, Sproul (1980: 105–111) criticized bills-only as an unnecessary restriction on policy tools. On the other hand, it might have contributed to policy freedom by serving as protection from Treasury pressures to manipulate the yield curve. Bills-only was criticized by economists on the grounds of both technique and objectives. A review of their critiques of bills-only concluded:

> Sizeable price changes and difficulty in selling securities – both conditions which would not exist in a market with depth, breadth, and resiliency – may at times be of great help in achieving credit policy objectives.... Difficulties in completing security transactions and in financing dealer positions – in a word, impairment of the bond market's ability to function, temporarily at least – are an essential part of a restrictive credit policy. Thus the "bills only" policy was not only poorly designed to achieve its purpose; its very purpose was wrong.
>
> (Ahearn 1963: 65–66, 69)

It appeared to interventionists that the FOMC was less concerned with effective policy than the welfare of securities dealers – similar to the "paternalistic support accorded to the bankers' acceptance market" in the 1920s, when, according to Seymour Harris (1933 i: 428), "credit policy [was] jeopardized by the assumed need of protecting" that market. His Harvard colleague, Alvin Hansen (1955), also thought the FOMC's concerns were misplaced. "The notion that Fed intervention in the market has the effect of increasing risk and uncertainty is certainly one of the most curious arguments I have ever encountered."

Harris and Hansen were typical of economists in expecting the Fed to ignore the banking interests that were its chief political supporters and provided the environment through which it influenced the economy. Economists and their textbooks presumed the apolitical policy rules derived from their monetary theories. Sidney Weintraub (1955) of the University of Pennsylvania dismissed as "cajoling oratory" Martin's statement that "the credit and money of this country is at the grass roots," and that "the composite judgments which come up through [the] various towns and hamlets [have] more to do with the credit basis of this country than the influence of the Treasury and the Federal Reserve put together." Weintraub believed "the job of controlling monetary phenomena still remains with the Reserve System and cannot be farmed out to the mythical 'grass-roots'."

Martin and the economists differed in their dynamics. Macro-policy models after Keynes were static equilibria. Consumption depended only on current income instead of the expected wealth restraint over time as in the classics (Fisher 1930: chs. 5, 10), and investment decisions equalized the marginal productivities of capital goods with the fixed cost of capital. High (low) interest rates discouraged (encouraged) the purchases of capital goods. Countercyclical implications of these so-called Keynesian models included raising rates (costs) to moderate demands in boom times and reducing rates when demand was weak, within, for example, the popular IS-LM versions of Hicks (1937), Hansen (1949: ch. 5), and Ackley (1961: ch. 14). Most of these models assumed fixed (exogenous) prices, divorcing them from one of the Fed's primary interests and flouting the reality of one of the greatest peacetime inflations in history. The purpose of their monetary policy was to accommodate fiscal deficits while inflation was blamed on wage-and-price-setting unions and corporations. Chairman of the president's Council of Economic Advisors (1964–8), Gardner Ackley (1971: 5–6) believed that inflation was "deeply rooted in the economic structures of modern Western societies," and described his job as "President Johnson's principal agent in attempting to hold down wages and prices by 'jawboning'." Money and its relation to prices did not find their way back into the mainstreams of economic theory and policy until Friedman and Schwartz's *Monetary History of the United States* (1963) and the realization that Congress was too cumbersome and otherwise interested to engage in and undertake serious countercyclical fiscal policy (Wood 2009: ch. 4).

The static equilibrium nature of economists' models also meant abstraction from the questions of credibility that were so important to Martin, as to the pre-1914 Bank of England. A cut in interest rates might or might not encourage demand, depending on expectations of future changes. A reduction would depress demand if it were believed to be a step on the way to still lower rates.

Keynes, unlike the Keynesians, had understood the importance of expectations to credible policies. To stop the post-World War I inflation, he advised a "very stiff dose of dear money" for a long time, an approach that he held throughout his life (Howson 1973; 1975: 19–20). He wanted a model that could deal with money, time, and uncertainty, but the analysis was too complex for those wanting clear interventions with certainty-equivalent effects (Wood 2014). The resulting Keynesian policies were a confusion of short-term interventions in the context of static-equilibrium models such as the Phillips Curve inflation–unemployment trade-off that collapsed practically and theoretically in the 1970s.

Leaning against the wind

Martin was not an academic economist and he avoided their jargon. He preferred to describe his policy as in the above statement to a congressional committee, although he regretted in public and in FOMC meetings (e.g., June 22, 1955) that the leaning had been more against deflation than inflation. The major difference between monetary policy in the decades following the Accord and earlier periods is reflected in the nearly continuous inflation in the later years. The Consumer Price Index was about the same in 1914 as in 1824. In comparison, the 1980 index was more than triple that in 1950.

That inflation needs to be explained. As a matter of arithmetic, it is the difference between the public's desire for government benefits and its willingness to pay (be taxed) for them, resulting in deficits that are inflated away. A common economic rationale for these deficits is the stimulation of demand in order to prevent a repeat of the Great Depression, hence the Employment Act of 1946. An objection to this rationale is that Keynesian stabilization does not imply constantly rising debt because deficits during recessions should be offset by the surpluses supplied by prosperity. More logical is the Stagnation Thesis of Keynes (in another part of his *General Theory*, 1936: 378) and Hansen (1939), according to which declining demand, due especially to the exhaustion of investment opportunities, needs to be offset by government spending. Such pessimism in the 1930s is easy to understand, and with hindsight easily criticized, although the slow growth of the twenty-first century has prompted similar statements (Gordon 2012; Summers 2013). It is interesting that both these periods experienced record peacetime deficits. The push for budget deficits by the Council of Economic Advisors during the prosperous 1960s also suggests a belief in stagnation. On the other hand, the depressive effects of government debt suggest a logically more consistent explanation of our persistent deficits and inflation such that the various economic rationales are excuses for a policy whose cause must be found elsewhere, such as in the incentives of Congress and the Fed (Buchanan and Wagner 1977; Wood 2009: ch. 4).

The majority of Fed officials, led by Martin, preferred the price and financial stability valued by banks, with the policy consequence of the Fed digging in its heels as tenaciously as it dared against the easy-money pressures of Congress, the Executive, and academia. "No one but Mr. Martin knows," wrote Yale economist James Tobin (1958), soon to be a Nobel laureate and member of the Council of Economic Advisors, "how much slack the Federal Reserve is willing to force upon the economy in the effort to stop inflation." Wright Patman of the House Committee on Banking and Currency complained that the Fed's tight-money policy had "throttled" the economy – even though prices were rising and Martin regretted that policy had been too easy (US Congress 1964: 926). After the recession of 1957–8, he responded to criticisms of insufficient ease by members of the House Ways and Means Committee:

I do want to point out that in eight years of experience in the Federal Reserve System, I am convinced that our bias, if anything, has been on the side of too much money rather than too little.

(US Congress 1959: 185)

Note the negative real rates during the 1949–53 and 1954–7 expansions in Figure 5.1. The Accord was less important than commonly believed (Weintraub 1978; Selgin and White 1999). Deficit governments have traditionally used their influence over monetary institutions to borrow at artificially low interest rates, even negative real rates. The practice has been called "financial repression" in studies of politically weak developing countries without the ability or will to balance their budgets (McKinnon 1973: 66–68). Demands for government currencies are bolstered by increases in bank reserve requirements (as in the United States in the National Bank Act of 1862, and in World Wars I and II), and the cost of government borrowing is kept low by controls and/or central bank security purchases.

Referring to the "neo-colonial" practices of less-developed countries, Ronald McKinnon (1973: 70) wrote that

> favored private and official borrowers still absorb the limited finance available at low real rates of interest.... Again, the mass of small farmers and indigenous urban industry remain financially "repressed," although they own a significant proportion of the deposits on which the expansion of bank credit to the favored enclaves is based.

Developing governments have "used their central bank as a fiscal milch cow," a group including Goodhart concluded in a study for the Bank of England (Álvaro *et al.* 1996: 8).

That the practice has not been limited to the developing world is indicated by the fate of a buyer of 30-year, 2-percent US bonds in 1950, who experienced average annual inflation of 4.2 percent during the life of the bond, and collected less than 30¢ per 1950 dollar of his principal in 1980. Although the national debt more than doubled between 2007 and 2013, its interest component fell as the Treasury bill rate plummeted from 5 percent to virtually zero and long rates fell two-thirds. Figure 5.2 shows the nearly continuous deficit in the federal budget from the 1930s to the present, which is the primary explanation of Fed behavior and the equally continuous inflation.

Nor has the Bank of England been innocent. It was used by governments to repress private industry in favor of public programs for at least a quarter of a century after World War II. Limits on advances (bank loans) were a hopeful means by which a full-employment monetary policy might be reconciled with a fixed exchange rate, which, however, collapsed in the 1960s (Fforde 1992: 360–396, 298–323, 695–703; Wood 2005: 297–314). These experiences illustrate the continued truth of Adam Smith's (1776: 882) observation:

> When national debts have once been accumulated to a certain degree, there is scarce, I believe, a single instance of their having been fairly and completely paid. The liberation of the public revenue, if it has ever been brought about at all, has always been brought about by a bankruptcy, sometimes by an avowed one, but always by a real one, though frequently by a pretended payment ... [usually] the raising of the denomination of the coin.

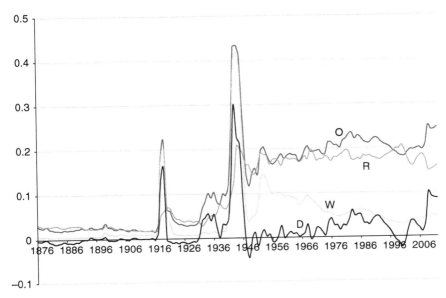

Figure 5.2 Federal government receipts (R), outlays (O), deficits (D), and military spending (W) relative to GNP, fiscal years, 1876–2012.

Neither the development of central banks nor Keynesian economics changed the practice, but rather provided another tool and another rationale. Even in the 1990s, after the public's reaction to the high inflation of the 1970s, cutbacks in military spending, and the advent of "independent" central banks avowedly dedicated to price stability, inflation was significant. The shift in standards was signified by New York Fed President William McDonough's comment on reported inflation of 1.9 percent: "If that isn't price stability, I don't know what is" (*New York Times*, October 1, 1999). Such an inflation doubles prices every 37 years. Vera Smith's 1936 (167–168) observation still applies, only more so as the evidence accumulates.

> Looking at the circumstances in which most [central banks] were established, we find that the early ones were founded for political reasons connected with the exigencies of State finance, and no economic reason for allowing or disallowing free entry into the note-issuing trade was, or could have been given at that time, but once established, the monopolies persisted right up to and beyond the time when their economic justification did at last come to be questioned. The verdict of the discussions round this problem vindicated the choice in favour of unity or monopoly in the note issue as opposed to competition, and thereafter the superiority of central banking over the alternative system became a dogma which never again came up for discussion and was accepted without question or comment in all the later foundations of central banks.

Patman still found the Fed insufficiently tractable. In 1964, he staged a critique in hearings on *The Federal Reserve System after Fifty Years.* To the congressional committee's question of "how much independence [the Fed] needs," all 23 academic witnesses answered "None." Four favored money rules and the rest would have subordinated monetary policy to the President. It was unthinkable, even "ludicrous," to suggest that monetary policy should not conform to the program of the elected representatives of the people, said the University of Washington's Dudley Johnson. MIT's Paul Samuelson said:

> Whatever may have been true in a few countries for a few decades in the 19th century, there can never be a place in American life for a central bank that is like a Supreme Court ... – truly independent, dedicated to the public weal but answerable for its decisions and conduct only to its own discretion, and to the consciences of its men in authority as they each envisage their duty.
>
> Lack of coordination between monetary, fiscal, and debt policies, as determined by the Executive and Congress, with monetary credit, interest, and debt-management policies, as determined by Federal Reserve policy, can lead to short-run crises and to costly long-run ineffectiveness.
>
> A central bank that is not responsible is irresponsible, rather than independent.

Samuelson recommended a Federal Reserve essentially like the Bank of England (although he did not mention the Bank by name or draw examples from its performance), which would conduct "day-to-day operations" and advise the Executive, but "be responsible to the Executive," who "should have the power to ask for their resignations." Stanford's John Gurley said Fed independence was

> like having two managers for the same baseball team, each manager independent of the other. The managers could get together for lunches once a week – that might help. Or one of them could try to offset the actions of the other – that might work a bit. Nothing of this sort, really, would correct the basic situation – the intolerable arrangement of having two managers.

An independent Fed meant the President would be forced to "design overall economic policy in the face of unnecessary uncertainty."

Bankers were rebuked by Patman when they indicated satisfaction with the Fed's organization and policies:

> The question before us, gentlemen, of course, is to consider these bills strictly from the standpoint of the public, the people. Although I am sure you keep in mind the public interest, you have a special interest.... It disturbs me to think that you gentlemen think that the private banks, with an ax to grind, with a special interest in money, the volume of money and interest rates, should be represented on boards to determine these questions for the whole country.

He castigated the "insincerity" and "hypocrisy" of arguments for independence. The Fed was

> insulated against the people all right, and the people cannot reach them. But they make no effort to insulate themselves against the bankers who profit the most by what they do.

When investment banker and Treasury Secretary Douglas Dillon warned against tinkering with a complicated, evolving institution that was performing satisfactorily, and said there was a good working relationship between the Treasury and the Fed, Patman dismissed their "buddy-buddy" luncheons as ineffectual because the administration was powerless to enforce its views (US Congress 1964: 926, 1444, 1105, 1309, 961).

Whatever their economic rationale, the suggestions that the Fed be formally subordinate to the President indicated misunderstandings of American government. Congress takes its constitutional responsibility for the currency seriously, as well as its own independence of the Executive. Few, if any, government agencies are more closely monitored by Congress. The Fed's chairman and other representatives are called to Capitol Hill several times a year to explain their actions to various committees of both Houses. In normal times, Congress is more intent on shielding the Fed from presidential influence than in relinquishing its own powers, even refusing (tongue-in-cheek?) requests by Chairmen Eccles (1935), McCabe (1949), and Martin (1957) to make the Chairman's term coterminous with the President's (US Congress 1964: 108). Congress has on several occasions chastised the Executive for trespassing on monetary policy, as we have seen. During hearings on the renewal of Chairman Martin's term in 1956, Senator Paul Douglas told him:

> I have had typed out this little sentence which is a quotation from you: "The Federal Reserve Board is an agency of Congress." I will furnish you with scotch tape and ask you to place it on your mirror where you can see it as you shave each morning."
>
> (US Congress 1956: 24–25; Kettl 1986: 84)

"In normal times" is a significant qualifier because Congress has yielded its authority over monetary policy in several emergencies, genuine or manufactured, including 1917–19, 1933–51, the 1970s, and since 2008. In the 1960s the Fed's battle for independence of the Executive received little help from Congress.

Operation twist

"Bills only" was terminated in 1961 when the new administration wanted to make full use of the Fed's powers. The 1960 Democratic platform promised "an end to the present high-interest, tight-money policy" that had produced "two recessions within five years" and "bankrupted many of our families." The deteriorating balance of payments was also a concern.

The peak of optimism concerning the powers of economic policy that came in the 1960s joined with active administrations that were eager to use them. All the New (Keynesian) Economists needed was an econometric model and as many instruments as goals (Tinbergen 1952; Smith 1965). The goals were numerous, external as well as the chief internal goals of economic growth and stable prices. The external goals included the balances of trade and payments, the gold reserve, and the international value of the dollar, complicated by the special place of the United States in the international payments system. The 1944 agreement at Bretton Woods, New Hampshire, had established a fixed-exchange-rate system based on gold, or rather the US dollar backed by gold. The country's gold reserve had fallen from $25 billion (of the world's monetary gold stock of $35 billion) in 1949 to $17 billion at the time of John F. Kennedy's inauguration in 1961, and was falling $2 billion a year.

The administration had a plan for the Fed to target these multiple and potentially conflicting objectives – particularly growth, the balance of payments, and price stability – by twisting the yield curve. The Fed would stimulate long-term investment by buying long-term securities while helping the balance of payments by attracting short-term investments through the higher short-term yields that would result from sales of short-term securities. The program would not be inflationary because the reserves created by long-term purchases would be offset by the sales of short-terms.

Kennedy had raised the possibility of replacing Martin during the 1960 presidential campaign, and when the chairman-designate of the Council of Economic Advisers, Walter Heller, called on Martin, the latter warned: "I'm not going to give up the independence of the Fed." Nevertheless, Heller recalled, Martin added that "There's plenty of room for cooperation" (*Banking*, September 1960: 90; Hargrove and Morley 1984: 189). Martin agreed to try to persuade his colleagues to nudge short-term rates up while keeping long-term rates low. Operation Nudge turned into Operation Twist, which would involve vigorous actions to reduce long rates. It was the end of "bills only." "This is an historic reversal of policy," Heller told the President, "for which Chairman Martin deserves our appreciation" (Kettl 1986: 98).

"Economics has come of age in the 1960s," Heller (1966: 1–5) wrote:

> Two presidents have recognized and drawn on modern economics as a source of national strength and Presidential power. Their willingness to use, for the first time, the full range of modern economic tools underlies the unbroken U.S. expansion since early 1961. [W]e have at last unleashed fiscal and monetary policy for the aggressive pursuit of those objectives.

The "Keynesian economic system," Nobel-laureate-to-be Lawrence Klein (1947: 153) had written a few years earlier "is essentially a machine which grinds out results according to where the several dials controlling the system are set."

It seemed straightforward, but the majority of the FOMC did not view markets this way. Chairman Martin, who liked to introduce himself as "just a bond man" – he had been a bond trader on the New York Stock Exchange – lived in a world of arbitrage in which Keynesian quantitative policies might be erased in a blink. More on this below, but Heller's satisfaction with Martin was premature. Several members of the FOMC "were strongly opposed to the end of 'bills only' [as] a step back toward political interference in monetary policy and a pegged bond market," and Martin managed to keep the majority's support for Operation Twist only by an execution that bordered on the imperceptible (Kettl 1986: 98–99). Heller remembered that

> we'd have a meeting with Kennedy ... and before the meeting Bill would be out there buying those long-term securities, but afterwards his buying would flag ... [fellow CEA member] Jim Tobin would keep track of this and he'd say, "Walter, you'd better ... arrange another meeting ... because Martin isn't buying enough long-term bonds." So I'd call a meeting and sure enough the purchases would rise again, and Martin would be able to tell Kennedy, "We're doing everything we can."
>
> (Hargrove and Morley 1984: 191)

A later Council Chairman, Arthur Okun (1968–9), remembered that "the change in the federal funds rate in the week preceding [meetings with President Johnson] was almost always negative ... Martin was always bringing the president the present of a little lower interest rate than he'd run in the interim" – to "a boy from Texas" who could not "see high interest rates as a lesser evil than anything else" (Hargrove and Morley 1984: 293, 274).

Yet the yield curve twisted in the desired direction during the period that it was proclaimed policy, and the 1966 *Economic Report of the President* (p. 50) pointed to the "remarkable stability" of long-term rates during a period of generally rising rates. In fact, rate movements were normal. Smaller rises in long than in short rates are characteristic of economic expansions, and consistent with the expectations theory of the term structure of interest rates, for which long rates are averages of current and expected short rates, and rates tend towards a normal level in the long term (Wood and Wood 1985: 629–636).

Yield curves during 1961–5 are compared with the two preceding expansions in Figure 5.3, which indicates that the twist was less than at least recent experience. The change in the difference between one- and twenty-year rates was 0.84 percent between 1961 and 1965, compared with 2.07 and 1.19 percent for 1954–7 and 1959–61, respectively. The twist in fact increased after it was no longer policy as interest rates continued their rise in the 1960s – as the 1966 yield indicates.

A good deal of evidence points to the futility of attempts to control more than one price of substitutable assets in the face of the "alert arbitrage of markets for issues that are out of line" (to repeat a phrase of the FOMC's Ad hoc Subcommittee). The dislocations arising from the World War II bond support program were an example (Table 4.6). Operation Twist could not have worked, and was hardly tried. Moreover, the Treasury acted contrary to declared policy by issuing

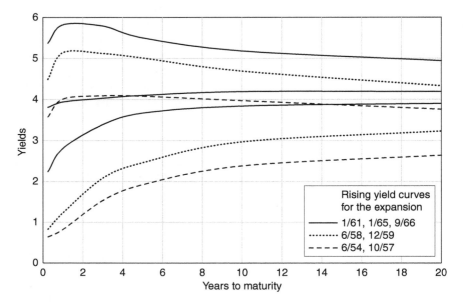

Figure 5.3 Operation Twist, 1961–5, compared with preceding expansions.

more long than short debt, a natural step when interest rates are expected to rise. "As a result, the maturity of the debt lengthened appreciably, instead of shortened as the policy would require" (Johnson 1963).

The Fed again became interested in twisting the yield curve a half century later as it tried to assist recovery from the Great Recession, with a similar lack of success. There were temporary announcement and quantity effects (Swanson 2011), but arbitrage erased quantity influences on the rates of return of substitutable investments, that is, on long terms in the presence of fixed short terms. The fact that long rates exceeded short rates already indicated the market's skepticism of the Fed's commitment to simultaneous low inflation and low short rates. The modern Fed seems less aware of arbitrage than in Martin's time.

Increasing inflationary pressures, 1965–79

Federal government spending of all kinds – social and military programs and for economic stimulus – rose after World War II while tax rates trended down from their wartime highs. Spending as a proportion of GDP nearly doubled, from 12 percent to above 20 percent, between the late 1940s and the late 1970s, and the budget turned from surplus to annual deficits of 2–4 percent of GDP (Figure 5.2). Legislated tax cuts were made possible by the inflation tax. Countercyclical policies attract most of the attention of Fed histories, but they should be understood against the more enduring background of the Fed's fiscal contributions. We can see why the true dual mandate has led to a trade-off between the monetization of the deficit and the support of financial institutions, although the goals join when the inflationary consequences of the former lead to bailouts of the latter.

Vietnam and the Great Society

The Johnson administration's reach for guns and butter put pressure on government budgets which it believed the Fed should help finance. The federal deficit rose from $5 billion in 1963 to $9 billion in 1967 and $25 billion in 1968. M2 money rose 7.6 percent per annum, and inflation from under 2 percent to over 6 percent.

"For four years there had been a widening difference of opinion within the Federal Reserve ... over the issue of how soon and how much to tighten monetary policy," new Board member Sherman Maisel (1973: 69) observed in 1965,

> This was a contrast to the situation which had prevailed during the Eisenhower Administration when, even on most of the critical votes, there had never been more than one dissenting member, and even that had been rare. Recent appointees of the Kennedy and Johnson Administrations, however, had brought new value judgments and theories to the Board.

Coming from the University of California at Berkeley, with a Harvard PhD, Maisel was the Board's first academic New Economist. He "had spent nearly twenty years studying and teaching monetary economics," and thought he "understood what the Fed did and how it affected the economy. I soon discovered how little I knew." He was unable to identify the theory behind monetary policy. In policy discussions, "words took on special connotations, and nuances were extremely important.... I was struck by surprising gaps in the arguments and presentations" (Maisel 1973: ix).

He could not have been referring to the staff's introductory presentations, which considered "everything" in the context of a large-scale econometric model (de Leeuw and Gramlich 1968). However, when the presentation was over, the economists left the room, and the Committee got down to business, its attention turned to the money markets. The money markets were barely evident, and certainly not crucial, in economists' models, but Maisel (1973: 78–79) found that his colleagues "used money market conditions simultaneously as a target, or measure, of monetary policy and as a guide for the manager of the Open Market Desk – all reflections of the importance of financial institutions to the Fed." Students of the Fed found that policy corresponded more closely with the open-market manager's report of money market conditions (from the New York Reserve Bank) than the staff's macroeconomic projections (Feinman and Poole 1989).

Maisel (1973: 69–70) saw the FOMC divided between "anti-inflationists" and those, including himself, who "favored a policy of furnishing the funds necessary for full employment." The weight of votes slightly favored the former, so decisions "generally favored restrictive targets," which, however, were moderated by the strong feelings of the minority, as well as the administration, which favored "broader objectives." It should be noted that annual inflation rose from about 1.5 percent at the beginning of Maisel's seven-year service (April 1965) to almost 6.5 percent when Arthur Burns became chairman in 1970.

Maisel also found disagreements over "the question of coordination with other government agencies versus the independence of the Fed, and the method of tightening money to be used." Although undermined by the administration's bad faith, he was heartened by offers "to coordinate monetary and fiscal policies," and grasped at assurances that the budget would be addressed. It should be noted that the 1960s saw the longest economic expansion in American history, although the Council of Economic Advisors was always able to find a worrisome gap between GNP and its potential, which if closed would produce a budget surplus. Nevertheless, the majority of the FOMC chose restraint in their terms, meaning less ease than the administration wanted.

How should it be applied? As quietly as possible – "No announcement effect" – urged Maisel and two colleagues. A slower rise in bank reserves would do the job. The majority, however, felt the announcement of an increase in the discount rate would have a favorable impact on foreign central banks, slowing their exchange of dollars for gold.

Also important was the Fed's desire to help banks break "President Johnson's stranglehold on the prime rate" (Maisel 1973: 76). The President had set low-interest guideposts, and since the banks wanted to avoid a political confrontation, "some Board members felt that it was up to the Federal Reserve to oppose him in order to avoid a threatened inflationary increase in bank credit." The increase in the Fed's discount rate from 4 to 4.5 percent in December 1965 was immediately followed by an equal rise in the banks' prime rate.

The Board also raised the maximum rate on short-term time deposits from 4 to 5.5 percent. It had been 2.5 percent from 1936 to 1957, when the Board began to allow banks to compete with rising open-market rates. The rise in December 1965 seemed large enough "to prevent the ceilings from having any effect on the market for the present and far into the future" (Maisel 1973: 77). Not very far, it would soon be learned.

A review of the Fed's model in the fiat system

Answers to Maisel's questions about the Fed's model might consider financial conditions, the relations between prices and economic activity, and federal deficits, modified, even dominated, by variable political pressures, although the case can be made that the complexity of monetary policy is mostly in the language. The record is simpler and summarized in a word: inflation. All the above influences are interpreted to produce that result. The political costs of leaning against expansions and the political benefits of ease during contractions combine to produce an upward trend in prices that fiat money makes possible.

Bankers like monetary order. They benefit from the realization of expectations that enable the repayment of loans. Central bankers operate in a bankers' environment and share their preferences. They dislike the monetization of deficits, which develop into inflation, speculation, and monetary disorder. This does not mean that bankers do not succumb to speculative fever, often accompanied by their central bankers, and when the bust comes, the fiat system allows them to be bailed out without tax increases (Kirshner 2007; Wood 2009: 155–161). So the real dual mandate of monetary policy involves the trade-off between bank and Treasury/congressional preferences, that is, between financial stability and the monetization of federal deficits, or between the institutions upon which the Fed depends. Governments always see the need for stimulus, but their influence on monetary policy fluctuates. For example, the inflation of the 1970s exceeded the public's appetite and raised the political strength of those desiring stability.

Subject to this trade-off, the Fed became, with the demise of the gold standard, a fiscal (tax-gathering) appendage of Congress whose purpose is to increase the size of government. A simple example of how this is done is shown in Table 5.1, which presents a case of private income and taxes of $80 and $20 in period 1 with a balanced government budget. Money $(M) = \$100$, velocity $(V) = 1$, and real output $(Y) = 100$ imply $P = 1$. If increased government spending of $10 per annum is financed by monetary expansion, MV and P rise $10 and 0.1 per period, respectively, nominal private income and taxes are unaffected, and real values fall in line with the expansion of government – and Congress need not ask for an increase in taxes. Figure 5.2 shows the growth of government despite the decrease in its revenue (relative to the size of the economy) since the 1960s.

Edward Phelps (1973) proposed that inflation, like other taxes, be part of the decision-making process of fiscal policy, and set according to their relative costs which are primarily economic distortions. However, it seems that the Fed's goal, admittedly under political pressure, is simply as much inflation as the public will stomach, other goals serving as cover. Its model is more political convenience than economic welfare. There have been many studies of Federal Reserve behavior, and most have been successful in finding statistically significant explanations for limited periods. The operative word here is "limited" because no model or relationship has been stable for a long period, with one exception, namely that between Fed credit and government deficits (Wood 1967; Khouri 1990).

The 1966 credit crunch was a consequence of this conflict

The Fed continued its pressure into 1966, and financial institutions experienced a "credit crunch." Many banks and savings and loan associations lost deposits as market interest rates rose above the legal maxima on deposit rates. The Fed tried to relieve the problem by offering banks easy access to funds through the discount window if they would "cooperate in the System's efforts to hold down the rate of business loan expansion" (*Federal Reserve Bulletin* September 1966). Beyond defying the principles of economics (you can borrow if you don't use it), banks avoided the discount window because, New York Fed President Alfred Hayes (1970) said, they feared it "might bring their portfolio decisions, and

Table 5.1 An example of deficits, inflation, and the growth in government

t	$				P	Real = $/P			
	Private income	Taxes	Disposable private income	Government spending		Real private income	Real taxes	Real disposable private income	Real government spending
1	100	20	80	20	1.0	100	20	80.0	20.0
2	100	20	80	30	1.1	90.9	18.2	72.7	27.3
3	100	20	80	40	1.2	83.3	16.7	66.7	33.3
4	100	20	80	50	1.3	76.9	15.4	61.5	38.5
5	100	20	80	60	1.4	71.4	14.3	65.1	42.9
6	100	20	80	70	1.5	66.7	13.3	53.3	46.7
7	100	20	80	80	1.6	62.5	12.5	50.0	50.0
8	100	20	80	90	1.7	58.8	11.8	47.1	52.9
9	100	20	80	100	1.8	55.6	11.1	44.4	55.6
10	100	20	80	110	1.9	52.6	10.5	42.1	57.9
11	100	20	80	120	2.0	50.0	10.0	40.0	60.0

Note
Note that M rises by the government deficit: 10, 20, 30,…, and P in the same proportion.

particularly their business lending policies under close scrutiny by the Federal Reserve." It was also "becoming increasingly apparent to bankers" that the Fed would not ease the pressure by raising the ceiling on deposit rates. Large banks relied extensively on large negotiable certificates of deposit for funds. "The bond market reached frightening lows on Friday, August 26. One observer described the market psychology as 'the coldest, bleakest I have ever experienced on Wall Street'." The "old timers" were "scared." On September 13, Hayes told the FOMC "that the financial community was experiencing growing and genuine fear of a financial panic."

Figure 5.4 suggests that the source of the problem – as Thornton and Bagehot would have known – was the sudden halt in money growth. The Fed was so bent on resisting the inflationary effects of the government deficit that it neglected its responsibility for the payments system. The credit crunch illustrated the Fed's trade-off. Maintaining the payments system necessary to prosperity in the face of persistent government deficits produces inflation. The Fed was playing chicken with the Executive and Congress. The experience showed why the Fed lobbies against deficits.

In late 1966, the Fed blinked. Open-market purchases accelerated, the administration of discount windows eased, and interest rates fell (Burger 1969). Hayes rationalized the backdown by saying the Fed had helped the administration

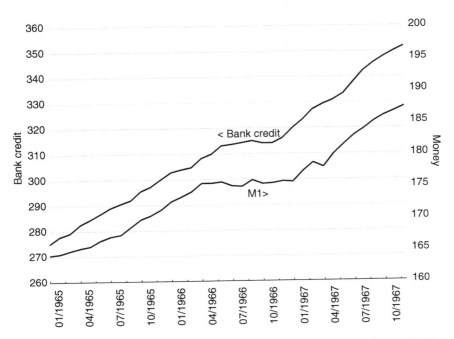

Figure 5.4 Bank credit and the money stock, 1965–7, billion dollars (source: Burger 1969).

accept its responsibilities. This turned out to be wishful thinking. The war continued, inflation rose, and when the Fed returned to the fray it was determined to show that, next time, it would keep its nerve (Hetzel 2008: 75–76).

Nixon and the Fed

The Nixon administration coming to office in January 1969 wanted to reduce inflation without raising unemployment. CEA Chairman Paul McCracken referred to their plan as "gradualism," which Paul Volcker called "a very comforting word meaning that nothing very drastic is going to happen" (Neikirk 1987: 98). A problem was the public's inflationary expectations, to which Martin's Fed, unlike the administration, was attuned. The Fed majority believed that the prevailing inflationary psychology needed to be broken by shock treatment, and got the ball rolling by raising the discount rate in December 1968. The Fed meant business, Martin told a group of bankers: "there is no gadgetry in monetary mechanisms and no device that will save us from our sins" (Matusow 1998: 25).

Martin apologized to the Joint Economic Committee for past errors and promised they would not be repeated. The Fed had been "overly optimistic in anticipating immediate benefits from fiscal restraint" (US Congress 1969: 648–651).

> We must deal with a heritage of cost and price increases that is continuing to generate further cost and price increases, and – importantly – has become deeply embedded in business and consumer expectation. After several years of rapidly rising prices, it is only natural that many spending decisions are motivated now by the fear that prices will be even higher next year, or by the conviction that inflation will bail out even the most marginal speculation.

Despite the recent temporary income tax surcharge, Martin observed, "consumers continued to increase their outlays at a rapid rate, drawing on their savings and borrowing heavily to finance both higher taxes and higher spending."[1] Measures seen as temporary are futile.

> Expectations of inflation are deeply embedded, ... and speculative fervor is still strong. A slowing in expansion that is widely expected to be temporary is not likely to be enough to eradicate such expectations. [W]e have had quite a credibility gap as to whether we meant business at the Federal Reserve.

The Fed had indicated, "perhaps unwisely," after the 1966 credit crunch that "we don't want a recurrence." However, "if you don't take some risk in policy you never get any result," Martin said. He addressed the administration's lack of resolve that "has raised the ghost of overkill at the first sign of a few clouds in the sky." The *New York Times* reported: "Martin strongly implied that this will not happen again and that restraint will persist even when there are clear signs the economy is slowing and in the face of some increase in unemployment" (US Congress 1969: 668–669; Bremner 2004: 253).

There has been much discussion of the Fed's increased sophistication following the "rational expectations revolution" of the 1970s, particularly its "new" understanding of the role of "credibility" and the discipline of "clear rules intended to ensure a stable standard of value," in place of the discretion "to serve whatever ends may seem most pressing at any given time" (Clarida *et al.* 2000; Romer and Romer 2002a; Woodford 2003: 2). This gives too much credit to economists, who see themselves as intellectual leaders. In fact, a comparison of the Fed's policies and statements with those of economists during the 1950s and 1960s suggests that the former's ideas led the latter's (Romer and Romer 2002b; Hetzel 2008: 58–59). A European central banker viewed "this episode – in which honest civil servants were ahead of their times in rejecting faulty propositions – as highly symbolic." It was "representative of the key but swinging and ambivalent relationship between cutting-edge economic research and long-established central banking principles," on which he quotes Martin. Jürgen Stark (2008) noted in Burkean terms that attention to long-established principles insured "against major policy failures that revolutionary ideas can inflict if applied untested." Although many central bankers understand the causes of inflation and the limits of monetary policy, their policies are governed by political forces.

Returning to the end of Martin's term, money growth slowed and unemployment rose as 1969 progressed, but inflation remained above 6 percent, and the Fed raised the discount rate. "We're going to have a good deal of pain and suffering before we can solve these things," Martin warned (Matusow 1998: 25). The Fed kept its word until February 1970, when in Chairman Burns' first meeting, "After the most bitter debate I experienced in my entire service on the FOMC," monetary policy changed direction (Maisel 1973: 250).

The 1970s

An esteemed student of the business cycle and long-time Nixon confidant, Burns succeeded Martin at the end of January 1970. The President expected a pliant Fed. "Eisenhower liked to talk about the independence of the Federal Reserve," Burns said at a cabinet meeting in February 1969. "Let's not make that mistake … again." In October, shortly after Burns' nomination to the Fed, Nixon invited him in for "a little chat." "You see to it – no recession," the President said. Martin is "six months too late," Burns replied. "I don't like to be late." Nixon continued: "Shultz says 'turn now'" [referring to a memo from Secretary of Labor George Shultz] (Matusow 1998: 20, 31).

Burns whipped and cajoled the FOMC into an expansive monetary policy. He was not the President's man unreservedly, however. He would do his part for economic stabilization, but he expected the administration to do its part. Credibility in the fight against inflation required fiscal discipline, Burns argued, and he made a cutback in government spending a condition of monetary ease.

Among the reductions found for a small projected surplus was the postponement of a scheduled pay raise for federal employees. When New York City postal workers went on strike in March, Nixon called out the army but finally yielded to a "budget-busting wage settlement." He said Burns "had brought on the strike" (Matusow 1998: 59).

Burns had much in common with Marriner Eccles. Neither was a central banker in market outlook, and unlike Martin and Benjamin Strong, neither saw the payments system as a primary concern. Burns and Eccles wanted to help the President run the country. Neither offer was appreciated by Presidents who simply wanted money on demand. Burns was more strongly positioned than Eccles, however. Thanks to Martin, Burns came to a respected Fed that Presidents were unwilling to challenge openly.

Shultz observed that

> Arthur has a way of holding the money supply as a hostage – saying that "if you don't behave, I'll tighten up on money," and in fact in that way he's trying to run the whole executive branch with the Federal Reserve
> (Matusow 1998: 62)

To those concerned with inflation, however, Burns was shirking his duty, blaming everyone and everything – government fiscal policy, union wage demands, business mark-up pricing, and consumer spending – for an inflation that could be traced to a single cause over which the Fed had complete control: too much money. "Burns seems to have a model," Ray Lombra (1980) wrote,

> where there are n causes of inflation, and monetary policy is the nth. Within this model monetary policy is totally endogenous; the nation must first deal successfully with the $n-1$ causes of inflation and only then can the nth – that is, monetary policy – be formulated and executed in a manner consistent with long-run price stability.

To critics who said the way to reduce inflation is to reduce money growth, Burns replied: "The rules of economics are not working the way they used to." He told Congress' Joint Economic Committee in July 1971 that "Despite extensive unemployment in our country, wage rate increases have not moderated. Despite much idle industrial capacity, commodity prices continue to rise rapidly" (Burns 1978: 118). Throughout his term at the Fed, he blamed inflation on the economic structure. "In recent decades, a new pattern of wage and price behavior has emerged," he told a university audience in 1975. "The average level of prices ... hardly ever declines.... Wage reductions are nowadays rare even in severely depressed industries.... Lenders ... expect to be paid back in cheaper dollars, and therefore hold out for higher interest rates," which they are able to obtain "because the resistance of borrowers to high interest rates is weakened by their anticipation of rising prices.... Structural reforms of our economy ... deserve more attention ... than they are receiving," especially from economists, who "have tended to concentrate excessively on over-all fiscal and monetary policies" (Burns 1978: 218–224; Lombra 1980).

It is one thing for administrations and legislatures to choose to believe in non-monetary causes of inflation. That is in the interests of big government. It is another thing for central banks, whose task is purported to be monetary stability, to share those beliefs. A consequence of the shared beliefs on this occasion was the Great Inflation of the 1970s.

In any case, Burns's denigration of the possibility of a credible monetary policy took place in the context of four decades of continuous, recently rising, inflation. What else but a continuation could economic agents reasonably have expected? Martin had seen the best, but still painful, course in striving for credibility. Burns and his Fed, on the other hand, wanted less inflation without the costs of a significant reduction in money, and certainly no shock to expectations – a sequence of events that had few, if any, precedents. The rules of economics had in fact continued to apply, not least in the modest responses of wages, prices, and interest rates to changes in policy, relations so familiar that the historian's candor is suspect. The high interest rates during the long deflation of the late nineteenth century were a source of farmers' distress and hostility to the gold standard. Fisher (1930: ch. 19) wrote extensively of the sluggishness of interest rates. In Britain, William Ashley (1903) urged a "sliding scale" to overcome the downward rigidity of wages. The resistance of wages to falling prices during the Great Depression was well-known. Burns was unwilling to take, or be seen to take, actions strong enough to break inflationary expectations. Easy money in the 1970s has been blamed on overestimates of the output gap and the benefits of inflation (Clarida *et al.* 2000; Lindsey *et al.* 2005; Orphanides 2003), but monetary policy was consistent with the ever-present goal of monetizing the deficit.

The Burns Fed is best explained by politics, first supplying monetary ease for Nixon's reelection in 1972, then preventing interest rates from rising because of fear of the short-term costs of disinflation (Figure 5.1) (DeLong 1997; Meltzer 2005). They also gave up on help in budget surpluses. Burns indicated that if he did not get a tight budget, Nixon would not get easy money. On the other hand, he joined Shultz in opposing the policy of a modest surplus as standard practice. That "seems to me unworkable and represents an unrealistic expectation," Shultz said. Congress would spend it or give it away in a tax reduction, he felt. Burns called the idea "a little romantic" (Matusow 1998: 52–53).

Burns' logic is difficult to follow here. Central banks have supplied easy money for fiscal deficits. Easy money with surpluses suggests a Keynesian approach in which fiscal and monetary policies are substitutes, although Burns did not usually talk like a Keynesian. His approach really came down to structural changes or controls. He was not the first or last Fed chairman for whom money was at the back of his toolbox.

The administration was in no position to force the structural changes that Burns wanted, even if the President had wanted, and he would not risk the economic or political costs of tight money. There was nothing left but to pretend that, somehow, wages and prices could be held in check by exhortation and legal action without cutting money growth or government spending. The businessmen in Nixon's cabinet were enchanted by the prospect. On February 18, 1969, "[Secretary of Housing and Urban Development George] Romney shattered the usual false harmony by challenging the lack of policy in the wage-price field" at a time when "some very inflationary wage settlements" were looming. "What wage-price policy ever worked?" Nixon asked. "The British Plan," Romney replied. "Oh, no. Now, George," Nixon said. "[D]on't tell me about British wage-price policy. I know about that. It didn't work" (Matusow 1998: 66–67).

Polls showed a majority for controls, and in August 1970, the democratic Congress tried to force the President's hand, or embarrass him, by giving him discretion to impose mandatory controls on wages and prices for up to six months. The President held out, and was displeased when Burns publicly indicated that controls might be needed (Matusow 1998: 70). Nixon's understanding of the appropriate economic policy never changed. His *Memoirs* (1978: 521) stated that the

> August 15, 1971, decision to impose [controls] was politically necessary and immensely popular in the short run. But in the long run I believe that it was wrong ... and there was an unquestionably high price for tampering with the orthodox economic mechanisms.

He regretted that "the *politics* of economics has come to dictate action more than the *economics* of economics."

The Nixon package

The administration's problems did not end with domestic inflation and unemployment. The international monetary system, which depended on a stable dollar, was in danger. The gold standard had broken down in the 1930s, and although many said "good riddance to its rigidities," leading governments, at least their bankers, yearned for its pre-1914 stabilities. In 1944, a conference at Bretton Woods, New Hampshire, founded the International Monetary Fund to oversee a new monetary system that was intended to achieve the advantages of the gold standard, particularly the steadiness of fixed exchange rates, without its rigidities. Changes in rates under stress could be agreed without provoking rate wars – competitive devaluations – like those that disrupted trade in the 1930s. Gold was the ultimate reserve, but since most of it was held by the United States, the dollar became the main international currency.

It is not clear whether the postwar boom in international trade was helped or hindered by the Bretton Woods system, but it contained inconsistencies that were bound to bring about its demise, which came in 1971. First, the primary macroeconomic goal of the postwar world was full employment. This meant fiscal stimulation and easy money, resulting in inflation differences that were inconsistent with fixed exchange rates. Second, the so-called fixed rates also lacked credibility because, under the Bretton Woods rules of adjustment, they were not binding on monetary and fiscal policies. The third inconsistency followed from the general price increases relative to the fixed $35 per ounce price of gold that discouraged gold production and additions to gold reserves. The increase in international reserves needed for the growth in international trade required additional dollars which the United States supplied by running trade deficits. Countries began to lose confidence in the dollar and increasingly converted it to gold as the gold/dollar ratio fell (Triffin 1960).

The end of the Bretton Woods system looked near when Nixon came to office. In June 1969, a Treasury group laid out three options that necessarily resembled the alternatives considered on earlier occasions of international monetary stress, modified by the dominant role of the dollar: suspension (close the gold window), devaluation, and a general realignment of currencies (Volcker and Gyohten 1992: 67–68).

Nothing was done at the time because there was no urgent pressure for a change despite the threats to the fixed rates of Bretton Woods. International trade was thriving and the dollar system benefited the United States. The fundamental solution of bringing inflation under control was not seriously considered. Action would wait until the issue was forced by a crisis, presumably a run on the dollar, which came in 1971.

Nixon and his Secretary of the Treasury, John Connolly, were ready, having decided to "go for a long bomb," in Nixon's words, that would turn the looming economic defeat into political victory. Connolly had found the sources of America's problems in foreign capitals and financial centers, where restrictions on American exports were hatched and speculators planned the destruction of the dollar. "My basic approach is that the foreigners are out to screw us," Connolly told a group of Treasury consultants. "Our job is to screw them first" (Odell 1982: 263).

On August 15, 1971, the President announced a 90-day wage and price freeze, a 10-percent import surcharge, and "closed the gold window." The program ended the Bretton Woods fixed-exchange-rate system and signaled that the United States would not address inflation. Controls were extended to April 1974, but wages and prices continued to rise. The main effect of the controls was to cause shortages by disrupting supply chains. The long lines of cars at gas pumps provided iconic photos of the period.

In addition to the Price Commission and the Pay Board, it seemed reasonable to add a Committee on Interest and Dividends, headed of course by the Fed chairman. Burns found himself explaining to Congress that raising interest rates was part of fighting inflation while at the same time pressuring bankers into not raising loan rates in line with money market rates. "To a large degree, we are chasing shadows here," he told the Joint Economic Committee (1973: 429). "What an ugly tree has grown from your seeds," the unsympathetic President said (Wells 1994: 113).

The 1970s inflation was not due to the oil-price shock. Rather, the reverse was true. Crude oil prices had risen 7 percent between 1963 and 1970, a quarter of US inflation, and the Organization of Petroleum Exporting Countries (OPEC) stepped up plans to coordinate prices and take control of their production and distribution. Noting industrial inflation, OPEC announced a price hike in February 1971, and a month after the announcement of the Nixon package, which effectively stated that nothing would be done about American, and probably Western, inflation, OPEC resolved to offset foreign costs. The West's assistance of Israel in the 1973 Yom Kippur War unified the Arab countries sufficiently to enable them to put their 1971 plan into operation.

Congress' response

Politicians were not unhappy with the monetary expansion of 1972 – although it came to be regarded as one of Nixon's dirty tricks – but were dismayed by its consequences. The high interest rates and recession of 1973–5, the severest since the 1930s, led to cries for the reform of monetary policy, strengthened by the post-Watergate unhappiness with government. There was sentiment in Congress to take back the direction of monetary policy, strengthened by the democratization of the selection of committee chairmen and the reform-minded freshman class elected in 1974. One victim was the 82-year-old Patman, whose long but intellectually shallow opposition to the Fed had been ineffective.

His successor took up Patman's "populist attack on the Fed," Kettl (1986: 143–144) wrote, but instead of simply complaining about tight money and banker control, Wisconsin Democrat Henry Reuss "was very concerned about exerting congressional dominance over the Federal Reserve," first through "a resolution to lower the interest rate by increasing the money supply." This was dropped, but Congress imposed substantial reporting requirements on the Fed. House Concurrent Resolution 133 of March 24, 1975, required Fed officials to "consult with Congress" four times a year, twice with the banking committee of each House, and to reveal its "objectives and plans with respect to the ranges of growth or diminution of monetary and credit aggregates in the upcoming twelve months." For the first time, "Congress had voted to require Fed officials to testify regularly and publicly on past policies and future plans." Friedman called the resolution "the most constructive change in the structure for the formulation of monetary policy" since the Banking Act of 1935 (Woolley 1984: 144; Kettl 1986: 145–146; Friedman 1975: 34).

Monetarists and populists believed they had gained leverage over the Fed even though their objectives diverged. The monetarists wanted predictability, price stability, and neutral money (Friedman 1960), while modern populists never find money easy enough, although they manage at the same time to complain of inflation. Populism has had many meanings, but in monetary histories the word typically refers to the grassroots movement of small farmers of the South and Midwest in the late nineteenth century who opposed banks, railroads, corporations, and other large money interests, particularly in the cities of the East. They were suspicious of "big government," but increasingly looked to that body for protection and low interest rates, which they believed the Fed should provide. In 1920, when Fed credit and commodity prices were rising more than 20 percent per annum, and the Fed had raised its discount rate to 6 percent, Oklahoma Senator Robert Owen, who had managed the Federal Reserve bill in the Senate, wrote a letter of protest to the Federal Reserve Board. The Fed should set interest rates by the same criteria as commercial banks, he wrote. The latter were

> justified in charging six and seven percent because they pay two and three percent for deposits.... If the Reserve Banks would be content with the same margin of profit, ... they would be charging a rate of between three and four percent.
>
> (Harding 1925: 195–200)

The connections between populism and easy money have varied. The majority of small farmers of the early nineteenth-century South and West were conservative, monetarily and otherwise, opposed to banks, easy money, and inflation. Their spokesmen included the hard-money Jefferson and Jackson. The latter part of the century saw a shift to easy money in a reaction to the long deflation. A recent development has been the return to conservatism evidenced by the Red States. Easy money is now more closely associated with the cities and the East and West Coasts, with Christopher Dodd and Barney Frank of New England and Henry Waxman and Maxine Waters of California, although Senators Richard Durbin of East St. Louis and Carl Levin of Detroit, both educated at eastern private schools, should not be forgotten. Easy money is now associated with Keynesian interventionists and the politically Liberal supporters of big government, although "populism" is still a valued political currency and the language is "the same as if they were all back on the farm" (Hammond 1957: 328–329, 628–630).

A logical hurdle in the way of constructive dialogue between easy-money groups, called populists or not, and the Fed has been the former's commitment to the cost-push story in which high interest causes inflation, with the blissful prospect of simultaneously low interest rates and stable prices (Horwich 1966). Much of the testimony of Fed officials consists of attempts to educate congressional committees of the contradictory nature of these goals.

The new reporting disappointed its architects because it failed to elicit the answers desired. Reuss and William Proxmire of the Senate Banking Committee wanted numerical money and interest targets, preferably high and low, respectively, and time frames for their achievement. However, the Fed led by Chairman Burns, gave them "general objectives." Representatives of the Fed "appeared before the banking committees armed with growth rate ranges for five different measures of money and credit aggregates," enabling them

> to create confusion and to direct attention away from policy objectives and toward the technical question of the best M. Furthermore, the growth rate ranges for the aggregates were enough to guarantee that at least one fell within the target range

a member of the Fed's staff has written (Pierce 1978). In any case, the Fed could not be confronted with misses since with rolling predictions (from the previous meeting) outcomes were constantly in the future. Moreover, money was at least a step removed from the variables of interest, such as output, employment, and prices, for which the Fed could not be held fully accountable.

The resolution was converted to law in the Federal Reserve Reform Act of 1977, and the Humphrey–Hawkins (Full Employment) Act of 1978 further mandated that within 30 days of the President's transmission of the *Economic Report* to Congress, the Fed inform Congress of its own policy goals and explain their relations to the President's. In addition, the Fed would issue semi-annual reports of its projections of GNP, inflation, and unemployment for the coming year. "For the first time," the Fed's ever-hopeful critics noted, the institution "faced regular and permanent congressional oversight on the substance of monetary policy, how policy matched fiscal policy, and what economic effects Fed officials expected these policies to produce" (Kettl 1986: 149–150).

Disappointed again, members of Congress and economists found the Fed's reporting "fuzzy," a smokescreen, and "disgraceful sham" that "has not altered the conduct of monetary policy" (Meiselman interview, *Wall Street Journal*, March 22, 1984). The last phrase tells us the true source of disappointments with the Fed. Congress' reporting requirements were themselves mostly a smokescreen. The Fed is actually an open book. Its monetary actions – open-market operations and changes in the discount rate – are public information. Future actions are unknown – to the Fed as much as to Congress – except that they will be complicated reactions of the kinds seen in the past, such as combinations of "leaning against the wind" and monetizing deficits. Neither members of Congress nor Fed officials were prepared to discuss the niceties of an econometric model with conditional probabilities of monetary reactions to uncertain shocks. There were no hard questions.

Congress did not just want numbers. It wanted particular numbers. Fed appearances on Capitol Hill gave committee members a public forum in which to stage their mostly easy-money preferences, to which officials usually replied that low interest today means inflation and high interest later. The Fed's model under Martin, "leaning against the wind with credibility" (Hetzel 2012: 197), was straightforward and familiar to those who knew the classics (Wood 2014). Nevertheless, self-styled populists, Keynesian interventionists with their Phillips Curve, the Executive, congressional spenders, and other easy-money interests, no longer restrained by the gold standard, exerted continuous pressure on the Fed.

There have been many such confrontations, including the Hearing before the House Subcommittee on Domestic and International Monetary Policy on the *Report of the Federal Reserve Board pursuant to the Full Employment and Balanced Growth Act of 1978* on July 22, 1998. Times were good, Greenspan informed the Committee. The economy was strong, although no longer in a boom, and prices were stable.

So far this year, our economy has continued to enjoy a virtuous cycle. Evidence of accelerated productivity has been bolstering expectations of future corporate earnings, thereby fueling still further increases in equity values, and the improvements in productivity have been helping to reduce inflation. In the context of subdued price increases and generally supportive credit conditions, rising equity values have provided impetus to spending, and, in turn, the expansion of output, employment, and productivity-enhancing capital investment.

The essential precondition for the emergence and persistence of this virtuous cycle is arguably the decline in the rate of inflation to near price stability.

The unemployment rate was 4.5 percent and falling, and the federal government deficit had turned to surplus. The first speaker after the chairperson, Boston congressman Barney Frank, was still not satisfied with monetary policy. Although, "for the first time in my memory we do not meet under ... the imminent threat of a rate increase being rattled by some of the Chairman's tellings," Frank complained about the Fed's tendency to be more concerned with inflation than economic growth, and its "predisposition to raise interest rates." He lumped this complaint with the trade recommendations of economists who conceal the negative effects of free trade (and by implication the damages of anti-inflation policies) because "they are afraid of populistic viewpoints [and] are afraid that if we learn what was happening, we might kind of slip the traces."

Frank was one of several committee members who made statements but asked no questions. Others said:

Mel Watt (D, NC): I hope you [Greenspan] will specifically comment on one concern that I have and certainly not professing to be an expert in this area, but there is a clear interplay between unemployment and interest rates and inflation.... [U]nemployment in the aggregate has been very low, but in some parts of our communities, inner cities in particular, unemployment continues to be in double digits. And so I hope you will address your approach to deciding when to raise interest rates taking that into account.

Joseph P. Kennedy II (D, MA): [A]fter reading today's papers and hearing of your testimony yesterday on the Senate side, I am concerned that we are in the midst of a dilemma where, when it comes to the major overriding concern of the U.S. economy, we talk about the threat of inflation, which seems driven by the idea that somehow there is an unemployment number that threatens to create increased prices, and I worry that we essentially put the poorest of the poor in an untenable position...

We cut the housing budget [and] raise interest rates, therefore cutting off the very stepladder [needed] to get a job. [W]e say, "Oh, sorry, gang." I guess the overall economy is going to be threatened [by] inflation, so therefore we are going to cut off the ability of these people to ever get out, thereby creating this sort of perpetual hamster-like treadmill of economic life for the poor.

Carolyn Maloney (D, NY): [Y]our comments [that] the potential for accelerating inflation is probably greater than the risk of protracted, excessive weakness in the economy ... seem to sound like there is a bias toward raising interest rates.

We see thousands of people "walking around who are unemployed," especially minorities, Maxine Waters and Barbara Lee (D, CA) said. Other committee members made similar statements, although interest rates were their lowest during any economic expansion since the 1960s. There had been vaunted changes in economic theory, Keynesianism and the Phillips Curve were dead or in their last throes, succeeded by rational expectations and the conviction that the central bank ought to pursue the single goal of price stability. Yet Congress, at least their statements, had not changed. The same may be said of their silences. Sound-money members hoped for the best and let the Fed bear the unpopularity of tight money (Timberlake 1993: 393, 409). If we look for consistency in their policy statements, conscious or not, we find it in inflation's erosion of government debt, which, it should be noted, cannot be for the benefit of the poor, who are the most vulnerable to inflation. The inflation tax is among the most regressive, and does not help growth (Sturzenegger 1992; Romer and Romer 1998; Glanville 2013: ch. 5).

Fed officials were not always at odds with these congressional sentiments, as suggested by the following statements of Federal Reserve Bank presidents (Weintraub 1978):

Phillip Coldwell (Dallas): The Federal Reserve has normally taken a position that it should support the credit of the United States in its issuance of any securities.... And we monetized the Government's efforts to spend during the Vietnam War.

Robert Mayo (Chicago): The Treasury has to borrow in a real market. The Federal Reserve, I think, has a responsibility – I wouldn't call it a compulsion – to see that a Treasury offering when properly priced in the given market environment is not thwarted by tightening up on monetary policy.

Robert Black (Richmond): You know you pretty well have to underwrite those deficits unless you are going to crush out of the private economy an equal amount of spending.

The government is unwilling to pay the market rate of interest. The private sector is going to be "crushed" (crowded out) one way or another by government spending. These Bank presidents were among the more conservative members of the FOMC in their voting (Chappell and McGregor 2000), and publicly opposed inflation, but did not always see, or choose to see, the consequences of their policies. Perhaps the only difference between the groups is in their rhetoric – central bankers are proud to fight inflation while members of Congress oppose tight money on behalf of their constituents – while they pursue the same objective.

Although the Executive dominates monetary policy by its budget policy (Weintraub 1978), Congress wants to appear to be in control. But they don't work at it. Congress salves its conscience by passing laws, James Pierce (1978) wrote, and they enlist the time of many people in hearings, or political shows, but little in the kind of work that might be translated into meaningful oversight of the Fed. Of course they should also seriously consider how much inflation they want. In the meantime, matters are out of their hands and inflation persists until public dissatisfaction compels restraint, such as in 1979.

New operating procedures, 1979

President Jimmy Carter declined to reappoint Burns at the end of his term in February 1978, choosing businessman G. William Miller, who shared the President's belief in a monetary policy that was at once "accommodative" and "credible" (*Economic Report of the President* 1981: Introduction). Carter followed Nixon in looking for painless, non-monetary, direct solutions through successive inflation czars, whom William Buckley likened to directors of the Soviet Civil Liberties Union (Universal Press Syndicate October 16, 1980). In mid 1979, amid rising inflation, oil prices, and interest rates, a falling dollar, and the general loss of confidence expressed in his "malaise" speech, Carter was in political trouble. He trailed Ted Kennedy in the polls for his party's presidential nomination the next year. He reshuffled his administration and appointed a hard-money man to lead the Fed.

The markets responded to Volcker's appointment – stocks, bonds, and the dollar rallied – but soon resumed their declines. An appointment was not enough. The markets would have to be shown. "In September 1979," Volcker recalled, "the markets seemed confident of only one thing: bet on inflation. Even if the cost to do so was rising, that cost lagged inflation, and there always seemed to be enough money to finance whatever you wanted to buy" (Volcker and Gyohten 1992: 166).

Figure 5.5 shows that increases in the fed funds rate had been too little and too late to prevent the need for further rises. The Fed had underestimated the strength of inflationary expectations and/or would not take the political risk of raising the rate sufficiently to reduce the rate of inflation. (Burns' calls for controls and structural changes can be interpreted as symptoms of that political fear.) No one could know what that rate was, particularly in light of the Fed's lack of credibility, but the inflation had to be brought down sometime.

The opportunity for action grew as inflation became stagflation and Public Enemy No. 1 (*Time* January 17, 1978), so that Volcker felt the Fed possessed almost a free hand. Its signals were uncertain, however. Volcker hoped that the

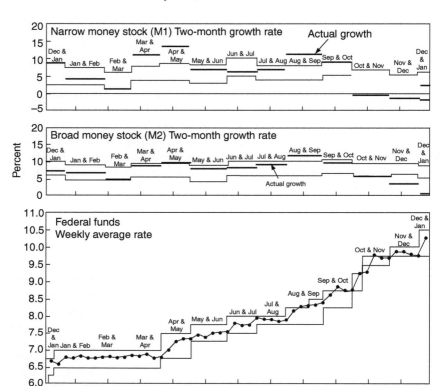

Figure 5.5 FOMC ranges for short-run monetary growth and for the Federal funds rate, 1978.

Notes

Shaded bands in the upper two charts are the FOMC's specified ranges for money supply growth over the two-month periods indicated. No lower bound was established for M1 at the October and November meetings. In the bottom chart, the shaded bands are the specified ranges for Federal fund rate variation. Actual growth rates in the upper two charts are based on data available at the time of the second FOMC meeting after the end of each period.

* Seasonally adjusted annual rates.

half-percent increase in the discount rate in mid-September, the second in a month, would impress the markets. However, the Board's vote, announced with the rate, was four to three. "Ordinarily, I might have been reluctant to move with such a split Board," Volcker writes,

> but I knew from the discussion the four votes were solid.... There was no reason for me to believe that further steps to tighten could not be taken when and if I was prepared to make the case for them.

(Volcker and Gyohten 1992: 165–166)

The press and the market didn't see it that way. To them, the split vote spelled hesitation and left the impression that this would be the Board's last move to tighten money. Volcker found a solution in Carter's question: "Why can't you control the quantity of money without raising interest rates?" (Greider 1987: 120). That could not be done but the Fed might find a use for monetarism, after all. It could fix the quantity of money and let the market find the right interest rates without incurring blame for their increase.

Volcker found the Bank presidents "eager to proceed," but he wanted more support from the Board. Surprisingly, the inflation hawks who had voted with him on the last discount rate increase were the most reluctant, while the doves saw the New Operating Procedure (NOP) as a way off the hook. As a president put it: "Everyone could say: 'Look, no hands'." The hawks went along in the interests of consensus (Volcker and Gyohten 1992: 107, 169; Greider 1987: 111–113; Hetzel 2008: 97).[2]

They didn't know what they were in for. Interest rates reacted strongly to Volcker's announcement of the NOP on October 6 (T bill rates rose a full percentage point the first business day), and continued to climb the next six months. The prime rate exceeded 20 percent most of the next two years.

Excerpts from FOMC Directives to the manager of the Open Market Desk in New York are shown in Table 5.2. The first, on September 18, 1979, directed the

Table 5.2 FOMC Directives before and after October 6, 1979

September 18, 1979. Early in the period before the next regular meeting, System open market operations are to be directed at attaining a weekly average federal funds rate slightly above the current level. Subsequently, operations shall be directed at maintaining the weekly average federal funds rate within the range of 11.25 to 11.75 percent. In deciding on the specific objective for the federal funds rate, the Manager for Domestic Operations shall be guided mainly by the relationship between the latest estimates of annual rates of growth in the September–October period of M1 and M2 and the following ranges of tolerance: 3 to 8 percent for M1 and 6.5 to 10.5 percent for M2. If rates of growth of M1 and M2, given approximately equal weight, appear to be close to or beyond the upper or lower limits of the indicated ranges, the objective for the funds rate is to be raised or lowered in an orderly fashion within its range.

April 22, 1980. In the short run, the Committee seeks expansion of reserve aggregates consistent with growth over the first half of 1980 at an annual rate of 4.5 percent for M1A and 5 percent for M1B,[a] or somewhat less, provided that in the period before the next regular meeting the weekly average federal funds rate remains within a range of 13 to 19 percent...

If it appears during the period before the next meeting that the constraint on the federal funds rate is inconsistent with the objective for the expansion of reserves, the Manager for Domestic Operations is promptly to notify the Chairman who will then decide whether the situation calls for supplementary instructions from the Committee.

Source: *Federal Reserve Bulletin*, November 1979 and June 1980.

Note
a M1A and M1B were new monetary aggregates, the first being currency and transaction (mainly checking) accounts in all depository institutions, the second limited to those in commercial banks.

manager to conduct open market purchases and sales to keep the Fed funds rate between 11.25 and 11.75 percent, and the annual rate of growth of narrow money (M1) between 3 and 8 percent. The narrow interest range and the wide money range suggest that, because of its importance or attainability, the interest rate was the principal target. The post-October 1979 directive reversed the relative importance of money and interest.

More surprising than the volatility of interest rates, which were expected to fluctuate under the new procedure, was the increased volatility of money. Money was supposed to be controlled, but it was more volatile after October 1979 than before. Milton Friedman (1982) complained about the bad name the Fed was giving monetarism, which for him meant a constant rate of money growth. Nevertheless, money growth came down, and so did inflation, although with more variability and greater economic cost, including two short but sharp recessions, that surprised even those who had warned of the inevitable pain of ending inflation. The fall in interest rates to politically acceptable levels allowed a return to interest targets in 1983.

Almost price stability, 1979–99

> [P]rice stability ... is to be treasured and enshrined as the prime policy priority; that objective is inextricably part of a broader concern about the basic stability of the financial and economic system.
>
> (Volcker 1994)

> Monetary policy basically is a single tool and you can only implement one goal consistently.
>
> (Greenspan 1994)

Following the joint occurrence of inflation and unemployment – stagflation – in the 1970s, several countries gave increased emphasis to price stability, formalized in the late 1980s by inflation targeting. Central banks were given more independence to pursue low-inflation targets assigned by or negotiated with their governments. These political choices reflected the unpopularity of inflation and a renewed understanding of credibility. The high real rates in the 1980s and 1990s in Table 5.3 resulted from the slow responses of expectations to changes in inflation. Markets did not believe the central bankers. Inflation targeting hoped to anchor those expectations. "We really, really mean it, this time."

Fed Chairman Greenspan explained the policy to a congressional committee:

> Variations in the stance of policy ... in response to evolving forces are made in the framework of an unchanging objective – to foster as best we can those financial conditions most likely to promote sustained economic expansion at the highest rate possible. Maximum sustainable growth, as history so amply demonstrates, requires price stability. Irrespective of the complexities of economic change, our primary goal is to find those policies that best

Table 5.3 Inflation (*p*), government long-term bond yields (*R*), and real rates (*r*)

	1880–1913	1953–62	1963–72	1973–82	1983–92	1993–2002	2003–10
p							
UK	−0.33	2.54	4.96	14.19	5.50	2.44	2.31
NZ		3.09	5.07	13.96	8.00	2.01	2.71
US	−0.15	1.33	3.29	8.74	3.81	2.52	2.44
Germany	−0.49	2.09*	3.24	5.37	1.85	1.85	1.52
Switzerland		1.32	4.04	4.92	3.19	1.12	0.88
R							
UK	2.76	5.61	7.53	13.39	10.01	6.38	4.41
NZ		5.09	5.37	9.68	13.19	6.92	5.73
US	2.34	3.44	5.45	9.36	9.11	5.89	4.02
Germany	3.60	6.46*	7.20	8.33	7.30	5.34	3.67
Switzerland		3.03	4.53	5.02	5.03	3.60	2.31
r=R−p							
UK	3.09	3.07	2.57	−0.80	4.51	3.94	2.10
NZ		2.00	0.30	−4.28	5.19	4.91	3.02
US	2.49	2.11	2.16	0.62	5.30	3.37	1.58
Germany	3.60	4.37*	3.96	2.96	5.45	3.49	2.15
Switzerland		1.71	0.49	0.10	1.84	2.48	1.43

Sources: International Monetary Fund, *International Financial Statistics*; Homer and Sylla (2005); Mitchell (2007).

Note
* 1956–62.

contribute to a non-inflationary environment and hence to growth. The Federal Reserve, I trust, will always remain vigilant in pursuit of that goal.

(Chairman Alan Greenspan presenting the Federal Reserve's *Report on Monetary Policy* to the Senate Committee on Banking, Housing and Urban Affairs, July 20, 2000)

At a Federal Reserve conference a quarter-century after October 1979, then-Governor Bernanke (2005a) reflected on "What have we learned since" that reform. Mostly, he said, we have learned the importance of the central bank's credibility to the effectiveness of monetary policy – a credibility that Volcker did not enjoy. The Fed's success in bringing down inflation was due to its determination over many years. The high real rates in Figure 5.1 and Table 5.3 indicate that the inflationary expectations of a skeptical public remained unbroken into the next century. Bernanke attributes the growing importance of credibility to the academic work of Kenneth Rogoff (1985), Finn Kydland and Edward Prescott (1977), and Carl Walsh (1995), although we have seen its importance to Chairman Martin in the 1960s, as well as to Baring in 1797 and Hankey in 1867. Bernanke and Volcker deplored the Fed's lack of credibility, as we have seen, and their statements above are examples of Volcker's and Greenspan's attempts to achieve it.

It is ironic given this purported lesson that the Fed's deviation from it has grown in recent years. Its unprecedented behavior, such as the composition and massive growth of its balance sheet, rates on bank reserves, and the tremendous overhang of excess reserves, have made monetary policy unnecessarily inexplicable and unpredictable, and must bear a large part of the responsibilities for the Great Recession and the weak recovery.

Bernanke in fact applauded the lack of continuity necessary to credibility when he said that the real significance of the Volcker experience was the presence of "one of the rare individuals tough enough and with sufficient foresight to do what had to be done." The possibilities are endless. During the 1980s and 1990s, the FOMC dropped the "reasonable" qualifier from "price stability" in its Directive of March 1988, and told Congress that it was "committed to the achievement, over time, of price stability," an "objective [which] derives from the fact that the prospects for long-run growth in the economy are brightest when inflation need no longer be a material consideration in the decisions of households and firms."[3] The Fed's confidence in its strength vis-à-vis the Executive was demonstrated in 1988, when Greenspan publicly "objected quite strongly" to a letter from the Treasury's Chief Economist urging it to spur the economy (Havrilesky 1993: 37).

Fed officials have indicated a desire for inflation targeting,[4] although the American version would have to differ from others. Inflation targeting elsewhere is enacted and administered by legislatures that are not distinct from executives, and are political commitments. Congress is unlikely to give the Fed the power to choose the target, it would not allow the Executive to be involved, and Congress presently has no executive body to fix the goal and monitor its achievement. Structural changes would be needed in Congress and the central bank.

There were also indications that the Fed had not completely committed to the single target. It had not forgotten the Phillips Curve. Chairman Greenspan told the House Budget Committee during the 1990–1 recession:

> The conduct of monetary policy ... has involved a careful balancing of the need to respond to signs that economic activity was slowing perceptibly, on the one hand, and the need to contain inflationary pressures on the other.
>
> (*Federal Reserve Bulletin* January 1991)

John Taylor (1993) explained the Fed's behavior during 1987–92 as a trade-off between output and inflation, and the "Taylor rule" became a standard way of looking at and even judging monetary policy. This public "dual mandate" was expressed by the FOMC (November 15, 2000) during the next recession a decade later, and in its January 2012 "statement of principle regarding longer-run goals and monetary policy strategy."

> The FOMC is firmly committed to fulfilling its statutory mandate from the Congress of promoting maximum employment, stable prices, and moderate long-term interest rates...
>
> In setting monetary policy, the Committee seeks to mitigate deviations of inflation from its longer-run goal and deviations of employment from the Committee's assessments of its maximum level. These objectives are generally complementary. However, under circumstances in which the Committee judges that the objectives are not complementary, it follows a balanced approach in promoting them, taking into account the magnitude of the deviations and the potentially different time horizons over which employment and inflation are projected to return to levels judged consistent with its mandate.

We have seen that these promises have been subject to the interests of fiscal policy and financial institutions. Regarding the former, another Treasury–Fed accord has been urged, one which clarifies the boundary of responsibilities for monetary and credit policy, and in 2009 it was agreed that

> (i) Fed credit policy should aim to improve financial conditions broadly, and not allocate credit to narrowly defined sectors or classes of borrowers, (ii) government decisions to influence the allocation of credit are the province of the fiscal authorities, (iii) Fed credit policy should not constrain monetary policy needed to foster maximum sustainable employment and price stability, (iv) the Treasury will remove or liquidate the Maiden Lane facilities [created in June 2008 for Bear Stears' assets] on the Fed's balance sheet, and (v) the Fed's independence with regard to monetary policy is critical for ensuring that monetary policy decisions are made with regard only to the long-term economic welfare of the nation.

This statement had all the signs of another "we won't do it again" posture while the regretted activities continued. "The joint statement was welcome and had much to recommend it," Marvin Goodfriend (2011) observed, but "did not provide a set of *principles* that could serve comprehensively to clarify the boundary of responsibilities between the Treasury and the Fed." Maiden Lane was paid off in 2012, but the Fed continued to buy more mortgage-backed than Treasury securities.

In the depths of the Great Recession, Bernanke rejected suggestions that the Fed pursue a monetary policy strategy aimed at pushing up inflation expectations to reduce real rates and stimulate spending and output. His response was based on a concern for the Fed's credibility. "[T]hat theoretical argument," Bernanke said (notice the disparagement of "theory," which suggests a rational system) "ignores the risk that such a policy could cause the public to lose confidence in the central bank's willingness to resist further upward shifts in inflation, and so undermine the effectiveness of monetary policy going forward."

Paul Krugman (2009) called Bernanke's position "fundamentally absurd – as absurd as the inflation fears that paralyzed the Bank of England [and the Fed] in the early 1930s even as the world went into a deflationary spiral." A problem with the arguments on both sides is that the Fed, like the post-1914 Bank of England, has no credibility to lose. Before 1914, the Bank could respond to shocks with minimal damage to the economy because of its commitment to convertibility. After 1918, its pursuit of an overvalued pound was supported – barely, from 1925 to 1931 – by deflation, unemployment, and foreign borrowing.

There is as little basis today for predictions of Fed policy. Every day is new. There is no policy, that is, no pattern of decisions guided by a rational principle. There have been times when the Fed appeared to have a policy: leaning against the wind with credibility under Martin (Hetzel 2012: 197) and what must be called reduced inflation (actually a return to pre-1965) under Volcker and Greenspan. Shifts, however, raise the question of whether "policy" is the right word. Small sets of incentives and interests govern policy, but their relative strengths fluctuate with administrations, budgets, and politics.

The complex outcomes of these forces were illustrated in an interview with Charles Plosser. President of the Federal Reserve Bank of Philadelphia (*New York Times* December 9, 2013). He was asked how he thought the Fed should "explain to investors exactly how the current bond-buying program is going to end." "Just do it," he effectively said. "Pick a time and reduce the ... constant uncertainty about what we'll do at each and every meeting." We created (the QE3) "program with the idea that somehow we could fine-tune the rate of purchases to adjust to the economy. [W]e've learned it's not that easy. We're getting a lot of volatility and a lot of uncertainty meeting after meeting."

> I've been talking for a few years now about how complicated we've made monetary policy, all this stuff on the margins in which we're trying to make decisions and influence markets and change expectations. I've become concerned that we've made it so complicated that we're getting in our own way.

The objective function is uncertain – some goals are more important than others, but not always in the same degree – and the path even more so. The next chapter describes remarkable examples of these forces during the recent Great Recession.

Notes

1 See Eisner (1969) for the ineffectiveness of the 1968 tax-surcharge.
2 Advisor Stephen Axilrod (2011: 108) has a somewhat different view of Volcker's "cover."
3 *Monetary Policy Report to the Congress*, pursuant to the Full Employment and Balanced Growth Act of 1978, February 20, 1990. Timberlake (1993: 391) noted the shift to the single goal of price stability in 1988.
4 For example, Bernanke in his Fed chairmanship nomination hearing, Senate Banking Committee, November 2005.

Plate 3 A bread line at Sixth Avenue and 42nd Street, New York City, during the Great Depression (©CORBIS; Photographer: H.W. Fechner).

Plate 4 A gas line, 1973 (©Bettmann/CORBIS).

Plate 5 USA-economy-rally to stop foreclosures, 2011 (©Max Whittaker/Reuters/Corbis).

Plate 6 Federal Reserve Centennial Advisory Council, December 16, 2013

Notes

Back row from left to right: Paul A. Volcker (honorary co-chairman), Eugene White, professor of economics, Rutgers University; G. William Beale, CEO of Union First Market Bank; Marvin Goodfriend, professor of economics at Carnegie Mellon University, Tepper School of Business, and chairman of The Gailliot Center; George Kaufman, professor of finance and economics, Loyola University; James Leach former US Congressman and current visiting professor of law, University of Iowa; *Middle row from left to right*: Paul Sarbanes, former US Senator; Alan Greenspan (honorary co-chairman); John Wood, professor of economics, Wake Forest University; Allan Meltzer, professor of political economy, Carnegie Mellon University, Tepper School of Business; Jeffrey Gerhart, chairman, Bank of Newman Grove; Denis Hughes, senior operating partner for government relations, Stonepeak Infrastructure Partner; Charles Calomiris, professor of financial institutions, Columbia University; Eileen Fitzgerald, CEO, NeighborWorks America; *Front row from left to right*: Richard Sylla, professor of history of financial institutions and markets and professor of economics, New York University, Stern School of Business; David Cowen, president and CEO, Museum of American Finance; Michael Bordo, professor of economics and director of the Center for Monetary and Financial History, Rutgers University; Ben S. Bernanke, chairman, Board of Governors of the Federal Reserve System; Nan J. Morrison, president and CEO, Council for Economic Education; E. Gerald Corrigan, managing director, Goldman Sachs Group, Inc., and chairman, Goldman Sachs Bank, USA; Roger W. Ferguson, Jr., president and CEO, TIAA-CREF.

6 The Great Recession

The Great Recession, dated from the December 2007 peak to the June 2009 trough, deserved its name. The 4.7 percent fall in real GDP exceeded all previous post-World War II declines (the next largest, 1973–5, was 3.2 percent), although it did not approach the one-third fall of the Great Depression of 1929–33, or the 10-percent fall of 1937–8.

The responses of government were as memorable as the decline itself, and perhaps more dramatic. They included massive stimulus packages, record peacetime budget deficits, and the acceleration of the Federal Reserve's transformation from central bank to fiscal adjunct, that is, from support of the payments system to allocator of credit even beyond the inflation tax that was already its chief function. The shifts in Fed credit from government securities to toxic mortgages and the bailouts of financial and even manufacturing firms were significant developments in government as much as in economic policy. It had been thought appropriate that monetary policy be free of politics because the payments system facilitates free choices that benefit the general public, while the government's assistance to particular firms and activities requires the approval of taxpayers acting through their legislators.

This may not be the worst of it. Most of the costs are yet to be borne. The development is inefficient as well as undemocratic. The Fed's power to print money is being used to direct resources to underperforming firms and unproductive activities in ways that interfere with payments and markets, undermining the competitive system in the process.

Boom and bust

The Great Recession is known for the housing boom and bust, the collapse and government bailouts of large financial institutions, and its weak recovery. After doubling from the beginning of the decade, house prices stabilized in spring 2006, and broke a year later, falling 30 percent over the next two years. Speculation on rising house prices had been facilitated by easy terms to low-income borrowers by financial institutions able to pass on the risk of subprime mortgages through securitization. Government-sponsored enterprises (Fannie Mae and Freddy Mac) bought risky securities under the pressure of Congresses and administrations dedicated to increased homeownership. Regulators failed to restrain leverage or loan risk, understandable in a period of high bank earnings and few problem banks. Risky behavior was also encouraged by the conflicted rating agencies' practice of awarding high grades to securitized subprime mortgages.

The boom was fueled by easy Fed credit. Real interest rates were negative early in the decade (Figure 5.1), and there was considerable feeling that the Fed would not let asset prices fall. This was the so-called "Greenspan Put" (*Financial Times* 2000: December 8), although protections for risk-takers went even farther. Over 60 percent of the liabilities of US financial institutions, including all those of the 21 largest banks, were explicitly or implicitly guaranteed (Walter and Weinberg 2002).

> [T]he extraordinary risks taken by managers of large financial firms ... were the result, not of 'random mass insanity' but of moral hazard resulting in large part from the Fed's willingness – implicit in previous practice – ... to rescue creditors of failed firms.
>
> (Calomiris 2009; Selgin *et al.* 2012)

Many of these hopes were disappointed when the Fed responded belatedly and inadequately to the recession.

After ease early in the decade, the Fed reacted to fears of inflation and maintained tight money until late 2008, even through the mid-year crisis. "[S]hocks to energy prices and the housing sector started a moderate recession in December 2007, [which a] contractionary monetary policy ... intensified ... in summer 2008." The recession's "severity derived from the combined contractionary monetary policy of all the world's central banks," who worried about inflation (Hetzel 2012: 208, 220). Instead of the ease called for by the recession, the Fed decided to reallocate credit in ways that disrupted the markets they hoped to save. Throughout the period the Fed departed from its traditional policy of "lean against the wind" and accentuated economic fluctuations.

Some at the Fed attempted to deflect guilt by pointing to an over-abundance of saving in the world economy that put savers in a weak position to demand risk premia. "They made us do it," Bernanke's "global saving glut" hypothesis asserted. This explanation must be dismissed, however, because there was no such glut. Negative saving in the United States more than offset positive saving elsewhere. Global saving was low by historical standards in the early 2000s, and the somehow always surprising small risk premia during booms are an old story. Risk premia often appear to have been too small after default (Bernanke 2005b, 2007; Taylor 2009; Mintz 1951; Madden *et al.* 1937).

Four years after the trough, in mid 2013, real GDP differed little from the preceding peak, and private fixed investment and the employment rate remained depressed. It is the slowest recovery since the Great Depression, and probably for the same reason: the government's reinforcement of uncertainty and its interference with market adjustments (Higgs 1997; Cole and Ohanian 2004).

It is claimed that the collapse was unforeseen. The story is told that Queen Elizabeth II asked her guide at the LSE, whose answer accepted the premise of her question, "If these things are so large, how come everyone missed it?"[1] It is true that the regulators were caught by surprise. A few days before Bear Stearns' collapse in March 2008, an on-site inspection of its position by the US Securities and Exchange Commission staff revealed no significant issues. Its capital position was "fine." The Federal Reserve attributed increases in Bear Stearns' cost of funds to "misinformation in the press" (McKinley 2011: 9–12). At the same time, individual investors and institutions were reducing their exposure to the company. A few of those who saw the collapse coming are listed with their alarms in Table 6.1. The regulators, on the other hand, demonstrated a combination of ignorance bordering on lack of interest and a belief in their patriotic duty to promote the boom. When in 2005 Chairman Bernanke of the Council of Economic Advisors was asked about the housing bubble, he replied that "the fundamentals are also very strong," and the rise was "supported by the strength of the economy." As Chairman of the Fed in May 2007, he saw "no serious spillover to banks or thrift institutions from the problems in the subprime market; the troubled lenders, for the most part, have not been institutions with federally insured deposits." When in July 2007 Treasury Secretary Henry Paulson was asked about the meltdown in the mortgage market, he said: "I don't think it poses any threat to the overall economy" (McKinley 2011: 120–121).

The course of Federal Reserve policy

Beginning in early 2007, banks and hedge funds reported increasing losses on subprime mortgages and mortgage-backed securities. This was especially true of adjustable-rate mortgages as interest rates rose through July 2006, and did not begin to fall until a year later. The crisis appeared in interbank lending markets in August 2007, when the London Interbank Offered Rate (Libor) and other funding rates spiked (Wheelock 2010). The Fed began to auction funds to banks against a "wide variety of collateral" in December.

The Fed's *Term Auction Facility* (TAF) was addressed to "elevated pressures in short-term funding markets" (Armantier 2008). It was a response to what was already called the subprime mortgage crisis and the widening spread between rates on overnight and term interbank lending that indicated a retreat from risk-taking. The Fed began to shift its credit from governments to mortgages, as shown in Table 6.2. US securities were reduced from 91 to 23 percent of Fed credit between November 2007 and November 2008. Surprisingly, in view of the announced purpose to enhance liquidity, the monetary base was held virtually constant until October 2008, and even afterwards the Fed's effect on money was slight because the increase in its credit went mainly into Treasury balances at the Fed and bank excess reserves. The program was simply a shift of Fed credit from US securities to "troubled" private assets.

Table 6.1 Unsurprised by the housing crisis and recession

Name	Affiliation	Quote
Dean Baker	Center for Economic and Policy Research	"… plunging housing investment will likely push the economy into recession." (2006)
Wynne Godley and Gennaro Zezza	Levy Economics Institute	"The small slowdown in the rate at which US household debt [is] resulting from the house price decline will immediately lead to a … recession." (2006)
Fred Harrison	Economic commentator	"The next property market tipping point is due at end of 2007 or early 2008.… The only way prices can be brought back to affordable levels is a slump or recession." (2005)
Michael Hudson	University of Missouri	"Debt deflation will shrink the real economy, drive down real wages, and push our debt-ridden economy into Japan-style stagnation or worse." (2006)
Eric Janszen	Investor and commentator	"The US will enter a recession within years." (2006)
Stephen Keen	University of Western Sydney	"Long before we manage to reverse the current rise in debt, the economy will be in a recession. On current data, we may already be in one." (2006)
Jakob Madsen	Copenhagen University	"We are seeing very large bubbles and if they burst, there is no backup. The outlook is very bad." (2005) "The bursting of this housing bubble will have a severe impact on the world economy and may even result in a recession." (2006)
Kurt Richebächer	Investment newsletter	"The new housing bubble – together with the stock and bond bubbles – will invariably implode in the foreseeable future, plunging the U.S. economy into a protracted, deep recession." (2001)
Nouriel Roubini	New York University	"Real home prices are likely to fall at least 30% over the next 3 years." (2005) "By itself this house price slump is enough to trigger a US recession." (2006)
Peter Schiff	Investment advisor and commentator	"The U.S. economy is like the Titanic.… I see a real financial crisis coming for the U.S." (2006) "There will be an economic collapse." (2007)
Carl Case and Robert Shiller	Yale University	"There is significant risk of a very bad period, with rising default and foreclosures, serious trouble in financial markets, and a possible recession sooner than most … expect." (2006)
Nassim Taleb	Writer/investor	"Banks are now more vulnerable to the Black Swan … than ever before.… Likewise,… Fanny Mae … seems to be sitting on a barrel of dynamite, vulnerable to the slightest hiccup." (2007, p. 225n)

Sources: "No One Saw This coming," Bezemer (2009); Madsen in *Boersen*, December 4, 2008 (trans. Soerensen); Richebächer in *The Daily Reckoning*, August 24, 2007.

Table 6.2 Factors affecting the reserve balances of depository institutions, 2007–9 (Federal Reserve Board release H1; billion dollars)

Weekly average ending	November 28, 2007	February 28, 2008	November 5, 2008	November 4, 2009
Reserve bank credit	866	867	2,056	2,147
US securities	780	713	490	777
Repurchase agreements	46	43	80	0
Federal agency securities	0	0	0	147
Mortgage backed securities[1]				774
Term auction credit[2]	0	60	301	139
Discount loans	...	...	110	22
Broker/dealer credit			77	0
Term asset backed securities[3]				43
Credit to AIG				45
Asset-backed commercial paper money market mutual fund liquidity facility			92	0
Other credit extensions[4]			80	0
Commercial paper funding facility			226	14
Portfolio holdings of Maiden Lane[5]			27	66
Float	−1	−1	−1	−2
Central bank liquidity swaps[6]				32
Other Federal Reserve assets[7]	41	51	574	90
Gold stock and special drawing rights	13	13	13	16
Treasury currency outstanding	39	39	39	43
Total reserve funds	919	919	2,108	2,206
Currency in circulation	821	815	861	918
Reverse repurchase agreements	34	40	95	61
Deposits with FR banks other than reserves	12	12		
US Treasury	5	5	590	97
Depository institutions clearing balances	6	7	6	3
Other	...	...	16	1
Other liabilities and capital	42	44	45	63
Reserve balances with FR banks (excess)	8	8	494 (453)	1,062 (1,002)

Notes
1 Guaranteed by Fannie Mae, Freddie Mac, and Ginnie Mae.
2 Reserves auctioned by the Fed to depository institutions (see text).
3 Loans to investors in asset and mortgage backed securities. "Citigroup, Ford, and JPMorgan Chase are among companies that have sold auto and credit-card debt through the TALF."
4 Emergency loans to institutions including AIG
5 "To facilitate a prompt acquisition of Bear Stearns by JPMorganChase, the FRBank of NY created a limited liability company, Maiden Lane LLC, to acquire and manage them." AIG was added.
6 Dollar values of foreign currency.
7 Accrued interest and accounts receivable; Reserve Bank premises and operating equipment; Term Asset-Backed Securities Loan Facility.
   Maiden Lane is a street in New York's financial district; the original name in New Amsterdam meant "footpath used by lovers."

The program was revised in March 2008 to the *Term Securities Lending Facility* (TSLF), still

to relieve liquidity pressure in the credit markets, specifically the mortgage-backed securities market, by which primary dealers (including banks and Fannie Mae and Freddie Mac) can access highly liquid and secure Treasury securities in exchange for the far less liquid and less safe eligible securities. This helps to increase the liquidity in the credit market for these securities.

The Fed's terminology was careless. "Liquidity" is the ready accessibility of cash on terms approximating normal market values. In times of panic – shortages of cash often caused by hoarding – nothing is liquid, and even high-grade securities cannot be sold. This characterized the panics of the nineteenth century, but not 2007 and 2008, when there was plenty of cash. The spreads seen by the Fed were risk premia. "The cash investors who had provided the short-term financing for the securitized markets did not disappear," Robert Hetzel (2012: 224) observed. "They put their funds into the insured deposits of banks (whose guarantees had been raised) and government money-market funds."

Bagehot's advice to the Bank of England in times of panic had been to lend liberally at high interest rates on good security. The Fed violated both conditions. The confusion of liquidity and solvency, along with the incredible assumption that markets are less informed than regulators, led on an expanded scale to another episode of too-big-to-fail bailouts. George Kaufman explained them to a congressional committee (US Congress 1991: May 9):

> systemic risk is ... a phantom issue. It is a scare tactic.... The runs on Continental Bank in 1984, the large Texas banks in 1987–89, and the Bank of New England in 1990–91 were rational runs on economically insolvent institutions that moved funds not into currency to start systemic risk, but to safer banks. The delayed resolutions by the regulators did little more than increase FDIC losses substantially. The small depositors are the only ones you need to worry about because they are the only ones who could run into currency. The big depositors can't. The only way that systemic risk, if there is such a thing, can occur is if there is a run on all banks into currency.

In fact, bank deposits were rising in 2007–8. Despite loose talk of the credit markets "freezing up" (or "melting down"), bank credit continued and mortgages were available to the credit-worthy at historically attractive interest rates. Figure 6.1 indicates that the abrupt increase in the three-month Libor rate relative to the overnight federal funds rate in August 2007, after the failures of banks heavily involved in mortgage-backed securities, as well as the jump in September 2008, after the failure of Lehman Brothers, were due to risk rather than illiquidity. Certificates of deposit (CDs) were in the same risk category as Libor, while overnight Fed funds were low risk (Taylor and Williams 2009). TAF probably "increased the risk premium ... because market participants interpreted the announcement by the Fed and other central banks as a sign that the financial crisis was worse than previously thought" (Thornton 2011).

Also in March 2008, the Treasury decided to bail out the investment banking firm Bear Stearns, which was heavily exposed to mortgages. Rather than seeking a congressional appropriation, it got the Federal Reserve Bank of New York to lend $30 billion to J.P. Morgan Chase (collateralized by Bear Stearns' mortgages

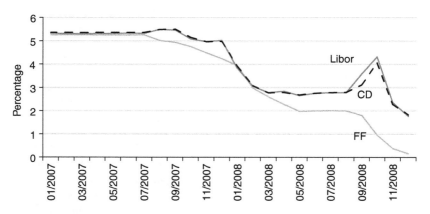

Figure 6.1 Fed funds and three-month Libor and CD rates, monthly averages 2007–8.

rather than Morgan assets) to enable a merger with Bear Stearns while guaranteeing a selection of its obligations. Bernanke, Chairman of the Fed since February 1, 2006, made the unsubstantiated claim that a Bear Stearns bankruptcy would have affected the real economy and caused a "chaotic unwinding" of investments across the nation's markets (Bloomberg news service, April 2, 2008). Intervention was necessary, he said, because "market participants would not be adequate to deal in an orderly way with the collapse of a major counterparty," even though risk spreads indicated that orderly market adjustments were underway (Bernanke 2008).

New York Fed President Timothy Geithner testified to the Senate Banking Committee that widening credit spreads were evidence that markets were not working, he called insolvency illiquidity, likened the situation to the currency crises of the nineteenth century, and called "the extensions of credit to Bear Stearns ... in keeping with the traditional role of lender of last resort" (US Congress 2008: April 3; McKinley 2011: 138–139, 310–312).

There was no basis for any of these claims. Nor was there any logic behind the idea that taxpayer credit directed to failing firms would reverse the falling course of house prices and make mortgages whole. The bailouts' main effect was to prevent market adjustments. The blow to wealth had occurred. The government's policy was to transfer that blow from those who stood to profit if things had gone well to the taxpayers. Anna Schwartz observed that saving the banking system was confused with saving the banks (Carney 2008). "We've told the world we're not going to let any of our major institutions fail," Geithner reminded his colleagues. "We're going to have to make it really clear we're standing behind Citigroup" (Paulson 2010: 407).

The Housing and Economic Recovery Act, signed into law July 30, 2008, authorized the Federal Housing Administration to guarantee up to $300 billion of new 30-year fixed-rate mortgages for subprime borrowers if lenders wrote down loans to 90 percent of current appraisal value. It was intended to restore confidence in FannieMae and FreddieMac, and encourage the flow of funds into the housing market. However, as of February 2009, only 451 applications had been received and 25 loans finalized, instead of the 400,000 homeowners that had been expected to participate. The shortfall demonstrated the emptiness of the government's promise to help Main Street borrowers, and followed from the program's high fees and interest rates, the required reduction in principal on the part of the lender, and the requirement that the federal government receive half of any appreciation in value of the house. FannieMae and FreddieMac were placed in government conservatorship on September 7, 2008.

On September 16, the Federal Reserve Board authorized the New York Fed to lend $85 billion to American International Group (AIG), rising to more than $180 billion in May 2009. AIG had sold hundreds of billions of dollars' worth of credit default swaps (CDSs) insuring collateralized debt obligations (CDOs), many backed by subprime mortgages. The Fed's loan allowed AIG to pay $53.5 billion to CDS counterparties by December 2008, the largest being Société Générale, Deutsche Bank, and Goldman Sachs.[2] Regulators had encouraged the CDS market by raising the credit ratings of bank loans insured by them, and thereby reducing required bank capital – even though they purported to insure the systemic risk of mortgages, violating the risk-independence principle of insurance.

On September 21, the Fed granted requests by the last two major investment banks, Goldman Sachs and Morgan Stanley, to change their status to bank holding companies. This gave them greater access to Fed funding in exchange for the fictional tighter regulation of banks (Saunders and Cornett 2012: 414).[3]

Summarizing the Fed's activities during the subprime crisis, former Fed economist and monetary historian David Humphrey (2010) wrote that it "deviated from the classical model in so many ways as to make a mockery of the notion that it is a lender of last resort," specifically by accepting "toxic assets" (mortgage-backed securities) above their market values as collateral for loans or buying them outright and supplying funds directly to firms understood to be insolvent. Until September 2008, the Fed also sterilized its direct lending operations through offsetting Fed sales of Treasury securities, in effect transferring some $250 billion in liquid funds from presumably solvent firms to potentially insolvent ones – a strategy precisely opposite Bagehot's, and one that tended to spread rather than to contain financial stress.

Since the excesses were confined mainly to the financial and household sectors, Willem Buiter (2008) argued, "it should have been possible to limit the spillovers ... without macroeconomic heroics. Measures directly targeted at the liquidity crunch [which we have seen was not substantial] should have been sufficient." The bailout of Bear Stearns might have been "effective in dealing with the immediate crisis, [but it was], quite unnecessarily, structured so as to maximize moral hazard by distorting private incentives in favour of excessively risky future borrowing and lending," which came home to roost later in the year.

The cuts in the discount rate penalty, the extraordinary arrangements for pricing the collateral offered to the Fed by the primary dealers through the

TSLF and the PDCF [Primary Dealer Credit Facility], the proposals for bringing forward the payment of interest on bank reserves, the terms of the Bear Stearns bailout and the "Greenspan-Bernanke put" rate cut on January 21/22, 2008, 75 basis points at an unscheduled meeting and out of normal hours, are most easily rationalized as excess sensitivity of the Fed to Wall Street concerns, reflecting (cognitive) regulatory capture of the Fed by Wall Street.

Industry capture of regulators takes many forms (Stigler 1971). Buiter's "cognitive" twist refers to "an excess sensitivity of the Fed to financial market and financial sector concerns and fears and in an overestimation of the strength of the link between financial sector [problems] and the stability and prosperity of the wider economy." "Capture" may not be the best word since the Fed, like many regulators, was established by and for their industry. The Fed was born in captivity. The chief cause of its aggressive errors during the Great Recession was not the importance it attached to the financial markets but its determination to enhance the wealth of particular individuals at the expense of those markets.

The Fed's strategy may have harmed even the troubled enterprises it was intended to assist, for if instead of reallocating credit the Fed had increased the total in the customary way, "the failures of Bear Stearns, Lehman Brothers, and AIG may have been avoided, and, so too, the need for" the massive bailout called TARP (Thornton 2009). It was thanks to TARP itself, or rather to the gloom and doom warnings of Bernanke and Paulson in their efforts to obtain TARP, that a "relatively modest contraction of economic activity due to … the deflation of house prices became the Great Recession," John Taylor (2009) wrote, giving as much blame to central banks' effects on uncertainty as to their tight money (also Goodfriend 2011).

In September 2008, the Fed at last turned from sterilized to unsterilized lending, on a scale that doubled the monetary base in eight months. "At the same time, however, it began paying interest on excess reserves, thereby increasing the demand for [them], while also arranging to have the Treasury sell supplemental bills and deposit the proceeds in a special account. Thanks in part to these special measures, bank lending, nominal GDP, and the CPI, instead of responding positively to the doubling of the monetary base, plummeted" (Selgin *et al.* 2012).

Everything about the monetary policies of the 2000s – the return to the stop–go policies of the 1960s and 1970s at the beginning, the bailouts of selected firms, credit reallocations, and gratuitous assaults on confidence – suggests that financial and economic problems would have been less serious if the Fed had stayed with what Hetzel (2012: 128–148) has called the "leaning-against-the-wind with credibility" rule of the Volcker and most of the Greenspan eras and their trust in market adjustments. The Fed possessed the powers to deal with the problems at hand, particularly in its ability to supply the needed liquidity by open-market purchases of government securities. The recession in homebuilding, with its effects on the wider economy, would have occurred, along with the problems of over-zealous lenders. Failing firms would have been allowed to disappear, potentially profitable activities would have been purchased and continued.

The *Troubled Asset Relief Program* (TARP) was the headline official response to the crisis, giving its name to the whole jumbled program because of its own mercurial adoption and implementation, and more than anything else, its inexplicable scale. On September 17, 2008, after the piecemeal actions of the preceding days and months, Chairman Bernanke and Secretary Paulson informed a meeting of congressional leaders that the financial system was on the verge of a "melt down," and if major funding was not forthcoming immediately, "there won't be an economy on Monday" – reminiscent of the Reconstruction Finance Corporation's power to buy preferred stock in banks that was introduced and acted upon in a day in 1933, with as little effect (McKinley 2011: 55–57).

The Treasury had developed a "Break the Glass Capitalization (*BTG*) Plan," typically named after an emergency metaphor, in which the US government would "recapitalize the banking sector by purchasing illiquid mortgage-related assets." The program was "designed to help banks resume lending and help stabilize the housing and mortgage markets" (Sorkin 2009: 83, 90–93; Wessel 2010: 176–177; McKinley 2011: 257–258). The author of the program admitted to the secretary that "there is no one metric I can point to. Ultimately, it's the combined judgment of Treasury and the Fed." Vincent Reinhart, former directory of Monetary Affairs at the Federal Reserve Board, summarized the situation in early October:

> Until now, the responses of government officials have been inconsistent and improvisational. The first impulse was to extend the federal safety net to investment banks. Thus, in March, the Federal Reserve rescued Bear Stearns, breaking a 60-year-old precedent by lending to a non-depository. That set in motion an uneven process of failure and intervention. The private sector lost its incentive to pump capital into troubled firms and gained an incentive to pick among the winners and losers of the government intervention lottery. Lehman Brothers or AIG? Washington Mutual or Wachovia? Rather than forecasting underlying values, financial markets were predicting government intentions. We should not be here, but we are.
> (McKinley 2011: 259)

This was a candid admission by a Fed official that the crisis, if there was one, was of the Fed's own making by its market interferences. The CEO of one of the majority of healthy banks tells the story from their viewpoint. The bailout of Bear Stearns "was a terrible message to the capital market. Since Bear Stearns was the smallest and least significant of the top six investment banks, the implication was that the larger investment banks had an implicit" government guarantee – making it less necessary to reduce their risks. However, one of those, Lehman, was allowed to fail on September 15. On September 25, after losing deposits of $16.7 billion in ten days, Washington Mutual was seized by the

Office of Thrift Supervision, which sold most of its assets, including its branch network, for what was discovered to be a low price to J.P. Morgan Chase.

The disappearance of these institutions, both larger than Lehman, was political (see below), but had no systemic effect on the system except to complete the demolition of the private market for bank capital. The greater than necessary losses to WaMu's bondholders and stockholders "destroyed the capital markets for banks," and prevented the troubled Wachovia Bank from finding a buyer at a market-relevant price. Most large institutions were healthy, and there were several potential buyers for those in trouble until the government interfered, when it became a game to see who could get the biggest subsidy. Private investors could not hope to compete with the government, particularly when it lacked recognizable criteria for action (Allison 2013: 162–163).

The regulators also were victims of their uncertainties. FDIC Chair Sheila Bair was "blindsided" ("The Wachovia Blindside" was a chapter in her 2012 book) by the Federal Reserve Bank of New York's attempt to arrange an "FDIC-assisted transaction for Citi to acquire Wachovia" when Citigroup itself was on the edge of failure. The idea was for Citi to buy Wachovia while the FDIC guaranteed the latter's subprime mortgages. "It sounded to me like a 'twofer' – a bailout for Wachovia and a bailout for Citi," Bair (2012: 96) wrote. The New York Fed's Geithner "did not want creditors, particularly bondholders, in those large, failing financial institutions to take losses. I did."

"For years, those poorly managed institutions had made huge profits and gains from their high-flying ways," while "their primary regulators, the NY Fed and OCC, had stood by." The large institutional bond investors had provided funding "on the implied assumption that if anything went wrong, the government would bail them out." But they hadn't bought insurance, the FDIC chair said. The well-heeled big-bond investors "can fend for themselves." "We charge banks a premium for [deposit] insurance…, which is inevitably passed on to consumers," who should not be expected to bail out "big banks and those who have invested in them" (Bair 2012: 99–100).

When the regulators backed out of their contract with Citi and turned to Wells Fargo, the capital markets knew "that the FDIC, the Fed, and the Treasury were not only incompetent but untrustworthy." They had no plan, and it was "clear that the rule of law no longer existed" (Allison 2013: 163–164).

Nothing can be found to justify TARP. "We should not be here, and we aren't," Reinhart should have said. Neither the payments nor the credit system was in jeopardy, no thanks to the government, which should have just pulled out. However, that was politically impossible.

A hearing before the Senate Banking Committee was arranged for September 23, where Paulson said bad loans "have created a chain reaction" that "froze the credit markets." The "root cause of this turmoil … is the housing correction which has resulted in illiquid mortgage-related assets that are choking off the flow of credit which is so vitally important to the economy so they can perform their mission of supporting future prosperity and growth."

Paulson, long-time partner and chairman of Goldman Sachs, had expected a difficult time from members of Congress suspicious that he was just seeking to bail out his friends. "They'll kill me up there. I'll be hung out to dry," he told Bernanke. It turned out to be no problem. There was "an eerie, jaw-dropping silence in the room," chairman of the Senate Banking Committee Christopher Dodd recalled. "I could hear everyone gulp," Senator Charles Schumer said. " 'People who talk for a living somehow couldn't think of anything to say,' Dodd marveled" (Kaiser 2013: 9).

The strategy was for Bernanke to lead off to exploit his academic credibility with the bonus of no vested interest in Wall Street. "This is only going to work if you scare the shit out of them," Paulson's aide said. "I kind of scared myself," Bernanke recalled. It's a matter of days before the next Great Depression, only worse. Our tools are not sufficient. We need hundreds of billions of dollars. To top off the presentation, "nothing like this [bank problems because of bad loans, complicated by nonbank involvement] has happened before" (Kaiser 2013: 8–9).

Couldn't anyone challenge even this assertion? The fast growing and unregulated trust companies were a factor in the panic of 1907, investment banks in 1929, and the Ohio Life Insurance and Trust Co. in 1858 (Myers 1931: 97; Friedman and Schwartz 1963: 159–160). Neither Paulson nor the congressional representatives knew the record (Bernanke should have known) – of economics, that is. That was irrelevant, anyway, because they understood the politics. Over 160 academic economists sent a letter opposing the plan as badly structured, unprecedented, and in violation of the rule of law and healthy economic incentives. "A whole lot of people made money supposedly by putting their capital at risk, and those are supposed to be the first line of defense. That's how capitalism works," said David Levine of the University of California at Berkeley. "It doesn't seem to me that a lot of decisions that we're going to have to live with for a long time have to be made by Friday," said the University of Chicago's Robert Lucas. Harvard's Jeffrey Miron objected to the "stunningly broad, aggressive government intervention without appropriate precedents." The normal process of business failure and bankruptcy ought to be allowed to run its course. Erik Brynjolfsson of the Massachusetts Institute of Technology objected to "the breathtaking amount of unchecked discretion [the bill] gives to the secretary of the Treasury. It is unprecedented in a modern democracy" (Bloomberg news service, September 25, 2008). Unfortunately, there was no Gallatin, Webster, Clay, Calhoun, Benton, Sherman, or Aldrich to carry economic ideas or knowledge of finance into political councils.

The simplicity of Paulson's plan ought to have revealed his purpose to the least suspecting: We need hundreds of millions of dollars to buy the banks' bad loans (mainly mortgages). It should also be remembered that only a few banks were troubled, the payments system was unthreatened, and credit continued to be available to the solvent. Bank depositors were not running to currency.

Treasury–Congress negotiations for the bill turned on politics. The "stickiest issue [was] the timing of the release of the TARP money," Paulson (2010: 308) recalled.

The Democrats were fairly certain Obama would win the election, and they didn't want the Bush Treasury to be able to use all the money.... Chuck [New York Senator] Schumer didn't believe Congress would give the Bush administration $700 billion. I told him the markets needed to know the money was available.

Schumer held back. "I asked what would happen if we urgently needed more funds and didn't have time to go back to Congress." Barney Frank, chairman of the House Banking Committee "quipped, 'Then you'll go back to Uncle Ben.'" They all laughed, and Schumer said: "If you need more than $350 billion before January 20, you'll use the Fed or call us back and ask for more."

"[B]ut we need to protect the American people from financial disaster," Paulson said. "You keep asserting that, but I don't hear persuasive reasons," Senate Finance Committee Chairman Max Baucus said, but only got a repeat of the assertions. Congress passed the Emergency Economic Stabilization Act of 2008, on October 3, signed into law by President George W. Bush the same day. The Act authorized the Secretary of the Treasury to buy up to $700 billion of undefined troubled assets from undefined financial institutions.

No reasoned case for TARP was made by the Fed or the Treasury. The original *BTG* plan had called for $500 billion, but just as arbitrarily became $700 billion. "It's not based on any particular data point," a Treasury spokesman said, "We just wanted to choose a really large number" (McKinley 2011: 262). Congress was not told what might happen if banks did not receive the cash, beyond more unreasoned predictions of doom, or what banks would be required to do with the cash when they received it. "Make a case," Congress should have said. On the other hand, maybe they knew a case could not be made – at least by the Fed or the Treasury, which had previously shown their unawareness of economic conditions and relations – but were simply driven, like those agencies, by the political need to show they were doing something. Congress was able to hide behind "the top two economic authorities in the world."

Paulson exalted know-nothingness – refused the possibility of learning – when he said: "There is no playbook for responding to turmoil we have never faced" (*New York Times* November 17, 2008). In fact, the failure of speculative loans based on the expectation of ever-rising prices has been the most common cause of financial crises. A recent account, *This Time is Different* (2009) by Carmen Reinhart and Kenneth Rogoff, gives eight centuries of examples. Official responses have also been repeated. Particularly since the 1970s, failures and threatened failures have inspired bailouts, followed by complaints and admissions that they were unnecessary, only to be repeated.

The absence of a careful rationalization of the bailout meant a scramble for surface explanations. The annual Jackson Hole Conference hosted by the Federal Reserve Bank of Kansas City in August 2008 had what seemed to Gary Gorton a real but unspoken undercurrent of anxiety. "On the one hand, participants did not act like we were in the middle of a terrible crisis that seemed out of control and not understood. On the other hand, the speed with which existing paradigms in economics were dropped as if they had never existed was breathtaking. In an instant, Keynesianism was revived, and the lender of last resort," formerly on the sidelines of monetary policy, became the focus. "By the time of the conference, central bankers had" developed what seemed like a coordinated narrative or rather catchphrase for the crisis, "the so-called *originate-to-distribute story*, which argued that securitization per se was bad because incentives were not aligned.... No serious evidence was offered for this viewpoint," and central bankers soon dropped it without offering another. Bernanke's introductory speech called for strengthening the financial infrastructure while the Fed was undermining it. "Soon the dominant narrative became that of the press and the politicians in which the crisis was due to a 'reckless few' who 'gamed the system' and got big bonuses," although ironically these were the very groups who supported the government's benefits to the culpable at the expense of the innocent (Gorton 2010: 9–10; Bernanke 2008).

The turndown of the economy after TARP may be attributed to the increased uncertainty of government actions. "Fear froze the economy, but that uncertainty itself might have a cost was something the young experimenters simply did not consider," Amity Shlaes (2007: 8) wrote of Great Depression policies.

A report card

"No one disputes that a few large banks were in danger of failing, but this does not justify a bailout," Jeffrey Miron (2009b) wrote.

> Failure is an essential aspect of capitalism. It provides information about good and bad investments, and it releases resources from bad projects to more productive ones. [H]ousing prices and housing construction were too high at the end of 2005. This condition implied a deterioration in bank balance sheets and a retrenchment in the banking sector, so some amount of failure was both inevitable and appropriate. Thus, an economic case for the bailout needed to show that failure by some banks would harm the economy beyond what was unavoidable due to the fall in housing prices.

The usual excuse is "systemic risk," where one bank's failure causes failure in others. That danger is often exaggerated and denies the substantial knowledge present in markets. Runs have historically been rational withdrawals from institutions known to be in trouble (Temzelides 1997; Walter 2005). Consider the case of Continental Illinois, the first rescue (1984) to be defended on the grounds that certain financial enterprises are 'too big to fail' (TBTF). The FDIC claimed during congressional hearings that Continental's failure would have exposed 179 small banks to high risks of failure. This figure was revised downward to 28 after investigation by the House Banking Committee and the GAO. George Kaufman found that only two banks would have lost more than half their capital. The 1990 failure of Drexel Burnham Lambert had no systemic consequences, nor did Long Term Capital Management when the Fed arranged a bailout in 1998 (Kaufman 1990, 2000).

Washington Mutual was five times larger than Continental Illinois in real terms. Yet the FDIC was able, after wiping out its shareholders and most of its secured bondholders, to sell it to J.P. Morgan Chase without inconveniencing its customers or disrupting the financial markets. Although Lehman Brothers was one of the largest dealers in credit default swaps, investigators found "no indication that any financial institution became troubled or failed" because of its failure. Lehman's inability to meet its obligations did not lead to the "contagion" that is the hallmark of systemic risk (Tarr 2010).

AIG's exposure was also easily settled (Wallison 2009). A greater danger to banks than size has been their rate of growth (discussed below in Chapter 7). WaMu's 2005 strategic plan called for "increasing our Credit Risk tolerance," and an examiner of Lehman's bankruptcy wrote that it "made the deliberate decision to embark upon an aggressive growth strategy, to take on significantly greater risk, and to substantially increase leverage on its capital." When loans began to turn bad, "Lehman made the conscious decision to 'double-down,' hoping to profit from a counter-cyclical strategy" (Stanton 2012: 33–34). Furthermore, the Bear Stearns example might have encouraged Lehman's expectations of a similar bailout, if needed.

This behavior had been seen before. Continental, WaMu, Lehman, Fannie-Mae, and Freddie Mac had grown too fast not to fail. Short of making them (and the regulators) learn from history that *This Time is [Not] Different*, the best public policy would have been to persuade them (managers, directors, stockholders, and creditors) that they would not be bailed out. That would have been difficult, however. They knew better, and their political, if not their economic, expectations were validated.

Even systemic risk would not have made bailout the right policy. "To see why, note first that allowing banks to fail does not mean the government plays no role," Miron noted. Federal deposit insurance prevents losses by insured depositors, and was expanded, Federal courts and regulatory agencies (such as the FDIC) supervise bankruptcy proceedings. The activities of bankrupt firms do not necessarily disappear. The personnel and facilities remain. Shareholders and bondholders take the losses required to make mergers and sales of potentially productive firms attractive. Taxpayer funds go only to insured depositors. Banking continues. The payments system and financial intermediation survive. Typical arguments for the bailouts of Boeing, Chrysler, General Motors and other manufacturing firms sound as if their facilities are in danger of disappearing. Not so, of course. What might be changed are their ownership and direction. The same is true of banking and financial intermediation (Miron 2009b).

There would have been takers for operations and assets at market prices because problems were limited to a few badly managed and/or unlucky firms. The governance of firms that withstood the crisis possessed certain features in common: "(1) discipline and long-term perspective, (2) robust communications and information systems, (3) the capacity to respond effectively to early warning signs, and (4) a process of constructive dialogue between business units and risk managers" (Stanton 2012: 14). These imply collegial/open rather than dictatorial/overbearing management. "Jamie and I like to get the bad news out to where everybody can see it ... to get the dead cat on the table," a J.P. Morgan Chase executive said of his CEO. The Fed–Treasury policy was to perpetuate the practices of those firms that had behaved oppositely, who lacked communication, suppressed news of risk, and were surprised by the bad news when it came, as the Treasury and Fed were surprised.

Lehman Brothers, which was allowed to go bankrupt, had many assets for which investors were willing to bid. "Some creditors didn't want to wait for their money, or take a chance that they wouldn't get paid at all." They sold to investment firms who had sent "teams to study Lehman's balance sheet to identify potentially valuable assets they could buy at discounts." In 2013, Paulson & Co. was more than a billion dollars up on these investments, and Elliott Management $700 million (*Wall Street Journal*, September 13, 2013). So where was the illiquidity?

Other institutions were saved with taxpayers' money under the mistaken (to be generous) notion that redistributing losses would make them disappear. In reality, in its purpose and effects, the "stimulus was not about improving economic efficiency but about distributing funds to favored interest groups" (Miron 2009a).

Official decisions were based more on politics than economics. The looming bankruptcy of Lehman Brothers at the end of summer 2008 was as threatening (or not) to the economy as Bear Stearns, Fannie Mae, and Freddie Mac had been a few months earlier. However, the growing backlash against bailouts caused a rethinking of strategy. "I'm being called Mr. Bailout. I can't do it again," Paulson said. His chief of staff e-mailed him that "bailing out Lehman [w]ill be horrible in the press." Federal Reserve statements showed the same attitude (Wessel 2010: 14–15; McKinley 2011: 159–161).

Lehman was allowed to file bankruptcy on September 15, but on September 23 Bernanke and Paulson came to Congress with their $700 billion scare. The need was so urgent, they said, Congress should act without hearings or debates (Isaac 2010: 148). A few members of Congress resisted, but President Bush urged the measure's necessity in a broadcast to the nation, and presidential candidates Barack Obama and John McCain issued a joint statement that "The effort to protect the American economy must not fail." The House's initial rejection catered to the popular opposition to which Congressman Watts referred (among the book's opening quotations). Its acceptance the second time around was in response to the determination of the congressional leadership than to any changes in the bill. Or perhaps the rejection was merely a token signal to the voters back home. "Monday I cast a blue-collar vote for the American people," Tennessee Republican Congressman Zach Wamp said. "Today I am going to cast a red, white and blue-collar vote with my hand over my heart for this country, because things are really bad and we don't have any choice."

TARP's purpose of jump-starting the system was not only bound to fail, it was counterproductive. The purchase of "$700 billion of toxic assets would have been a colossal waste of taxpayers' money," former FDIC Chairman William

Isaac (2010: 149) wrote. It looked like a "plan concocted by Wall Street for the exclusive benefit of Wall Street." Banks would not sell the assets to the government unless it offered more than they were valued by the market, investors would not buy them from the government unless they could get them cheap, the difference to be made up by the taxpayers.

As already indicated, the use of "illiquidity" in official circles the last half-century has been a cover for funds to the insolvent. Illiquidity, which is a system term, was not a problem. Funds were available for profitable activities, and defaulted mortgages could have been sold at freely negotiated prices.

In fact, even as TARP was before Congress, its authors recognized that the plan was unworkable. Who would decide what would be bought and at what prices? Within two weeks of passage, the plan that had been necessary to save the world was scrapped, and the Treasury announced that the funds would be used to buy capital instead of toxic assets. The money went to banks, insurance companies, finance companies, and even General Motors and Chrysler after Congress had rejected a proposal to bail out the auto companies.

The second financial collapse, on top of the first, was caused not by a turn-around in prices but by the fear of trading in the presence of policy uncertainty: who would be bailed out, in what amounts, in what forms, with what restrictions, and so on. Contradictions piled on top of one another. Informed market initiatives were impossible and the economic decline accelerated with TARP's adoption (see Table 6.3 and Figure 6.1.)

The claim that TARP had to be passed because of fear of a run on money market funds was specious, Isaac said, because the Treasury had already announced a blanket guarantee. The FDIC had recently managed the sale of the country's largest (and fastest growing – the Walmart of banking) savings and

Table 6.3 Percentage changes (per annum) of real GDP and nonresidential fixed investment, and percentage rate of unemployment

Quarter	GDP	Investment	Unemployment
2007			
II	3.2	11.4	4.5
III	3.6	9.6	4.7
IV	2.1	6.7	4.8
2008			
I	−0.7	1.9	4.9
II	1.5	1.4	5.4
III	−2.7	−6.1	6.1
IV	−5.4	−19.5	6.9
2009			
I	−6.4	−39.2	8.1
II	−0.7	−9.6	9.3
III	2.8	−4.1	9.6

Source: Federal Reserve Bank of St. Louis, *National Economic Trends*, December 2009.

loan association, Washington Mutual, without disruption. The further justification that depositors might run on banks also revealed the lack of knowledge of even recent history. Three thousand banks and thrifts failed because of failed loans during the 1980s without threatening the payments system (Miron 2009b; Isaac 2010: 154).[4]

> Thus, the bailout had huge potential for counterproductive impacts and at best an uncertain prospect of alleviating the credit crunch or ameliorating the recession. This means that allowing further failures would have been a price worth paying. In particular, the process of failure and bankruptcy would have countered the financial sector's temptation to "bank" on government largesse, so the bankruptcy approach would have created better incentives going forward.
>
> (Miron 2009b)

The Act's passage was due in large part to Congress' understanding or hope that distressed borrowers would be relieved and credit restored. No such luck. The bulk of the funds used under the Act, less than half of those initially appropriated, simply went into corporate coffers.[5] It should not have been expected that banks having just incurred significant losses in a new and uncertain environment would throw good money after bad. Survival understandably came first. A review of investor presentations and conference calls by executives of two dozen US banks by the *New York Times* found that "few [banks] cited lending as a priority. Further, an overwhelming majority saw the program as a no-strings-attached windfall that could be used to pay down debt, acquire other businesses or invest for the future." Several bank chairmen viewed the money as available for strategic acquisitions in the future rather than to increase lending to the private sector, whose ability to pay back the loans was suspect. One chairman saw the government's cash infusion as "opportunity capital," noting, "They didn't tell me I had to do anything particular with it." There was no serious government oversight over the use of public funds, and despite politicians' talk of "helping Main Street," banks passed little along as credit (Barofsky 2012).

A 1946 Brookings study stated that government regulations of "the investment market and security issues is a reflection of Main Street's opposition to Wall Street" (Atkins *et al.* 1946). During the Great Recession, as on other occasions, Main Street found the guns of regulation turned on itself.

The effects of these programs on Fed credit and its uses are seen in Table 6.2. Fed credit was $1,200 billion greater in November 2008 than February, although the effect on loans to the public was small. Treasury balances with the Fed (unspent funds) made up almost $600 billion of this amount, and bank excess reserves almost $500 billion. Bank credit, including loans, continued its downward path until mid 2009, not turning up until well into 2010.

The bulk of TARP and other Fed loans and Treasury appropriations went to favored firms, pension funds, and political entities, but little to the credit markets or distressed borrowers. They had no effect on bank credit or financial intermediation, except in the wrong direction. They interfered with market adjustments by propping up failing firms and reducing confidence in the system. The Bernanke/Paulson prophesies and Congress' stampede increased uncertainty and reinforced financial and economic declines in September 2008 (Blinder 2013: 19).

Officials went out of their way to undermine confidence in the system

> when Secretary Paulson called the CEOs of nine of the largest financial companies into his office with great fanfare and ordered them to take TARP money, which several of the banks did not need or want. Hundreds of smaller banks were pressured by their regulators to take the money "just in case."

The publicity associated with what were in fact routine "stress tests" of the 19 largest TARP recipients in February 2009 continued the attack that had no apparent purpose other than to undermine confidence (Isaac 2010: 158; Allison 2013: 167–168).

Squeals of pain emanate from Congress, but nothing has been learned. They voted vast sums to institutions, allegedly to benefit Main Street, with no effective oversight (which had been given to the Fed and the Treasury, who had asked for and dispensed the largesse), and have sought to preserve their political positions by toothless criticisms of executive salaries and mortgage foreclosures.

As always, new legislation criticized past emergency actions and directed agencies, existing and some created for the purpose, to prevent their recurrence. The Dodd–Frank Wall Street Reform and Consumer Protection Act of 2010 consisted of reforms intended, among other things, to protect taxpayers by ending TBTF bailouts. This must be viewed with considerable skepticism. "The idea that a present-day Congress can prospectively prevent a future Congress from the standard response of passing an ad hoc bailout in the midst of a crisis is fanciful," Geithner observed, even as he advocated the bill: "The size of the shock that hit our financial system was larger than what caused the Great Depression. In the future we may have to do exceptional things again if we face a shock that large" – regulatory reforms notwithstanding (McKinley 2011: 283).

Geithner was doubtless correct about the likelihood of future responses. All we can do in the interests of Main Street is to try to improve the intelligence and responsibility of those responses, which in turn requires a change in Congress. If Congress does not wish to continue to be the prey of Wall Street, if it wishes to make decisions based on reason rather than panic, it will have to take its job seriously. It must become more informed and attentive.

Comparisons with the Great Depression

The Great Depression has been a continual excuse for action, generally erroneous because its causes differed substantially from subsequent downturns. Furthermore, many government responses to the Great Depression were ineffective or worse. The Great Depression was a consequence of the gold standard, or rather its mismanagement, which has not constrained money or the economy since that time (Mazumder and Wood 2013). In their discussion of banking panics, Charles Calomiris and Gorton (1991) pointed out the differences in the Great Depression. Unlike earlier panics (as well as 2008), those of the Great Depression "did not occur near the peak of the business cycle and did result in widespread failures and losses to depositors" – 20 percent of banks compared to 1.3 percent, and 5 percent of deposits compared to 2 percent in the worst cases. "[T]he Great Depression tells one less about the inherent stability of the banking system than about the extent to which unwise government policies can destroy banks" – repeated unfortunately in the next century.

The origins of the Great Depression are found in the World War I inflation, which under the gold standard had to be reversed. Gold had come to the United States during the war, and American prices were stable for most of the 1920s. Deflationary pressures were common abroad, however, and they finally came to the United States, helped by the Fed's tight money at the end of the decade (see Chapter 3). The bank failures of 1930–2 were caused not by bank runs but by insolvencies due to price declines, especially in real estate. Bank failures and price falls accelerated as depositors fled to currency. The Fed failed to supply the high-powered money that would have been necessary to prevent the falls in money and prices, although whether they could have prevented the price from falling to the level dictated by the gold standard – that is, a purchasing power of gold equal to that in 1914, before the war inflation – is doubtful (Mazumder and Wood 2013). It should be noted that increases in the monetary base beginning April 1932 went to excess reserves (Federal Reserve 1943: 99).

Nor can anything be said for the absence of (Keynesian) demand stimulation as a lesson. Demand could hardly have been maintained or restored in the deflationary environment. Even so, the Great Recession rejuvenated Keynesianism to support the Bush stimulus package of 2008 (Blinder and Zandi 2010). The temporary tax cut had little effect on spending, however, as implied by the permanent income hypothesis, and the Obama deficits later in the year went to subsidies unrelated to demand, and in fact were associated with programs that promoted uncertainty and discouraged economic activity.

A similarity between the official policies of the two periods was the greater interest in allocating credit than supporting the payments system. The most obvious comparison is with the Reconstruction Finance Corporation that was established in January 1932 at President Hoover's request, with the primary objective of providing liquidity to, and restoring confidence in the failing banking system. There was no great rush on the part of banks for RFC funds primarily because of the continued fall in the value of potential collateral, to which might be added bureaucratic red tape, Congress' decision to publicize loan recipients, and accusations of political favoritism (Butkiewicz 2013).

A particularly unsuccessful program was the Fed's support of individual problem banks, especially country members. During most of 1932, for example, when their deposits fell by one-eighth, these banks were in debt to the Fed as their borrowings exceeded their reserve deposits. The effect on bank credit was probably negative because the weak banks that were propped up (and failed at a high rate) were more interested in survival than extending credit, and stood in the way of new and potentially more useful banks (Schwartz 1992).

The Bank of England became interested in the "rationalization of industry" as early as 1919, when industries encountered hard times. It was "for twenty years involved in a succession of financial reconstructions ['bailouts' is a better word] from which it repeatedly emerged as a loser." They became Governor Montagu Norman's primary interest after the Bank lost control of monetary policy in the 1930s (Sayers 1976: 316, 634; Boyle 1967: 250–259). Fed Chairman Marriner Eccles also took more interest in fiscal than in monetary policy in the 1930s (Eccles 1951: 131–133, 310–323; Meltzer 2003 i: 420, 612). Central bankers have grown increasingly unsatisfied with their traditional limited role as preserver of payments, and have wanted to branch out by influencing not only the rate but the distribution of activity.

Another difference between the two periods was the greater official interest in the public's problems in the earlier period, although help came late. Congress established various credit agencies, including the Federal Home Loan Bank System in 1932, with an initial capitalization of $125 million and the ability to borrow in order to lend to savings and loan associations, comprising 3.5 percent of the latter's assets in 1937. It established the Home Owners' Loan Corporation in 1933 to purchase and refinance delinquent home mortgages, including those that had recently been foreclosed. By 1936, HOLC had provided refinancing, usually with restructuring, of about a fifth of nonfarm, owner-occupied dwellings in the United States. Only 20 percent ended in foreclosure (Wheelock 2008). Much of the success of these programs was due to the general rise in prices, including house prices, after they had returned to their 1914 levels and the gold content of the dollar was reduced.

Starting in September 2012, the Federal Reserve further increased policy accommodation by purchasing additional MBS at a pace of $40 billion per month in order to support a stronger economic recovery and to help ensure that inflation, over time, is at the rate most consistent with its dual mandate.

Federal Reserve press release

The slow pace of the latest recovery threatens to match that of the Great Depression, when unemployment did not recover its 1929 rate until the command economy of World War II. The ineffectiveness of the bailouts is reflected by the FOMC's statement in January 2013 that its purchases of mortgage-backed securities would continue.

In a speech at the University of Chicago on Milton Friedman's 90th birthday (November 8, 2002), Federal Reserve Board Governor Bernanke said:

Let me end my talk by abusing slightly my status as an official representative of the Federal Reserve. I would like to say to Milton and Anna

[Schwartz]: Regarding the Great Depression. You're right, we did it. We're very sorry. But thanks to you, we won't do it again.

On the contrary, Bernanke's commitment to countercyclical credit instead of monetary policy is of long standing. His reputation as an economist rests on his 1983 paper on the "Nonmonetary effects of the financial crisis in the propagation of the Great Depression." The Great Depression continues to be an active field of enquiry because it was special. Its severity exceeds the predictions of otherwise useful economic models, which therefore must be missing something. That something was intermediary services, Bernanke hypothesized, meaning that the depression's bank failures interfered with output beyond their effects on money. His basic premise was that "intermediation ... requires nontrivial market-making and information-gathering services." He interpreted the data to support the hypothesis because changes in money captured no more than half the decline in output, and a good part of the gap was filled by variables relating to bank failures.

The implication for countercyclical policy drawn by Bernanke was that Friedman and Schwartz's emphasis on money should be supplemented by direct credit support. Unfortunately, Bernanke's study had several statistical and observational flaws. Regarding the former, Masahiro Hori (1996) showed that Bernanke's positive result was due to a single observation – the month of bank closings upon Franklin Roosevelt's inauguration on March 4, 1933. The following month saw the beginning of the recoveries of money and output discussed by Christina Romer in "What ended the Great Depression?" (1992).

A further illustration of the correlation between money and output during this period, and of the lack of correlation between output and bank loans, is shown in Figure 6.2. I do not mean to belittle financial intermediation, but there was little connection between bank loans and economic activity between 1933 and well after World War II. The significant 1933–6 increase in output proceeded without direct help from the cautious banking system, as bank assets continued to take the form of government securities. Traditional loan/investment ratios did not begin to be restored until the 1950s (Wood 1975: 2).

Federal Reserve actions in the first decade of the twenty-first century show no evidence of learning from mistakes. The first six years repeated the familiar tardy responses that have exacerbated economic fluctuations – negative real rates persisting well into an expansion followed by tight money after the economy turned downwards. Instead of concentrating on easy money once it had recognized the recession, the Fed, with the Treasury, decided to bailout selected banks and other firms that had become insolvent or near insolvency. These actions were sold to the public under the guise of liquidity, but we have seen that that was not the problem. Rather, it was a continuation of the bailout policy that began in the 1970s.

Instead of monetary policy, the Fed participated in a massive fiscal transfer from taxpayers to firms engaged in counterproductive activities. Its actions had nothing to do with the payments system, which had not been threatened. Unlike the primary purpose of the central bank as understood by Mill in 1857 (the

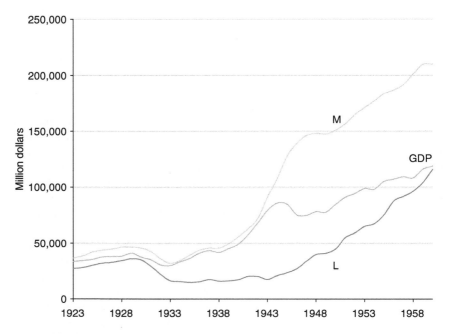

Figure 6.2 M2, bank loans, and real GDP (million dollars, annual).

continuity of the financial system) and the Federal Reserve Act in 1913 (an elastic currency), but rather like the Bank of England in the 1920s (after it had become a government agency during the war) and the Fed in the 1930s, the primary concern of today's Fed is the survival of favored groups, despite long-term effects contrary to its intentions. Bailouts bring more bailouts. Although there has been much theoretical work on moral hazard and the inconsistency of optimal plans, the Fed's recognition of these concepts has not improved.

Another familiar mistake in the making may be the eventual erasure of the massive excess reserves resulting from the increase in high-powered money shown in Figure 6.3. In its meeting on June 21–22, 2011, the FOMC agreed on the principles expected to guide the normalization of monetary policy sometime in the future, specifically raising the Fed funds rate and the draining of reserves. The first "key element of the strategy that they expect to follow when it becomes appropriate to begin normalizing the stance and conduct of monetary policy" is: "The Committee will determine the timing and pace of policy normalization to promote its statutory mandate of maximum employment and price stability."

> The timing and pace of [securities] sales will be communicated to the public in advance, that pace is anticipated to be relatively gradual or steady, but it could be adjusted up or down in response to material changes in economic outlook or financial condition.

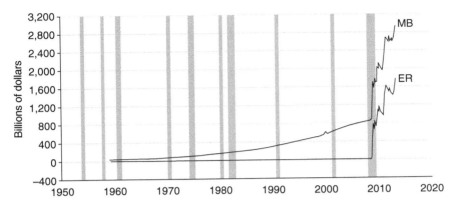

Figure 6.3 Monetary base and excess reserves, 1959–2013.

Note
Shaded areas represent US recessions.

The belief that either a monetary change or its effects can be controlled flies in the face of logic and experience. We know that the Fed's effort to reduce excess reserves in 1936–7 produced unexpected and disastrous results as banks reduced loans to hold on to their excess reserves. Ricardo's 1819 plan to increase the gold value of the pound in stages broke down in deflation as market expectations accelerated the process. The Fed cannot know beforehand the effects of an attempt to restore the monetary base and/or excess reserves to "normality."

Notes

1 Professor Luis Garicano responded: "At every stage, someone was relying on somebody else; and everyone thought they were doing the right thing" (*Telegraph*, November 5, 2008).

2

> A "credit default swap" (CDS) is a credit derivative contract between two counterparties. The buyer makes periodic payments to the seller, and in return receives a payoff if an underlying financial instrument defaults or experiences a similar credit event. The CDS may refer to a specified loan or bond obligation of a "reference entity," usually a corporation or government.
>
> (Federal Reserve Bank of Atlanta 2008)

3 Of the five largest investment banks existing before the crisis, Bear Stearns was acquired by J.P. Morgan, Merrill Lynch by the Bank of America, and Lehman was allowed to fail.

4 WaMu was seized September 25, 2008, by the US Office of Thrift Supervision and placed into receivership with the FDIC after the withdrawal of $16.7 billion (9 percent of its deposits) during a nine-day period. The FDIC sold the banking portions (minus unsecured debt and equity claims) to J.P. Morgan Chase for $1.9 billion, which the latter had been planning to acquire. WaMu branches were rebranded as Chase branches.

5 For TARP's implementation, see Webel (2013).

7 Bank regulation

> Although bank supervision under the National Banking System exercised a light hand and panics were frequent, the cost of bank failures was minimal. Double liability induced shareholders to carefully monitor bank managers and voluntarily liquidate banks early if they appeared to be in trouble. Inducing more disclosure, marking assets to market, and ensuring prompt closure of insolvent national banks, the Comptroller of the Currency reinforced market discipline. The arrival of the Federal Reserve weakened this regime. Monetary policy decisions conflicted with the goal of financial stability and created moral hazard. The appearance of the Fed as an additional supervisor led to more "competition in laxity" among regulators and "regulatory arbitrage" by banks. When the Great Depression hit, policy-induced deflation and asset price volatility were misdiagnosed as failures of competition and market valuation. In response, the New Deal shifted to a regime of discretion-based supervision with forbearance.
>
> Eugene White, " 'To establish a more effective supervision of banking':
> How the birth of the Fed altered bank supervision" (2010)

Banks have been more heavily regulated than other firms for two reasons: fear of market failure in an essential economic activity (payments) and the government's pursuit of revenue. The latter has been part of governments' fiscal exploitation of the monetary system, and was seen above in their extraction of credit from the Bank of England, the Banks of the United States, national banks, and the Federal Reserve, all chartered for the purpose.

The demand nature of banks' liabilities together with their fractional reserves continuously expose them to the risk of failure. Even the suspicion of a bank's insolvency might instigate a run, that is, a shift of its deposits to other banks or into currency. Risk may be systemic because the nature of the payments system means that banks hold substantial claims on one another. Banks have been a prime source of finance for expansions, which, in the event of collapse, leaves them with bad loans, insolvencies, runs, suspensions or closings, and threats to the payments system.

State and federal regulators seek to limit bank risks by supervision, capital requirements, and portfolio restrictions. Unfortunately, they have increased those risks by their credit demands, perverse regulations, and adverse incentives, before and especially since the creation of the Fed. The following highlights of the Fed's role in bank regulation will be enough to show that its failures in this area stem from the same misconceptions and lack of principles, especially of incentives, that haunt its monetary policies.

Before the Fed

A striking difference between national banking structures has been the much larger number of banks in the United States that can be traced to its political structure. Banking requires a charter; most American banks are state chartered, states did not permit banks chartered elsewhere to conduct business in their jurisdictions until the failures of the 1980s, and branching was limited even within states. Before the Civil War, only the short-lived Banks of the United States did not have state charters.

The Civil War added national charters conditional on investing in federal debt (discussed in Chapter 4), just as state banks were required to invest in state bonds (Figure 7.1). These requirements had pervasive effects on the country's financial and legal experiences. "As agents of the state [Illinois chartered banks] were expected to lend money by issuing their notes to finance the railroads and the other public works" favored by the legislature. Banks' zeal in this practice often resulted in failure or its expectation. In 1842, "A. Lincoln, debtor-creditor lawyer" (Billings 2010) accepted a case in which his client had tendered $400 in State Bank of Illinois notes in payment of a debt of that amount. The creditor refused to accept the notes at face value because they were circulating at a discount of 40–50 percent, and went to court to collect. Lincoln lost the case. "The

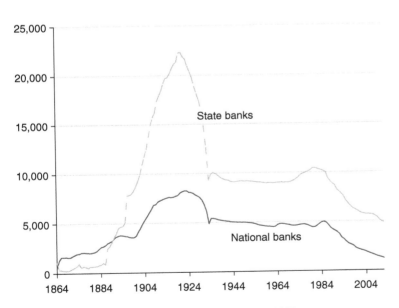

Figure 7.1 State and national banks, end-year 1864–2012.

court found that [the lender] could not have had in mind that the debt could be repaid at 50 cents on the dollar." What was considered theft, or at least sharp practice, on the nineteenth-century frontier is common under the Federal Reserve.

In 1914, there were about 7,500 national banks and 18,000 state banks, mostly small, undiversified, and vulnerable. Nebraska, for example, with a population of about 1,000,000, had about 1,000 banks. Suspensions were frequent, especially in the farm depressions of the 1890s, 1920s, and 1980s, as falling agricultural prices brought down borrowers and their banks (Federal Reserve Board 1943: 20, 22; 1959: 625; Cottrell *et al.* 1995). The number of banks rose to 30,000 during the agricultural boom and inflation accompanying World War I, before falling to 25,000 in 1929 and 14,000 in 1932 (Figure 7.2). The Bureau of Labor Statistics index of agricultural prices rose from 44 to 96 between 1913 and 1919, fell to 61 in 1927, and 30 in 1932. These price changes were primary consequences of the Federal Reserve's first 20 years, which must bear most of the responsibility for the massive bank failures of the Great Depression. Regulators nevertheless focused on shortcomings in bank management.

The undiversified banking system was not the end of risk-increasing regulations. With their preponderance of demand deposit liabilities, it has been assumed that good banking practice requires investments primarily in short-term liquid assets, such as commercial paper and Treasury bills. However, we know that a prime purpose of the Bank of England and of the Banks of the United States was long-term credit for their governments. That was also true of American state and national banks. The general incorporation laws of banking in the

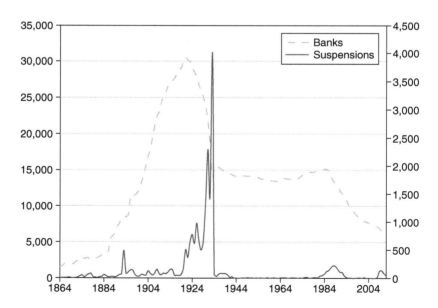

Figure 7.2 Banks and bank suspensions, 1864–2012.

first half of the nineteenth century required banks to deposit state bonds with the state auditor as security for their notes. Consequently, the periodic falls in state bond prices became a significant cause of bank failures (rather than the largely fictional accounts of fraudulent "wildcat" banking). High interest rates (low bond prices) corresponded with other weaknesses at business cycle peaks (Rolnick and Weber 1984). State bank notes were taxed out of existence to make way for a uniform currency in 1868, but national bank notes were secured by US bonds.

The banking system before the Fed contained features that limited the damage of panics, including double liability and discretionary restrictions of cash payments. Double liability is the obligation of shareholders at the time of a bank's failure to pay assessments up to the par value of their stock to compensate depositors and other creditors. The National Bank Act of 1863 imposed double liability, which, Senator John Sherman argued, provides security to creditors and "tends to prevent the stockholders and directors of a bank from engaging in hazardous operations." Most state banks were also subject to double liability (White 2010; Macey and Miller 1992).

Events confirmed Sherman's expectations. Over four times the number of troubled national banks were voluntarily liquidated than closed as insolvent (2373/501) between 1864 and 1913. Unlike the years since 1913, the authorities were quick to close insolvent banks, and creditors' losses were small (White 2010). Nevertheless, "public dismay" concerning bank failures in the Great Depression led to the repeal of double liability at the state and federal levels. "Despite its venerable heritage, [double liability] seemed 'inadequate as a means of protecting the depositing public'," and was replaced by deposit insurance despite its obvious adverse incentives (Golembe 1960; Macey and Miller 1992).

Banks restricted payments on several occasions before 1913. "To the best of our knowledge," Friedman and Schwartz wrote, "in these earlier restrictions, no substantial number of banks closed down entirely even for a day, let alone for a minimum number of six business days" as during the Bank Holiday of March 1933. During the pre-Fed restrictions, banks

> continued to make loans, transfer deposits by check, and conduct all their usual business except the unlimited conversion of deposits into currency on demand. Indeed, the restriction enabled them to continue such activities and, in some instances, to expand their loans by relieving them from the immediate pressure to acquire currency to meet the demands of their depositors
>
> (Friedman and Schwartz 1963: 328)

Hammond (1957: 713) wrote of the bank restrictions of 1857:

> As usual, the immediate effect of stopping specie payments … was ease. The banks, relieved of having to pay their own debts, ceased their harsh pressure on their borrowers. The general understanding that specie payments must sooner or later be resumed impelled a continuation of liquidation but of milder sort.

State regulations imposed penalties, even the loss of charters, for failing to pay notes in specie. They were seldom enforced, however, and legislation often postponed or relieved banks of the penalties (Warburton 1958).

Enter the Fed

Payments restrictions were considered a less than satisfactory solution to panics, and brought pressures for reform. The Federal Reserve was created to solve the problem, but it failed its first test in the Great Depression. Banks were closed or had restricted payments in all 48 states when Franklin Roosevelt assumed the presidency on March 4, 1933.

The 1933 banking panic started with the difficulties of two large Detroit banks whose real estate loans had deteriorated (Wicker 1996: 116–120). The Reconstruction Finance Corporation (RFC) was instituted to help banks in need, and the Glass–Steagall Act of 1931 empowered the Fed to lend to banks on their promissory notes if they lacked acceptable assets to obtain normal accommodation. However, negotiations between the RFC and a Detroit bank broke down, and the Governor of Michigan declared a bank holiday on February 14, 1933.

Bank holidays had been used on several occasions to avert crises, as in five western states in 1907, and several cities after serious fires, including Chicago in 1871 and San Francisco in 1906. Legislation in several states, beginning with Oregon in 1930, enabled banks to suspend cash payments partially or in full during the Great Depression (Wicker 1996: 121). Where was the Fed in all this? It hindered instead of helped the elasticity of the currency. The actions of J.P Morgan, clearing houses, and others before 1913 failed to develop afterwards because the Fed with its stated purposes and great resources was expected to take the lead. The result was a gap in the traditional responses to panic. When a Detroit bank asked the Federal Reserve Bank of Chicago for a $35 million loan under Glass–Steagall, it was refused because of the "dangerous precedent" of lending to a closed bank. The Chicago Fed chose to conserve its resources for existing banks. It also doubted the legality of lending to a closed bank that planned to reopen by paying depositors less than in full (Friedman and Schwartz 1963: 327–332; Wicker 1996: 122).

The Michigan holiday spread to contiguous states, which quickly placed restrictions on deposit withdrawals. By the end of February, bank holidays in one form or another had been declared throughout the United States. The Fed joined the panic, and instead of providing assistance, sought protection for itself. The New York Reserve Bank raised its discount rate on March 3, after gold drains had reduced its reserve ratio below its legal requirement, and Governor Harrison informed the Board that "he would not take the responsibility of running this bank with deficient reserves in the absence of legal sanction." The Board suspended reserve requirements for 30 days but Harrison appealed to Treasury Secretary Ogden Mills for a nationwide bank holiday. When this was unsuccessful, he joined the New York Clearing Banks and the state superintendent of banks in requesting New York Governor Herbert Lehman to declare a state bank holiday, which he did on March 4, along with Illinois, Massachusetts, New Jersey, and Pennsylvania. Neither the Federal Reserve Banks nor the leading exchanges opened on March 4.

> The central banking system, set up primarily to render impossible the restriction of payments by commercial banks, itself joined the commercial banks in a more widespread, complete, and economically disturbing restriction of payments than had ever been experienced in the history of the country.
>
> (Friedman and Schwartz 1963: 327–328)

No one took charge. On February 14, President Hoover proposed that clearinghouse scrip be issued by member banks under the direction of the Federal Reserve Banks, but was strongly opposed by the Board and the New York Fed "on the grounds that the issue of scrip would reflect negatively on the 'adequacy and flexibility' of the Federal Reserve." The Treasury had the authority to implement the Hoover Plan with or without the Fed (as Secretary McAdoo had done successfully in 1914), but that "would not have been in keeping with Hoover's distaste for imposing a decision on a recalcitrant Fed" (Wicker 1996: 124).

Hoover also proposed that all banks be closed, and reopened with a statement of solvency, but the Attorney-General ruled the President did not have the necessary power without the approval of Congress. With the end of his term rapidly approaching, Hoover would not make further proposals without the expressed approval of the incoming administration. Roosevelt refused any joint action, although he implemented Hoover's plan shortly after assuming office when he closed the banks on March 6 using emergency powers granted during World War I, confirmed by the Emergency Banking Act of March 9, 1933.

"The period between the closing of the Michigan banks and the declaration of a national bank holiday has to be the most exasperating two and a half weeks in twentieth century financial history," Wicker (1996: 125) wrote. There was no shortage of plans to reopen the Michigan banks, close and open banks nationally, issue currency, modify reserve requirements, and/or suspend gold convertibility. "What was lacking was the element of leadership that would have commanded the cooperation of the interested parties. Neither President Hoover, the Federal Reserve, the RFC, nor the bankers themselves had the necessary clout [or will] to impose a viable solution." Congress did not enter the picture.

The Fed also diluted regulatory responsibilities in normal times. Before 1913, there were two bank regulators: states for state banks and the Office of the Comptroller of the Currency (OCC) for national banks. The Federal Reserve Act added a third by authorizing the Fed to supervise state member banks. The Fed competed for members by relaxing requirements and subsidizing services. This induced reactions by states anxious to keep their clientele, leading to regulatory arbitrage as banks sought to minimize the costs of regulation (White 1983: 127). The free but primitive Fed services (large transfers used faster private means) slowed innovation, although Congress seeking revenue eventually required the

Fed to charge fees commensurate with the costs of services (Wood and Wood 1985: 93–94).

The net effects of competition in regulation are unclear. It is not as simple as "a race to the bottom." For example, the FDIC *Banking Review* noted that States were often readier than the OCC (for national banks) to allow "their banks to introduce new ideas and innovations, with the result these institutions have been able to experiment" with new ideas, which were "subsequently adopted by national banks." This process was reinforced

> starting in the late 1970s [by] a spate of innovations [that] took root in state-chartered banks: interest-bearing checking accounts, adjustable-rate mortgages, home equity loans, and automatic teller machines.... During the 1980s the states took the lead in deregulating the activities of the banking industry. Many states permitted banks to engage in direct equity investment, securities underwriting and brokerage, real estate development, and insurance underwriting and agency. Interstate banking began with regional compacts at the state level. The OCC followed by expanding the powers of national banks, as long as they could be considered 'incidental to banking.' "
>
> (Blair and Kushmeider 2006)

A US Treasury (1991: XIX-6) study commented that "Diversity increases the chances that innovative approaches to policy problems will emerge.... A sole regulator, not subject to challenge from other agencies, might tend to become entrenched, conservative, and shortsighted." Chairman Greenspan also argued that the absence of the dual (state and national regulators) system could harm consumers and the economy: "when there is no choice of regulatory agency, rigid policies and interfering regulatory micro-management can develop" (American Bankers Association 2005). The choice continues, unaffected by Dodd–Frank. Although banks became larger during the merger movement beginning in the late 1980s, the proportion with state charters rose from 67 percent to 80 percent between 1987 and 2012. Half the 100 largest banks were state banks.

Fed regulation has conflicted with its monetary policy. It worried about the growing severity of the "membership problem" as banks left the System for the lower reserve requirements of state banks when interest rates rose in the 1960s and 1970s. It must be remembered that reserve requirements are primarily taxes on banks in the form of forced currency holdings (which until recently paid no interest). The Fed responded with cuts in members' reserve requirements (matched by the states), which have fallen since World War II from 20 percent and 6 percent on most demand and time deposits to 10 and zero (Lown and Wood 2003).

A conflict between monetary policy and the Fed's idea of bank stability, especially in the 1920s and 1980s, was the use of the discount window to help troubled banks. In November 1929, 60 percent of the reserves of banks outside New York and Chicago were borrowed from the Fed (Federal Reserve Board 1943: 398–399). A Fed study reported that in August 1925, 593 member banks had been borrowing from the Fed continuously for at least a year, 239 since 1920. At least 80 percent of the 259 national banks that had failed since 1920 had been "habitual borrowers." One-seventh of 457 continuous borrowers during 1926 disappeared by the end of 1927 (Shull 1971). That experience of lending to insolvent institutions was "eerily similar to the current episode," Anna Schwartz wrote in 1992. Regulators graded banks on a descending scale from 1 to 5, made up of five measures known as CAMEL (Capital adequacy, Asset quality, Management, Earnings, Liquidity). Of 530 borrowers between 1985 and 1991 that failed within three years of the onset of their borrowing, 437 had the lowest CAMEL rating of 5, and 51 borrowers had the next worst rating of 4.

In May 1991, for example, the House Committee on Banking, Finance and Urban Affairs asked for the Fed's rationale for lending to the Madison National Bank of McLean, Virginia, known to be on the verge of bankruptcy. Madison borrowed from January 22, 1991 (continuously from February 12) until its closing on May 10, when the loan totaled $125 million. "Until May 1, the bank had not been found to be insolvent by the primary regulator," the deputy-associate director of the Fed's Division of Banking Supervision and Regulation testified: "efforts were under way by new management to restructure the bank and attract new capital." The Fed was able to defend its action by the lack of an efficient information flow between regulators. Communication from the national banks' chief regulator (OCC) to the Fed has never been good, although in this case the Fed treated the problem as a virtue, and even the receipt of hard information did not prevent the use of the discount window for purposes for which it had not been intended under law.

The OCC began a full-scope examination in early February, the Fed official testified, the final results of which were made available to the Federal Reserve on May 1. The examination findings revealed that the bank was "in imminent danger of insolvency. At that point we notified the FDIC that the Federal Reserve's discount window would be limited to the purpose of effecting a prompt and orderly resolution of the bank."

Question: Did Federal Reserve loans permit Madison to stay open beyond the point when it became insolvent?

Answer: The bank was not declared insolvent until its closing on May 10, although we were aware on May 1 of its imminent insolvency. Failure to extend credit from May 1 through May 10 before the FDIC was ready to effect an orderly resolution might have disrupted the local payments system, denied insured depositors access to their funds for a period of time, possibly increased the FDIC's cost of resolution, and preempted the bank's attempt to respond to an OCC request for a capital plan.

(*Federal Reserve Bulletin*, July 1991)

The Fed's discount rate was generally below the Fed funds rate, more a bank subsidy than an instrument of monetary policy, between the mid 1960s and the early 2000s (Madigan and Nelson 2002). "[W]ith federal spending at an all-time high," Schwartz (1992) suggested, "policy makers see the discount window as a mechanism for providing funds off budget." The practice was less than fully effective, however, as Congress had to bail out the FDIC in turn. The FDIC Improvement Act of 1991 directed the agency to pursue the least cost resolution of failed banks and amended the Federal Reserve Act to restrain credit to depository institutions with inadequate capital or low supervisory ratings (*Federal Reserve Bulletin*, November 1994). As we have learned, these after-the-fact regrets are forgotten with each new crisis, and even before that. Although bank failures were much less during 1993–2002 than the preceding decade, the average loss rate to the FDIC more than doubled (Kaufman 2004).

The decline in effective supervision after the coming of the Fed is not surprising because of the banking interests that brought the institution into being, although its impact was small initially. "A small but significant minority of banks became dependent on the discount window, voluntary liquidations were down, suspensions increased, and payouts declined." However, these changes were not sufficient to destabilize the system that had developed before 1913, and losses remained modest until the Great Depression.

New Deal reformers attributed the catastrophic losses of the depression, due in fact to a monetary policy of unprecedented volatility, to market failure. As much as politically possible, competition was displaced by a government cartel with controls on entry, pricing, and balance sheets. "Supervision abandoned efforts to reinforce market discipline and instead was given discretion to make independent judgments [including 'intrinsic' instead of market values of assets], permitting forbearance in closing insolvent institutions that might recover later" (White 2010). The coming deposit insurance and repeal of double liability ended voluntary liquidations, and banks closed only after, sometimes long after, they had become insolvent.

President Roosevelt initially criticized proposals of deposit insurance. A government guarantee of bank deposits, he said,

> would lead to laxity in bank management and carelessness on the part of both banker and depositor. I believe that it would be an impossible drain on the Federal Treasury to make good any such guarantee.[1]

Counting votes, however, Roosevelt effectively sided with deposit insurance over more liberal branching that would allow larger, more diversified, safer banks. Something had to be done to restore confidence in banking, and those opposed to a change in banking structure argued for deposit insurance. Marriner Eccles (1951: 269) was persuaded that Roosevelt's resistance to the consolidation of banking stemmed from his "nostalgic affection" for the existing system of many small independent banks.

Deposit insurance was credited for the low bank failure rate during its first half-century, and its moral hazard was blamed for the failures thereafter. Both are unlikely in view of the small insurance coverage – $10,000 or less per account until 1965, rising to $100,000 between 1980 and 2008 – offering little protection to the most active and informed depositors. Furthermore, most failures, which have been of small banks, have been due to agricultural depressions before and after deposit insurance, such as the 1920s and 1980s (Cottrell *et al.* 1995).

Bank failures have been caused primarily by insolvency rather than illiquidity, and deposit insurance has been irrelevant to the security of the payments system. Its other purpose, to protect the wealth of small depositors, is also unimportant considering the much less than 1-percent proportion that demand deposits contribute to the public's wealth.

Branching in and across states was liberalized after the bank failures of the 1980s, but its substitute, deposit insurance, continued. The only purpose of deposit insurance now is to subsidize investments in bank (and other intermediary) deposits, including, fantastically, time deposits.

Although bank failures were fewer after the Great Depression, losses (formerly to depositors, now to the FDIC and taxpayers) rose. "The incentive effects of these vast changes were, however, hidden for decades. The Great Depression had winnowed out" the weaker banks, and events (depression and war) led to the substitution of US bonds. "By the end of the war," White (2010) wrote,

> banks had become extremely safe institutions, and it would take them decades to unwind from their bond-saturated positions [until 1970, Table 7.1; and agriculture enjoyed unprecedented prosperity until the 1980s] and permit the full effects of the New Deal incentives to operate,... when inflationary shocks created a perfect storm that caused the New Deal regulatory system to collapse.

Despite the consensus that the bank regulatory system was ineffective before and during the last crisis, neither its principles nor form has been changed.

Table 7.1 Federal reserve member bank assets, 1929–70, and loans relative to assets, L/A

End June	Loans	L/A	US securities	Other secs	Reserves	Total assets
1929	25.7	0.56	4.2	5.9	2.8	45.5
1933	12.9	0.39	6.9	5.0	2.7	33.0
1939	13.1	0.25	13.8	5.7	10.7	51.9
1945	20.6	0.16	73.2	5.6	16.0	126.4
1950	37.7	0.28	55.8	9.3	17.2	133.7
1960	98.3	0.48	43.5	15.8	20.3	204.2
1970	240.8	0.56	37.3	54.8	27.1	433.1

Sources: Federal Reserve Board (1943, 1976).

Note
1 Total assets also include balances with banks, cash items in the process of collection, and bank premises.

Regulators have been added to watch the regulators, and prohibitions have been directed at recent failures – placing a fielder where the last ball was hit – and the most active regulations continue to be capital requirements. The international Basel Committee on Capital Regulation has come up with more-and-more complex capital requirements in Basel I (1988), Basel II (2004), and Basel III, scheduled for implementation in 2019 (Saunders and Cornett 2012: ch. 13). The problems with the changing Basle agreements are similar to the domestic "capital adequacy" indicator, particularly the difficulties of evaluating risk, finding a meaningful measure of capital (beyond suspect book values), and the lack of correlation between capital, however measured, and bank performance. These problems have been understood for decades. Sam Peltzman (1970) wrote:

> Bank examiners devote the greater part of their efforts to a determination of the "riskiness" of a bank's assets, on the one hand, and the "adequacy" of its capital, on the other.... However, the preponderant emphasis is placed on regulating bank capital rather than the details of the asset portfolio. While there is no specific reason for this emphasis on capital adequacy, it can be explained on institutional grounds. It is surely difficult for a bank examiner to judge accurately the riskiness of the many asset items he comes across, since they reflect a great variety of [changing local and national] market conditions, bank management judgments, and special circumstances. Instead of attempting an independent assessment of these details, a much easier course of action is to accept bank management judgment while substituting for this acquiescence a strong insistence that depositors be protected with adequate capital against the consequences of mistakes.

More capital might be thought to help, but researchers have failed to find a relation to bank failures (Thomas 1935). Bad loans, mistaken or unlucky, erode capital very quickly. Better predictors of failure are the same as the reasons for bad loans, particularly rapid growth and loans to directors. This knowledge has been reinforced by later studies. Studies at the Federal Reserve Bank of St. Louis, the OCC, and the FDIC all found "remarkably little evidence ... that links the level of capital or the ratio of capital to assets with bank failure rates" (Gilbert *et al.* 1985). Yet the emphasis on capital continued. A good part of the 1990–1 recession may be due to the effects of the application of the 1988 Basel capital accord on bank credit (Bernanke and Lown 1991).

Dodd–Frank

The chief regulatory response to the financial crises of 2006–2008 was the Wall Street Reform and Consumer Protection Act of 2010, called Dodd–Frank after the chairmen of the Senate Banking and House Financial Services Committees. It is sprawling and complex, desirous of reducing risk throughout the financial system, but its principles are "more of the same." It creates new agencies, including the Financial Stability Oversight Council, chaired by the Secretary of the Treasury, to oversee other regulators; a watchman to watch and correct the failures of existing watchmen, even though its remoteness from taxpayers and the regulated is even greater. The council has broad powers to collect information from and direct other agencies, it is exempt from the limitations of the Federal Advisory Committee Act, and has an almost unlimited budget in being able to draw on virtually any resource of any department or agency of the federal government.[2]

The perceived ineffectiveness of the existing system was illustrated by Congress' rejection of the administration's plan to make the Fed the chief coordinator of regulations, not only because of inter-agency jealousies, but also because of the Fed's failures within its previously limited scope. "Giving the Fed more responsibility," Senator Dodd admitted, "is like a parent giving his son a bigger, faster car right after he crashed the family station wagon" (Kaiser 2013: 56, 91, 95). However, instead of changing the approach from oversight and direction to incentives (which would have reduced agency budgets and powers), it was decided to pile another agency with the same approach on top of the existing failures. The idea of letting market disciplines operate – of letting failure impose costs on owners and creditors – seems never to have been taken seriously by the legislators. Not only is double liability a thing of the past, bailouts and the protections of "too big to fail" have lessened the incentives even of single liability.

The Act showed its lack of thought and study in its incompleteness. It consisted mainly of directions to agencies to revise their regulations and develop rules for financial insurance and advising, the trading of derivatives, consumer protection, the winding down of bankrupt firms, the Fed's extensions of credit in "unusual or exigent circumstances" (which, tongue in cheek, will require the approval of the Secretary of the Treasury), credit rating agencies, corporate governance, debit card fees, limits on bank investments which put their federally insured deposits at risk (the Volcker rule), and the meaning and application of "too big to fail," most of which remained undone years later. They remained to be negotiated among the regulators in turf battles and between the regulators and the industry. Several were subjects of legal battles as firms contested their implementation even before their formulation.

The special exemptions given by the Volcker rule to bank lending to governments fit the repressive practice of directing credit away from the private sector – without effect. The prohibition of specific investments or practices will not prevent banks whose incentives point to risk-taking from finding substitutes.

The contest over the Fed's application of the Dodd–Frank authority to fix bank credit card fees charged to retailers based on costs became *blood sport* (McGarity 2012). On July 31, 2013, US District Judge Richard Leon in Washington declared the Fed's rule an "utterly indefensible" interpretation of the Act's purpose to protect consumers and retailers (Dow Jones Business News, July 31, 2013). The stated purposes of the Act are

To promote the financial stability of the United States by improving accountability and transparency in the financial system, to end "too big to fail," to protect the American taxpayer by ending bailouts, to protect consumers from abusive financial services practices, and for other purposes.

In fact, it encourages the opposite. Most of the provisions that survive "negotiations" between the regulators and the regulated will be ineffective because they prohibit specific activities, such as over-the-counter derivatives and certain investments. This does not limit risk, which as the history of imaginative and evasive financial innovations shows, takes many forms – called the "regulatory dialectic" by Edward Kane (1981). The Act even promotes risky behavior by explicitly providing for the administration's bailout of large firms, formalizing the connection between political power and government assistance. The identification of firms as TBTF lowers their cost of funds and generally subsidizes risky behavior, raising the probability of financial crises and bailouts. The Act institutionalizes TBTF and bailouts, and substitutes political power for the marketplace, although as seen above it must still run the judicial gauntlet.

Summary

The special fragility of banks and the banking system (systemic risk) is largely a function of regulation, rather than the reverse. There is no question that banking deserves our attention. Half of every transaction is the exchange of money (current or promised). The interruption of that exchange ravages the economy, but in seeking stability governments have promoted the opposite. The instability of American banking has been due mainly to its thousands of undiversified banks and, since the establishment of the Federal Reserve, the promotion of moral hazard by supporting insolvent banks, large and small. Medium- and long-term loans financed by unrestricted, first-come first-served, demand deposits, with fractional reserves and imperfect information of bank values, imply a non-zero probability of runs and failures, as suggested in the oft-cited 1983 paper by Douglas Diamond and Philip Dybvig. Actually, just about any firm dependent on credit, directly or through its customers or suppliers, is continuously threatened with termination if it does not take defensive action. However, firms do seek credit protection, and that includes banks if their regulators let them. Instability "is not an intrinsic problem with banking per se" (Gorton and Huang 2003).

The coming of the Fed did nothing to stabilize the banking system, and much to destabilize it. In addition to the moral hazard and increased costs of propping up insolvent banks, the Fed ended bank restrictions and clearinghouse certificates. The latter were a form of private money that partially filled the payments gap on several occasions before 1913, and the former gave a minimum protection to bank depositors and permitted the continuation of bank credit. Access has different values for different depositors, and in a free market would command different rates of return (Dwyer and Gilbert 1989; Wallace 1990). The Fed's approach to bank regulation has been to discourage free-market adjustments to risk, promote the risks arising from moral hazard, and trust to the oversight of ill-informed and conflicted regulators – in short, to take away the costs of mistakes, just as in monetary policy.

Notes

1 From a letter to the *Baltimore Sun* in 1932, quoted in the *New York Times*, October 27, 1936.
2 A purpose of the Federal Advisory Committee Act is to increase transparency by requiring committees of the federal government, unless exempted, to hold open meetings, preceded by public notice, with records available to the public.

8 Conclusion

The necessity and possibility of replacing the Fed

The Fed's performance has been disappointing at every stage of its existence, to the point that the doubling of the price level the last quarter-century is considered a triumph. These diminished inflation expectations have been accompanied by increasing financial instability and bailouts culminating in the agency's massive and aberrant fiscal intrusions during the Great Recession. Some of these repeated its errors of the Great Depression, demonstrating once again the Fed's inability to learn from its mistakes because its remote and independent (of the taxpayers) position of the insulation of the consequences of its actions.

Yet inertia and its usefulness to the politically powerful continue to preserve the Fed with its lack of restraints. Serious critics continue their relegation to the political and academic fringes. Monetary policy should not, and need not, be allowed to go on like this. We have known how to do better. History amply demonstrates the possibilities of sound money and financial stability, and that they may be achieved not only without significant costs, but with benefits to the interests concerned. This chapter reviews the records of monetary authorities as governed by their incentive structures and draws lessons for the Fed's replacement

Responsibilities and methods of monetary policy

Congress is responsible for the currency, and consequently for the 96-percent fall in the value of the dollar the past century. It has inflicted this tragedy on the public and the economy by means of the Federal Reserve System that it created as an expert agency independent of the electorate. The Fed was sold to the congressional majority and the public as an apolitical body with limited goals, in particular, "to furnish an elastic currency" and "to establish a more effective supervision of banking." Less publicized but as important to its passage, the Federal Reserve Act benefited its primary supporters, the large banks, by extending and supporting their markets. Most important for the economy and the public, the Fed was endowed with the enormous power of printing money that, given its necessarily limited knowledge of economic relations and its susceptibility to political pressures, it could not help but abuse.

The Fed's direction has in fact varied with political pressures, but the organization that was established in 1913 has remained virtually unchanged. The point of its lowest repute, at the end of the Great Depression, coincided with an activist administration that still saw uses for a government bank.

The Fed's goals, on the other hand, have expanded greatly, explicitly and otherwise. The Employment Act of 1946 and the Full Employment and Balanced Growth Act of 1978 directed it to add variables beyond banking and finance to its objectives, particularly the price level, employment, and growth. The Fed's competence to achieve these numerous often contradictory goals with what is essentially a single tool – Fed credit, that is, the purchase of assets with newly printed money – has been questioned, not least, though intermittently, by the Fed. Notwithstanding these difficulties, the Fed has voluntarily added to these commitments by offering its money creation services to the Executive and Congress in their circumvention of the taxpayers as they direct public credit to their political favorites.

Although they are often disguised as questions of economic stimulus, battles over monetary policy essentially come down to the choice between sound and easy money, that is, between price stability and inflation, or more accurately since the end of the gold standard, between low and high inflation. The most rudimentary understanding of monetary policy, therefore, must focus on the reasons for the persistent inflation under the Fed, and for that we need to know who and what drive the institution.

Monetary policies in the public interest are typically recommended by economists in the form of rules, such as a fixed rate of money growth, trade-offs between prices and output according to estimates of the Phillips Curve, and targeted price stability (or low inflation). The Fed resists externally imposed rules in favor of discretion, although its actions have sometimes corresponded with "lean-against-the-wind" or free-reserve guides. Each of these rules/guides (except fixed money growth) describes the Fed's behavior for limited periods, but none has applied for long. One might have thought that a more promising approach to understanding the Fed, at least for economists, would be to apply the same economic principles as for other agents, that is, the pursuit of interests subject to constraints.

Monetary institutions and incentives

Central bankers, like the rest of us, pursue their interests. The privately owned Bank of England and the first and second Banks of the United States pursued profits and survival, which they found to depend on the well-being of their customers and the community. The good behavior of these privileged banks was also encouraged by the attention of skeptical legislatures and executives. The Bank of England narrowly survived on several occasions, and the US Banks were not rechartered. Their continuation was always an issue, not only because of competitive interests but because their necessity was doubtful under the gold standard and balanced budgets.

That incentives dominated experience in determining monetary policy is indicated by the Bank of England after World War I, during which it effectively had been made a government department with a permanent management. Its leading role in choosing deflation to force a return to convertibility at the 1914 par differed from its nineteenth-century concerns for financial stability and prosperity in the short term, including its resistance to a speedy resumption after Waterloo.

"I think myself justified in affirming that the mitigation of commercial revulsions is the real, and only serious purpose of the Act of 1844," J.S. Mill (1857: 657) wrote after the Bank and the government agreed to suspend the monetary rule prescribed by the Act. "No Government would hesitate a moment" to stop convertibility in order to assure the continuity of the Bank of England's support of the financial system. That was turned upside down in the 1920s and after 1945, when convertibility took precedence, along with the support of government finance at the expense of industry.

This is not to say the Bank did not make plenty of mistakes before 1914. Central banks have always been slow to respond to developments, although that was also true of banking systems without central banks, and of the price system generally. They tended to be honest mistakes, however, on the side of caution, unlike the aggressive shocks that independent central banks insulated from the rest of the economic system have been willing to force.

In the United States, former House leader James G. Blaine explained Congress' reversal of its rush to contraction after the Civil War in terms that anticipated Keynes' "We are all dead in the long run" criticism of the Bank of England's post-World War I policy of restriction. Although the "ultimate result" of the 1864 Contraction Act would be beneficial, Blaine (1886 ii: 328) wrote, "the people knew that the process would bring embarrassment to vast numbers and would reduce not a few to bankruptcy and ruin." We saw that before and after this episode, Congress and the Treasury provided financial relief within a stable price system – just like the Bank of England, which also departed from "the rules of the gold-standard game," that is, the subordination of domestic stability to international flows.

Congressmen took their oversight of the Independent Treasury seriously at least partly because the consequences of their actions were clear and direct. This was the period of what has been called congressional government, when a responsible Congress controlled budgets, genuinely monitored monetary policy, and were punished for their errors at the polls.

Of course the argument that monetary policy would be better – more supportive of the continuity of payments and the value of the currency – if it were more responsible to the electorate is subject to qualifications: first that Congress accepts the responsibility. It cannot be the same body that subscribes to massive current deficits and open-ended commitments like the current social security and health-care programs.

On the other hand, being responsible – including *being seen to be responsible* – for money and the price level might reduce those commitments. Congress used the Fed to see to it that an investor in a 25-year government bond in 1945 received half of his investment in real terms. The same was true in 1985, and it promises to be true today. A Congress that is genuinely responsible for the price level would have no third party to inflate its debt away.

Another qualification is that voters must dislike inflation (and deflation) sufficiently to prefer stable-price representatives. There is evidence that instability is electorally costly – ask Van Buren, Hoover, or Carter. An increase in responsibility – coming out from hiding behind the Fed – might improve that discipline.

It must be admitted that the chances of price stability in the modern world are small when we think of the incentives facing Congress and the public, indeed of all who derive more utility from receiving than paying. It has been done before, however, when the incentives were right.

The reader must have noticed that my method is an increase in democracy, which is the opposite of arguments that rely on dictatorships for stability, a position that is contrary to the evidence. The higher inflations in authoritarian systems, including after World War II, are well known. Democracies have had nearly continuous single-digit inflations, others well into the double digits. An explanation is that dictatorships, without the support of free electorates, tend to be weak and are forced to buy off powerful groups. This Jeffersonian notion of the primary source of effective government seems to apply at least as much to money as to other activities.

The incentive incompatibility of our present monetary framework is clear. The Fed is insulated from the disciplines of profits or votes, but dependent on the support of large financial institutions and congressional spenders. Interests therefore incline the Fed to deficits and bailouts, for which it need not pay politically or economically. There is no incentive structure through which mistakes from the public's standpoint lead to behavior adjustments. They are not even seen as mistakes. The Fed's public depredations do not register as mistakes today any more than during the Great Depression. Costs are not costs without pain and suffering.

The Fed's powers without knowledge ended the gold standard's restraints. When price and economic fluctuations seriously resumed in the 1960s (after the Fed had supposedly regained its independence), financial instability was intensified as bailouts prevented market adjustments and necessitated their repetition.

Matters have gotten worse as the Fed's relief of Congress from the political costs of spending has increased. The near-zero interest rates in the face of the expanding government debt constitutes financial repression to a degree that used to be associated with backward regimes.

The weak economy since 2008 is consistent with other periods of financial repression that have been found to undermine growth. "The growth-reducing effects of high public debt" are reinforced by the low interest rates that discourage productive investments, which is used as an excuse to increase government spending, which slows growth, and so on (Reinhart *et al.* 2012). The "Fed's real goal in keeping interest rates low is to finance government debt and deficits," just as was explicitly agreed between the Fed and the Treasury during the 1942–51 peg (Brenner and Fridson 2013).

Financial repression, including inflation and bailouts, are long-term problems that require long-term solutions. Most of the arguments for change, however, have failed to address institutions or incentives. The solutions to our monetary problems are technically simple – balanced budgets and the withdrawal of subsidies – but unchangeable without a revision of incentives, that is, of the institutions of money.

Two possible changes were successful in the past: the private, profit-seeking pre-1913 central banks that did not possess unlimited capacities for printing money, and the Treasury under the direction of Congress. Each required an expert and attentive legislature that only responsibility can bring.

The lack of monetary sophistication in Congress the last 100 years, evidenced by its susceptibility to panic in 2008 and its submissiveness to the Fed during the Great Depression, is not a random event nor due to the decline of the human race. The cause is institutional, specifically the abdication of responsibility and the work and attention that go with it, resulting in the lack of active and informed congressional experts, no Websters, Calhouns, Bentons, or Shermans.

The Bernanke–Paulson demands were dumped on an uninformed and intellectually defenseless Congress that was unprepared to engage in argument or even to reject the implausible. Congressman Barney Frank, Chairman of the House Financial Services Committee, who saw the situation as an excuse for more regulation, admitted that the bailouts opened "the greatest breach between elite and public opinion that I have ever seen" (Kaiser 2013: 37). "Elite" in what sense, one wonders. When the Republican leadership, under pressure, asked for a meeting to debate TARP, they had no argument even for the unsubstantiated claims of the bailout champions.

Responsible monetary policy

Reinstituting Congress' responsibility for monetary policy would be technically straightforward, although it might have to be more involved than before 1913. Under the gold standard, money and prices were determined by free markets, by the public's preferences, and the relative cost of producing gold. The responsibility of central banks was limited to maintaining the payments system in the short run. Bringing back the gold standard would risk potentially damaging shocks to the system (although I will suggest free-market possibilities below). There would have to be a wholesale rewriting of contracts along with the reconsideration of payments in specie and paper, changes that would take decades to develop. Nor do we know the dollar price of gold consistent with the current price level. It is probably not the current market price, which is subject to speculation about the monetary system. We need to avoid imposing the shocks of radically new institutions and arrangements that the founders of the Fed treated so cavalierly – notwithstanding their protestations. On the other hand, Congress would have to take more responsibility for money and prices than before 1913, especially at the outset.

The task would not be as difficult as those who desire government by expert bureaucracies like to believe. Most government agencies are not explained by the world's increasing complexity. Quite the reverse, the calculation problems that can be solved only by markets have grown with the economy. The Interstate Commerce Commission, for example, unnecessarily and unsuccessfully employed large staffs to calculate rates for thousands of goods shipped over thousands of routes (themselves to be approved), whereas giving free rein to supply and demand would have been sufficient (Hoogenboom and Hoogenboom 1976: 69–70). The substantial reporting requirements of the New Deal Securities Acts were also unnecessary (the losses during the Great Depression being almost entirely due to business losses because of the Great Deflation caused by the Fed) and unhelpful in a financial world dependent on reputation and the competition for information (Stigler 1964).

The Fed is comparable. Its origins also lay in a crisis mentality that failed to address the real problems of an overregulated financial system. We would not be giving up much by eliminating the Fed. All but one or two of its offices and over 90 percent of its employees were unnecessary to the Act's goals. There was a reason for the regional Fed banks at the beginning because most Fed credit was dispensed through discount windows. That has been replaced by open-market operations in New York. Other sources of bank credit, particularly interbank lending, are sufficient. The discount windows have served mainly to supply funds at below market rates, and should be ended. Most Fed employees have cleared checks or performed other services with which the central bank has no reason to be involved. The Fed's bank regulation was redundant, and turned out to be harmful. The purported dual mandate – the inflation–unemployment trade-off – was nothing more than a rationalization of the Fed's fiscal subservience along with the age-old argument that easy money is beneficial. The logical and practical failure of the Phillips Curve amounted simply to another not-very-novel chapter in the long conflict between sound money and inflation – from John Law (1705) (and before) to the Keynesians (and no doubt afterwards). Of course, the employment acts of 1946 and 1978 would have to be jettisoned – and a Congress again responsible for money can return to its skepticism of the notion that paper money is a road to wealth.

That leaves the primary monetary functions of assisting payments and deter-mining the monetary base. The former would be greatly helped by eliminating the Fed, so that the clearing house and other cooperative arrangements which it displaced may resume and develop. The elimination of bailouts (and their expec-tation) should induce caution. Not completely necessary but helpful measures would be the ending of deposit insurance and portfolio regulations. A substantial part of the history of crises has concerned the effects of regulations.

An unregulated monetary base might easily develop, but in the immediate future, thinking of the continuity of our fiat-money regime overseen by Con-gress, we need a rule for the monetary base, and for that we need a monetary theory. Remember that we are trying to remove the unrestrained power of an independent money monopolist without shocking the quantity of money or the continuity of payments. Congress is not primarily an administrative agency, although that has been changing. In any case, with the will, it should have little difficulty monitoring a simple rule. Happily, a path was suggested recently by central banks in several countries in their statements and sometimes performances in the 1990s – inflation targeting, under which the minister of finance and governor of the central bank agree on an inflation target.

Targeting the Consumer Price Index or its change (inflation) is tantamount to a commodity-money system that in some ways is superior to the gold standard. A dollar is defined not as the value of a weight of gold but in terms of a basket of goods. An agency would stand ready to buy and sell the basket at the price (create the currency necessary), or price range, desired.

There would be technical and political disadvantages. The basket of goods changes, and its specification has been the subject of political controversy among those interested in inflation, such as in adjustments to social security and wage contracts with escalator clauses. However, it can reasonably be expected that prices under this system would be more stable than under the Federal Reserve, or even the gold standard.

What if something happens? No one in authority, the Fed in particular, knew what to do during the Great Depression, and did not feel the need to take steps commensurate with the emergency. Many economists, members of the public, and a minority of Congress wanted to cut gold's constraint on money. President Hoover called the fight against depression equivalent to war, but was constrained by the Federal Reserve, which he called a "weak reed to lean on in a time of trouble." Similarities existed in 2008, but in neither case was Congress, the official body most exposed to the costs of actions and inactions, prepared to interfere with the expert agency. New problems, real and imagined, will arise in any system, and need to be addressed by an informed, intelligent, and responsible body. In a democracy, that means the legislature rather than an independent agency that in fact is independent only of the public.

The development of congressional oversight in its many committees and subcommittees, absolutely and relatively to the rapidly changing and highly politicized administrative agencies, has often been noted (Kirst 1969; MacNeil 1963: 125). That expertise and experience could be applied to money. Members inclined to maintain the value of money would be induced to oppose the spenders instead of waiting for the Fed to bear the unpopularity of tight money (Timberlake 1993: 393, 409).

Appendix A gives an example of how other monies might arise if the withdrawal of regulations permits. The government's monopoly has prevented the public from defending itself against the depreciation of the currency. The simple system described here might help, but making it a monopoly could be as dangerous as the present system. There may be a desire for other, potentially safer, monies. For example, banks might borrow and lend gold coin or ingots. The price (currency value) of gold would be market determined, banks could be hedged, and individuals would be free to shift to gold if they lacked confidence in the government. In the meantime, they would have access to a fiat system unsullied by a belief in monetary stimuli.

Must we change our monetary authority?

Our book began with this question, but it was already too late. Federal Reserve officials had already changed the institution beyond recognition, from a supporter of an elastic currency, with assistance to the Treasury, to primarily a government financial adjunct outside the electoral process. The Fed has stopped believing in monetary policy or even the relevance of money. Economic downturns are treated as shocks to financial institutions whose problems are solved by largesse from the Fed.

Charles Goodhart (1988: 85–86) argued that banks need a central bank because of informational asymmetries between banks and depositors, which together with the prospect of contagious bank runs, requires quality control, supervision, and a lender of last resort that can only be supplied by a modern central bank. In fact,

> The success of delegating the achievement of price stability to an operationally independent central bank has been regarded as so manifest in the OECD countries … the question is now often posed, why not also delegate fiscal policy to an independent fiscal authority. My answer is that almost every fiscal decision involves choices between priorities and objectives, among them macro stability, micro efficiency, and distributional effects, to name but three. The essence of politics is to make such difficult decisions, and that should not, in my view, be delegated to an unelected, primarily technical body.
>
> (Goodhart 2003)

Goodhart's argument rejects the well-documented finding that the reason for central banks is found in government desires for cheap finance rather than as a remedy for market failures, but even those accepting the possibility of a useful Fed are troubled (Smith 1936: 167–168; Dowd 1994; Selgin and White 1999). President Jeffrey Lacker (2012) of the Federal Reserve Bank of Atlanta observed that the Fed's large purchases of mortgage-backed securities tilted "the flow of credit toward one particular economic sector. Markets generally are a better judge of creditworthiness than any central authority, I believe, so the Fed's actions risk distorting credit allocation."

> If such purchases are to be made at all, they should be made with specific authorization from Congress. By purchasing MBS, the Fed conducts what is essentially fiscal policy without the checks and balances built into the normal appropriations process. The Fed has the ability to engage in credit allocation due to its operational independence – an important feature for protecting monetary policy decisions from short-run political pressures.... But by using that independence to favor specific sectors, the Fed opens itself up to criticism that could jeopardize that very independence in making … monetary policy.

The Fed has increasingly become like national banks in centrally planned economies – as an allocator of credit – which have poor investment records, with the difference that the Fed directs funds to known failures.

I hope Goodhart is as disappointed in the Fed as I am, although he may not agree that the observed perversions of central banking are inherent in unaccountable institutions. It is essential that we understand the reasons for their behavior because of the extensive effects on society. Edward Kane (2012) wrote:

> [T]hroughout the housing bubble and the long-lasting economic slowdown that the bursting of the bubble brought about, governments in the U.S. and Europe have put the interests of elite [politically powerful] financial institutions far ahead of the interests of society as a whole. Taxpayer interests were and are poorly represented because of regulatory hubris and regulatory capture. Influence-driven incentive conflict is a phenomenon that mainstream models of optimal macroeconomic and financial stabilization studiously ignore.

This is the "breach between elite and public opinion" seen by Congressman Frank, who after a nod to the latter, joined the former. We cannot expect monetary policy in the public interest without the necessary incentives that require direct and transparent responsibility/accountability. The chances of the example presented above being adopted, and if so, its chances of success, are subjects of further study. An important but difficult question concerns the incentives affecting Congress' choice between change and the institutional status quo.

Is Congress up to the job?

The major change in American national government since 1900, other than its size, has been in the power shift from Congress to the Executive. Legislation is initiated by the President, and Congress is judged on the basis of how well it follows his lead. The only questions for Congress are in the details. Harry Truman ran successfully against what he called the "do-nothing" 80th Congress that he said failed to pass his program. Harvard Professor Samuel Huntington (1965) noted:

> When in 1963 the 88th Congress seemed to stymie the Kennedy legislative program, criticism rapidly mounted. "What kind of legislative body is it," asked Walter Lippman, neatly summing up the prevailing exasperation, "that will not or cannot legislate." When in 1964 the same 88th Congress passed the civil rights, tax, and other bills, criticism of Congress correspondingly subsided. Congress's dilemma, Huntington argued, was that it could exercise power only by obstructing the president, which reduced its popularity and therefore its power

Huntington clearly favored the Executive activism of which he wrote, but his views are widely shared. It should also be noted in line with the theme of this book that Lyndon Johnson, the consummate politician who steered and pushed the Kennedy program through Congress, was not equally able or interested in getting Congress to pay for it; quite the opposite, as evidenced by the 1964 Kennedy (actually Johnson) tax cut and the administration's pressure on the Fed to monetize the deficit.

Huntington's explanation of Congress' decline is also interesting and relevant. The focal center of power in the national government most of the nineteenth century was Congress, which did not keep up with the economy and society. The twentieth century saw

> rapid urbanization and the rise of a post-industrial technological society; the nationalization of social and economic problems and the concomitant growth of national organizations to deal with these problems; the increasing bureaucratization of social, economic, and governmental organizations; and the sustained high level international involvement of the United States in world politics,

none of which has slowed since Huntington wrote. These changes have generated new forces and the redistribution of political power. Particularly important have been the "tremendous expansion of the responsibilities of the national government and the size of the national bureaucracy."

Looking at the downside of Huntington's observations, the dominance of the Executive has not led to the "insulation of Congress from other social groups and political institutions." In 1900, no gap existed between congressmen and other leaders of American society and politics. As the century progressed, however, Huntington claimed, congressmen remained rural and socially backward. Seniority became a prerequisite for leadership, which reduced the turnover necessary to keep pace with society. Interchange between administrations and Congress is rare (contrary to the nineteenth century, when, as we have seen, most Secretaries of the Treasury had been congressmen).

Congress' decline was hastened by procedural changes. Congressional power became less centralized, so that, although specialization has grown with tenure and the numbers of committees and subcommittees, its powers became more diffused. We see specialization without centralization, and a shift of the "aggressive spirit" cited by Woodrow Wilson from Congress to the Executive. Not legislation but its oversight has become the primary role of Congress, which may be a saving grace, to be discussed below.

The dominance of the Executive has not always had good effects, particularly in monetary affairs. Its continuous desire for spending for politically popular programs is well-known. We have given up a lot in Congress's diversity and deliberation. When the government's reaction to a problem, real or perceived, depends on one man, confronted with the label of savior or do-nothing, in danger of being linked in popular histories with Coolidge and Hoover, his choice is clear. He must not only be active; he must be seen to be active. If there is a lack of dramatic problems with politically possible government responses, the

President's current and future reputations demand that at least one be found, or manufactured. The result has been government by crisis. The reforms of the 1930s, particularly the securities Acts, addressed not the causes of the Great Depression or the problems of the financial markets, but the age-old unpopularity of bankers. The experience had more than a slight resemblance to the 1964 Gulf of Tonkin incident that the administration manufactured to gain Congress' support of an expanded war effort; as well as the Panic of 1907 and the claims of Paulson and Bernanke in 2008. Neither President Bush nor candidates Obama and McCain wanted to be seen anywhere but in front of the demand to *do something*, whatever that might be. The fall in the supply of legislation increased the demand for crises (Aberbach 1990).

It is Presidents and their followers who are the most removed and dependent on crises, contrary to the argument presented above. It is difficult to believe that the New Deal Brains Trust and other intellectual and Beltway groups have been closer than Congress to Americans. Crises are used to stampede Congress into ill-conceived programs for which it soon loses its appetite, as during and after FDR's 100 days, but still cause problems today (Patterson 1967). One might argue for the principle of immediate imperious reactions to events, but they have not worked well in the field of money and finance.

Successful policies in monetary and finance require interdependent knowledge, responsibility, and deliberation at the highest level, which means Congress – day-to-day and especially in crises, which, whatever the arrangements in place, will happen. Congress' direct involvement in money and finance might have beneficial effects even for the interests traditionally opposed. The budgetary discipline forced by monetary responsibility ought to make it easier to say "no" to pressure groups. We might even see the return of the budget watchers – the "great objectors" of the nineteenth century (MacNeil 1963: 131). The well-being of financial institutions, who value the stability that is encouraged by responsible monetary policy, would also be promoted, and make the need for bailouts less likely (Bordo and Wheelock 1998; Schwartz 1995). The creation of the Fed was a powerful example of the advice: "Be careful what you wish for."

Appendix

A free resumption of gold money[1]

An impediment to the return to gold money is the choice of an official dollar price of the metal. Costs are unknown and the current market price of gold is affected by the uncertainties of future monetary policies. Prices increased between 50 and 150 percent during the three suspensions shown in Figure 2.1, compared with more than 3,000 percent between the 1971 suspension and 2012, when the gold price rose from $35 to $1,200. We do not want a 97-percent deflation, nor is there much justification for selecting any other dollar price of gold.

These problems can be circumvented by allowing the free development of a price when the government's role is only permissive. It needs only to withdraw its restrictions on money and banking. Bank portfolios are freed, and although the government's money may continue, and it may even choose to transact only in its own money, it does not interfere with other, including gold, monies. The government money-monopoly is ended.

Money holders may choose claims on gold along with or instead of government fiat money. The example in Table A.1 shows how banks might accommodate them without taking on risk even in the initial stages of the new system.

Inflation (the inverse of the gold purchasing power of government fiat money) may be –1, 1, or 3 percent with equal probabilities, that is, an expectation of 1 percent during the next quarter. Fiat cash reserves of $40 at T_0 will be $40 at T_1, or (40.4, 39.6, or 38.8; $E=39.6$) in real terms, where E indicates the expectation.

Fiat loans of $400 at the nominal rate 2 percent will be worth $408 at T_1, or (412, 404, or 396; $E=404$) in real terms. If the fixed (promised) price of gold is $400 an ounce, the expected real return on loans is 1 percent.

So much for nominal bank assets. Its gold reserves (say an ounce) worth $40, will be worth ($39.6, $40.4, or $41.2; $E=$40.4$), or 40 in real terms at T_1. Gold loans of $400 (10 ounces) at 1 percent will be worth 404 in real terms, or ($400, $408, or $416; $E=$408$) at T_1.

The liability (borrowing) side of the balance sheet shows that the risks of fiat and gold loans can be offset by fiat and gold deposits. The spread between fiat loans and deposits is a constant 0.5 percent, and similarly for gold loans and deposits. Hedging will in practice be more involved than in this example. Loan and deposit maturities may not quite match, but banks can use gold futures and options.

Table A.1 Real (gold) and dollar balance sheets at beginning (T_0) and end (T_1) of quarter

T_1	T_0	Assets	Liabilities	T_0	T_1
40 (40.4, 39.6, 38.8)	40	Fiat reserves	Fiat deposits	400	406 (410, 402, 394)
408 (412, 404, 396)	400	Fiat loans			
39.6, 40.4, 41.2 (40)	40	Gold reserves	Gold deposits	400	398, 406, 414 (402)
400, 408, 416 (404)	400	Gold loans	Capital*	80	83.6, 84.4, 85.2 (84.4, 83.6, 82.8)

Notes

Initial price of gold $400 per ounce and inflation = -1 percent, 1 percent, or 3 percent, Dollar and alternative real outcomes on top and bottom lines (), respectively.

* Does not reflect operating costs.

Off balance sheet

Gold futures and options with expirations determined by maturity differences between gold deposits and loans.

   Interest on fiat loans is 2 percent; for equal chances of -1 percent, 1 percent, and 3 percent inflation, real returns are 3 percent, 1 percent, or -1 percent, giving real payoffs of $412, $404, or $396, with expectation of $404 and 1 percent.

   Fiat deposits pay 1.5 percent, or $406, giving in real terms 410, 402, or 394.

   Gold deposits pay 0.5 percent, giving $398, $406, or $414.

   This is only one bank on one decision date. Other banks may buy and sell gold contracts at other prices, and our bank may transact at several gold prices. The offsets described would enable the development of an equilibrium dollar price of gold without excessive risk-taking. The growth of gold money would depend on the public's (including banks') attitudes toward risk and the prospective value of government money.

Note

1 From Crook and Wood (2004).

References

Aberbach, J.D. 1990. *Keeping a Watchful Eye: The Politics of Congressional Oversight*. Brookings.

Ackley, H.G. 1961. *Macroeconomic Theory*. Macmillan.

———. 1971. *Stemming World Inflation*. Atlantic Institute.

Acres, W.M. 1931. *The Bank of England from Within, 1694–1900*. Oxford University Press.

Ahamed, L. 2009. *Lords of Finance: The Bankers Who Broke the World*. Penguin.

Ahearn, D.S. 1963. *Federal Reserve Policy Reappraised, 1951–59*. Columbia University Press.

Aldrich, N. 1909. "The work of the National Monetary Commission," speech to the Economic Club of New York, November 29 (National Monetary Commission). US Government Printing Office.

Allison, J.A. 2013. *The Financial Crisis and the Free Market Cure*. McGraw-Hill.

Álvaro, A., M.J. Fry, and C.A.E. Goodhart. 1996. *Central Banking in Developing Countries*, for the Bank of England. Routledge.

American Bankers Association. 2005. *The Benefits of Charter Choice: The Dual Banking System as a Case Study*, June 24.

Anderson, B.L. and P.L. Cottrell, eds. 1974. *Money and Banking in England*. David & Charles.

Anderson, C.J. 1968. *A Half-Century of Federal Reserve Policymaking, 1914–64*. Federal Reserve Bank of Philadelphia.

Andrew, A.P. 1908. "Substitutes for cash in the Panic of 1907," *Quarterly Journal of Economics*, August.

Armantier, O., S. Kreiger, and J. McAndrews. 2008. "The Federal Reserve's Term Auction Facility," *Federal Reserve Bank of New York Current Issues*, July.

Ashley, W.J. 1903. *The Adjustment of Wages*. Longmans, Green.

Ashton, T.S. 1948. *The Industrial Revolution, 1760–1830*. Oxford University Press.

Atkins, W.E., G.W. Edwards, and H.G. Moulton. 1946. *The Regulation of the Security Markets*. Brookings.

Attwood, T. 1817. *Prosperity Restored*. Baldwin, Cradock, and Jay.

———. 1828. "Famine," *Globe*, June 11; reprinted in T. Attwood, ed., *The Scotch Banker*. James Ridgway, 1832; Capie (1993).

Axilrod, S.H. 2011. *Inside the Fed*. MIT Press.

Bagehot, W. 1866. "What a panic is and how it might be mitigated," *Economist*, May 12; reprinted in M. Collins, ed., *Central Banking in History*. Edward Elgar, 1993.

———. 1873. *Lombard Street*. Henry King; reprinted John Murray, 1917.

Bair, S. 2012. *Bull by the Horns: Fighting to Save Main Street from Wall Street and Wall Street from Itself.* Free Press.

Baker, D. 2006. *Recession Looms.* Center for Economic and Policy Research, November.

———. 1989. "The estimation of prewar gross national product," *Journal of Political Economy*, February.

Bank of England. 1819. *Representation by the Directors to the Chancellor of the Exchequer*, May 20. *British Parliamentary Papers, Monetary Policy, General*, 2. Irish University Press.

Baring, F. 1797. *Observations on the Establishment of the Bank of England and on the Paper Circulation of the Country.* Minerva Press; reprinted with *Further Observations*, A.M. Kelley, 1967.

Barofsky, N.M. 2012. *Bailout.* Free Press.

Barrett, D.C. 1931. *The Greenbacks and Resumption of Specie Payments, 1862–79.* Harvard University Press.

Beard, C.A. 1915. *Economic Origins of Jeffersonian Democracy.* Macmillan.

Bernanke, B.S. 2002. "On Milton Friedman's ninetieth birthday," Remarks at a conference to honor Milton Friedman's ninetieth birthday, University of Chicago, November 8.

———. 2005a. "What have we learned since October 1979?" *Federal Reserve Bank of St. Louis Review*, March/April.

———. 2005b. "The global saving glut and the U.S. current account deficit," *Sandridge Lecture*, Virginia Association of Economists, Richmond, March 10.

———. 2007. "Global imbalances: recent developments and prospects," *Bundesbank Lecture*, September 11.

———. 2008. "Opening remarks," *Maintaining Stability in a Changing Financial System.* Federal Reserve Bank of Kansas City.

Bernanke, B.S. and C.S. Lown. 1991. "The credit crunch," *Brookings Papers on Economic Activity*, Fall.

Bezemer, D.J. 2009. "No one saw this coming: understanding financial crisis through accounting models," *Munich Personal RePEc Archive*, June.

Billings, R. 2010. *Abraham Lincoln, Esq.: The Legal Career of America's Greatest President.* University Press of Kentucky.

Blaine, J.G. 1886. *Twenty Years in Congress.* Henry Bill.

Blair, C.E. and R.M. Kushmeider, 2006. "Challenges to the dual banking system: the funding of bank supervision," *FDIC Banking Review*, 1.

Blaug, M. 1995. "Why is the quantity theory of money the only surviving theory in economics," in M. Blaug, ed., *The Quantity Theory of Money: From Locke to Keynes and Friedman.* Edward Elgar.

Blinder, A.S. 2013. *After the Music Stopped: The Financial Crisis, the Response, and the Work Ahead.* Penguin.

Blinder, A.S. and M. Zandi. 2010. *How the Great Recession was Brought to an End.* Ms. Princeton University and Moody's Analytics.

Bloomfield, A.I. 1959. *Monetary Policy under the International Gold Standard, 1880–1914.* Federal Reserve Bank of New York.

Bordo, M.D. and D.C. Wheelock. 1998. "Price stability and financial stability: the historical record," *Federal Reserve Bank of St. Louis Review*, September/October.

Bordo, M.D. and E.N. White. 1991. "A tale of two currencies: British and French finance during the Napoleonic Wars," *Journal of Economic History*, June.

Bordo, M.D., E.U. Choudhri, and A.J. Schwartz. 2002. "Was expansionary monetary policy feasible during the Great Contraction? An examination of the gold standard constraint," *Explorations in Economic History*, January.

Boyd, W. 1801. *A Letter to the Right Honourable William Pitt on the Influence of the Stoppage of Issues in Specie at the Bank of England on the Prices of Provisions and Other Commodities*. J. Wright; reprinted O'Brien, *Foundations of Monetary Economics*. W. Pickering, 1994.

Boyle, A. 1967. *Montagu Norman*. Cassell.

Bradford, F.A. 1935. "The Banking Act of 1935," *American Economic Review*, December.

Brandeis, L. 1913. "Letter to President Wilson, June 14," *Wilson Papers*, 27.

Bremner, R.P. 2004. *Chairman of the Fed: William McChesney Martin, Jr., and the Creation of the Modern American Financial System*. Yale University Press.

Brenner, R. and M. Fridson. 2013. "Bernanke's World War II monetary regime," *Wall Street Journal*, March 25.

Brown, E.H.P. and S.V. Hopkins. 1956. "Seven centuries of the prices of consumables, compared with builders' wage-rates," *Economica*, November.

Brunner, K. and A.H. Meltzer. 1964. *The Federal Reserve's Attachment to the Free Reserves Concept*, for the House Committee on Banking and Currency; reprinted in K. Brunner and A.H. Meltzer, eds., *Monetary Economics*. Blackwell, 1989.

———. 1968. "What did we learn from the monetary experience of the United States in the Great Depression?", *Canadian Journal of Economics*, May.

Buchanan, J.M. and R.E. Wagner. 1977. *Democracy in Deficit. The Political Legacy of Lord Keynes*. Academic Press.

Buiter, W. 2008. "Lessons from the North Atlantic financial crisis," *Financial Times*, May 28.

Burger, A.E. 1969. "A historical analysis of the credit crunch of 1966," *Federal Reserve Bank of St. Louis Review*, September.

Burgess, W.R. 1936. *The Reserve Banks and the Money Markets*. Harper.

Burke, E. 1790. *Reflections on the Revolution in France*; new imprint of the Payne edn. Liberty Fund, 1999.

Burns, A.F. 1978. *Reflections of an Economic Policy Maker*. American Enterprise Institute.

Butkiewicz, J. 2013. "Reconstruction finance corporation," *EHNet Encyclopedia*, October 18.

Cagan, P. 1969. "Interest rates and bank reserves: a reinterpretation of the statistical association," in J.M. Guttentag and P. Cagan, eds., *Essays on Interest Rates*. National Bureau of Economic Research.

Calomiris, C.W. 2009. "Banking crises and the rules of the game," *NBER Working Paper* 15403, September.

Calomiris, C.W. and G. Gorton. 1991. "The origins of banking panics: models, facts, and bank regulation," in R.G. Hubbard, ed., *Financial Markets and Financial Crises*. University of Chicago Press.

Cannan, E. 1925. *The Paper Pound of 1797–1821*. P.S. King & Son.

Cannon, J.G. 1910. *Clearing Houses*. (National Monetary Commission). US Government Printing Office.

Capie, F., ed., 1993. *History of Banking*. W. Pickering.

———, ed. 1994. *The Future of Central Banking: The Tercentenary Symposium of the Bank of England*. Cambridge University Press.

Carney, B.M. 2008. "Bernanke is fighting the last war: interview with Anna Schwartz," *Wall Street Journal*, October 18.

Case, K. and R. Shiller. 2006. "Full house," *Wall Street Journal*, August 30.

Cassel, G. 1928. *Postwar Monetary Stabilization*. Columbia University Press.

Catterall, R.C.H. 1902. *The Second Bank of the United States*. University of Chicago Press.

Chandler, L.V. 1958. *Benjamin Strong, Central Banker*. Brookings.

Chappell, H. and R.R. McGregor. 2000. "A long history of FOMC voting behavior," *Southern Economic Journal*, April.

Chernow, R. 1990. *The House of Morgan*. Atlantic Monthly Press.

Clapham, J.H. 1944. *The Bank of England: A History*, 2 vols. Cambridge University Press.

Clarida, R., J. Galí, and M. Gertler. 2000. "Monetary policy rules and macroeconomic stability: evidence and some theory," *Quarterly Journal of Economics*, February.

Clarke, M.S. and D.A. Hall. 1832. *Documentary History of the Bank of the United States*. Gales and Seaton.

Clarke, S.V.O. 1967. *Central Bank Cooperation, 1924–31*. Federal Reserve Bank of New York.

Cloos, G.W. 1966. "Monetary conditions from the 1937–38 recession to Pearl Harbor," *Financial Analysts Journal*, January/February.

Cole, H.L. and L.E. Ohanian. 2004. "New Deal policies and the persistence of the Great Depression: a general equilibrium analysis," *Journal of Political Economy*, August.

Cottrell, A.F., M.S. Lawlor, and J.H. Wood. 1995. "What are the connections between deposit insurance and bank failures?" in A.F. Cottrell, *et al.*, eds., *The Causes and Costs of Depository Institution Failures*. Kluwer.

Crook, M.W. and J.H. Wood. 2004. "Private paths to resumption," in W. Todd and J.H. Wood, eds., *Prospects for a Resumption of the Gold Standard*. American Institute for Economic Research.

de Leeuw, F. and E. Gramlich. 1968. "The Federal Reserve: MIT econometric model," *Federal Reserve Bulletin*, January.

DeLong, J.B. 1997. "America's peacetime inflation: the 1970s," in C. Romer and D. Romer, eds., *Reducing Inflation: Motivation and Strategy*. University of Chicago Press.

Dewey, D.R. 1910. *State Banking before the Civil War*. US Government Printing Office.

——. 1928. *Financial History of the United States*, 10th edn. Longmans, Green.

Diamond, D.W. and P.H. Dybvig. 1983. "Bank runs, deposit insurance, and liquidity," *Journal of Political Economy*, June.

Dowd, K. 1994. "Banking, bankers' clubs, and bank regulation," *Journal of Money, Credit and Banking*, May.

Dwyer, Jr., G.P. and R.A. Gilbert. 1989. "Bank runs and private remedies," *Federal Reserve Bank of St. Louis Review*, May/June.

Eccles, M.S. 1951. *Beckoning Frontiers*. Knopf.

Eichengreen, B.J. 1992. *Golden Fetters: The Gold Standard and the Great Depression, 1919–1939*. Oxford University Press.

Eisner, R. 1969. "Fiscal and monetary policy reconsidered," *American Economic Review*, December.

Feavearyear, A.E. 1931. *The Pound Sterling*. Clarendon Press.

Federal Open Market Committee (FOMC). 1952. *Report of the* Ad hoc *Subcommittee on the Government Securities Market*, in US Congress, *United States Monetary Policy: Recent Thinking and Experience*, 1954.

Federal Reserve Board. 1943. *Banking and Monetary Statistics, 1914–41*.

——. 1959. *All-Bank Statistics: United States, 1896–1955*.

——. 1976. *Banking and Monetary Statistics, 1941–70*.

Feinman, J. and W. Poole. 1989. "Federal Reserve policymaking: an overview and analysis of the policy process: comment," in K. Brunner and A.H. Meltzer, eds., *Carnegie-Rochester Series on Public Policy*, spring.

Feldstein, M. 2010. "What powers for the Federal Reserve?" *Journal of Economic Literature*, 1.

Fenstermaker, J.V. 1965. *The Development of American Commercial Banking, 1782–1837*. Kent State University Press.

Fetter, F.A. 1965. *Development of British Monetary Orthodoxy, 1797–1875*. Harvard University Press.

Fforde, J.S. 1992. *The Bank of England and Public Policy, 1941–58*. Cambridge University Press.

Fisher, I. 1920. *Stabilizing the Dollar*. Macmillan.

——. 1922. *The Purchasing Power of Money*, 2nd edn. Macmillan.

——. 1930. *The Theory of Interest*. Macmillan.

Friedman, M. 1960. *A Program for Monetary Stability*. Fordham University Press.

——. 1962. "Should there be an independent monetary authority?" in L.B. Yeager, ed., *In Search of a Monetary Constitution*. Harvard University Press.

——. 1975. "Testimony," in US Congress, *Second Meeting on the Conduct of Monetary Policy*, 1975.

——. 1982. "The Federal Reserve and monetary instability," *Wall Street Journal*, February 1.

Friedman, M. and A.J. Schwartz. 1963. *A Monetary History of the United States, 1867–1960*. Princeton University Press.

Fullerton, T.M., R.A. Hirth, and M.B. Smith. 1991. "Inflationary dynamics and the Angell-Johnson proposals," *Atlantic Economic Journal*, March.

Furlong, F.T. and R. Ingenito. 1996. "Commodity prices and inflation," *Federal Reserve Bank of San Francisco Economic Review*, 2.

Furlong, F.T. and S.H. Kwan. 2006. "Sources of bank charter value," *Federal Reserve Bank of San Francisco Working Paper*, September.

Gallatin, A. 1809. *Report on the Bank of the U.S., American State Papers, Finance II*.

——. 1830. "Considerations on the currency and banking system of the United States," *American Quarterly Review*, December (*Writings* iii).

——. 1879. *Writings*, H. Adams, ed., Antiquarian Press, 1960.

Giannini, C. 2011. *The Age of Central Banks*. Edward Elgar.

Gilbert, R.A., C.C. Stone, and M.E. Trebing. 1985. "The new bank capital adequacy standards," *Federal Reserve Bank of St. Louis Review*, May.

Gildea, J.A. 1992. "The regional representation of Federal Reserve bank presidents," *Journal of Money, Credit and Banking*, May.

Gilman, T. 1898. *A Graded Banking System*. Houghton Mifflin.

Girton, L. 1974. "SDR creation and the real bills doctrine," *Southern Economic Journal*, July.

Glanville, B. 2013. *Remembering Inflation*. Princeton University Press.

Glass, C. 1927. *An Adventure in Constructive Finance*. Doubleday, Page.

Godley, W. and G. Zezza. 2006. "Debt and lending: a cri de coeur," *Policy Note*. Levy Institute of Bard College, April.

Goldenweiser, E.A. 1925. *Federal Reserve System in Operation*. McGraw-Hill.

Golembe, C.H. 1960. "The deposit insurance of 1933: an examination of its antecedents and its purposes," *Political Science Quarterly*, June.

Goodfriend, M. 2011. "Central banking in the credit turmoil: an assessment of Federal Reserve practice," *Journal of Monetary Economics*, January.

Goodfriend, M. and J.M. Lacker. 1999. "Limited commitment and central bank lending," *Federal Reserve Bank of Richmond Economic Quarterly*, fall.

Goodhart, C.A.E. 1988. *The Evolution of Central Banks*. MIT Press.

——. 2003. "Whither central banking," in D.E. Altig and B.D. Smith, eds., *Evolution and Procedures in Central Banking*. Cambridge University Press.

Gordon, R.J. 2012. "Is U.S. economic growth over? Faltering innovation confronts the six headwinds," *NBER Working Paper* 18315.

Gorton, G. 1984. "Private clearinghouses and the origins of central banking," *Federal Reserve Bank of Philadelphia Business Review*, January/February.

——. 2010. *Slapped by the Invisible Hand: The Panic of 2007*. Oxford University Press.

Gorton, G. and L. Huang. 2003. "Banking panics and the origin of central banking," in D.E. Altig and B.D. Smith, eds., *Evaluation and Procedures in Central Banking*. Cambridge University Press.

Gouge, W.M. 1833. *A Short History of Paper Money and Banking in the United States*. Grigg & Elliott; reprinted A.M. Kelley, 1968.

Govan, T.P. 1959. *Nicholas Biddle*. University of Chicago Press.

Greenspan, A. 1994. "Discussion," in Capie, *The Future of Central Banking: The Tercentenary Symposium of the Bank of England*. Cambridge University Press.

Gregory, T.E., ed. 1929. *Select Statutes, Documents & Reports Relating to British Banking, 1832–1928*, 2 vols. Oxford University Press.

Greider, W. 1987. *Secrets of the Temple: How the Federal Reserve Runs the Country*. Simon & Schuster.

Griffin, G.E. 1995. *The Creature from Jekyll Island*. American Opinion.

Hamilton, A. 1961–79. *Papers*. H.C. Syrett, ed. Columbia University Press.

——. 1790. *Report on a National Bank*, December 13, in *Papers*, Columbia University Press, 1961–79.

Hammond, W.B. 1957. *Banks and Politics in America from the Revolution to the Civil War*. Princeton University Press.

Hankey, T. 1867. *The Principles of Banking, its Utility and Economy; with Remarks on the Working and Management of the Bank of England*. Effingham Wilson.

Hansen, A.H. 1939. "Economic progress and declining population growth," *American Economic Review*, March.

——. 1949. *Monetary Theory and Fiscal Policy*. McGraw-Hill.

——. 1955. "Monetary policy," *Review of Economics and Statistics*, May.

Harding, W.P.G. 1925. *The Formative Period of the Federal Reserve System*. Houghton Mifflin.

Hargrove, E.C. and S.A. Morley. 1984. *The President and the Council of Economic Advisors: Interviews with CEA Chairmen*. Westview Press.

Harr, L. and W.C. Harris. 1936. *Banking Theory and Practice*. McGraw-Hill.

Harris, R. 1994. "The Bubble Act: its passage and effects on business organization," *Journal of Economic History*, September.

Harris, S.E. 1933. *Twenty Years of Federal Reserve Policy*. Harvard University Press.

Harrison, F. 2007. "House prices: expect the worst," *Money Week*, November 7.

Havrilesky, T. 1993. *The Pressures on American Monetary Policy*. Kluwer.

Hawtrey, R.G. 1938. *A Century of Bank Rate*. Longmans, Green.

Hayek, F.A. 1932. "The fate of the gold standard," *Der Deutsche Volkswirt*, 6; reprinted

R. McCloughry, ed., *Money, Capital and Fluctuations: Early Essays of F.A. Hayek.* Routledge & Kegan Paul, 1984.

——. 1973, 1976, 1979. *Law, Legislation, and Liberty*, 3 vols. University of Chicago Press.

——. 1990. *The Denationalisation of Money: the Argument Refined.* Institute of Economic Affairs.

Hayes, A. 1970. "The 1966 credit crunch," in D. Eastburn, ed., *Essays in Honor of Karl Bopp.* Federal Reserve Bank of Philadelphia.

Heller, W.W. 1966. *New Dimensions of Political Economy.* Harvard University Press.

Hepburn, A.B. 1903. *History of Coin and Currency in the United States and the Perennial Contest for Sound Money.* Macmillan.

Hess, G.D. 2012. "The Federal Reserve and the crisis of confidence: the five unanswered questions," in M.D. Bordo and H. James, *The Economic Challenge: Learning from Crises*, Ms.

Hetzel, R.L. 2008. *The Monetary Policy of the Federal Reserve: A History.* Cambridge University Press.

——. 2012. *The Great Recession: Market Failure or Policy Failure?.* Cambridge University Press.

Hicks, J.R. 1937. "Mr. Keynes and the 'Classics'," *Econometrica*, April.

Higgs, R. 1997. "Regime uncertainty: why the Great Depression lasted so long and why prosperity resumed after the war," *Independent Review*, 561–590.

Highfield, R.A., M. O'Hara, and J.H. Wood. 1991. "Public ends, private means: central banking and the profit motive, 1823–32," *Journal of Monetary Economics*, October.

Hilton, B. 1977. *Corn, Cash, Commerce: The Economic Policies of the Tory Governments, 1815–30.* Oxford University Press.

Hofstadter, R. 1948. *American Political Tradition and the Men Who Made It.* Knopf.

Holdsworth, J.T. 1910. *The First Bank of the United States* (National Monetary Commission). US Government Printing Office.

Holt, M.F. 1999. *The Rise and Fall of the American Whig Party*, Oxford University Press.

Homer, S, and R. Sylla. 2005. *A History of Interest Rates*, 4th edn. Rutgers University Press.

Hoogenboom, A. and O. Hoogenboom. 1976. *A History of the ICC.* Norton.

Hoover, H. 1952. *Memoirs: The Great Depression, 1929–41.* Macmillan.

Hori, M. 1996. *New Evidence on the Causes and Propagation of the Great Depression*, dissertation at the University of California at Berkeley.

Horner, F. 1802–6. *Economic Writings in the Edinburgh Review*, F. Fetter, ed. Kelley & Millman, 1957.

Horsefield, J.K. 1946. "Review" of Mints (1945), *Economica*, May.

——. 1960. *British Monetary Experiments, 1650–1710.* Harvard University Press.

Horwich, G. 1966. "Tight money, monetary restraint, and the price level," *Journal of Finance*, March.

House of Commons. 1819. *Second Report from the Secret Committee on the Expediency of the Bank Resuming Cash Payments. (British Parliamentary Papers, Monetary Policy, General, 2.* Irish University Press. 1969).

——. 1832. *Report from the Committee of Secrecy on the Bank of England*, Charter (*British Parliamentary Papers, Monetary Policy, General, 4.* Irish University Press. 1969).

——. 1931. *(Macmillan) Committee on Finance and Industry: Evidence.* Cmd. 3897. His Majesty's Stationary Office.

House of Lords. 1848. *Report from the Secret Committee to Inquire into the Causes of the Distress which has for some Time Prevailed among the Commercial Classes, and how Far it has been Affected by the Laws for Regulating the Issue of Bank Notes Payable on Demand.* (*British Parliamentary Papers, Monetary Policy. Commercial Distress*, 3. Irish University Press. 1969).

Howson, S. 1973. "A dear money man? Keynes on monetary policy, 1920," *Economic Journal*, June.

———. 1975. *Domestic Monetary Management in Britain, 1919–38.* Cambridge University Press.

Hseih, C. and C. Romer. 2006. "Was the Federal Reserve constrained by the gold standard during the Great Depression? Evidence from the 1932 open market purchase program," *Journal of Economic History*, March.

Hudson, M. 2006. "Saving, asset-price inflation, and debt-induced deflation," in L.R. Wray and M. Forstater, eds., *Money, Financial Instability and Stabilization Policy.* Edward Elgar.

Hummel, J.R. 1978. "The Jacksonians, banking, and economic theory: a reinterpretation," *Journal of Libertarian Studies*, 2.

Humphrey, T.M. 1982. "The real bills doctrine," *Federal Reserve Bank of Richmond Economic Review*, 5.

———. 2001. "The choice of a monetary framework: lessons from the 1920s," *Cato Journal*, 2.

———. 2010. "Lender of last resort: what it is, whence it came, and why the Fed isn't it," *Cato Journal*, 2.

Huntington, S.P. 1965. "Congressional responses to the twentieth century," in D.B. Truman, ed., *The Congress and America's Future.* Prentice-Hall.

Huskisson, W. 1810. *The Question Concerning the Depreciation of Our Currency Stated and Examined*, 3rd edn. John Murray.

Isaac, W.M. 2010. *Senseless Panic: How Washington Failed America.* Wiley.

James, J.A. 1976. "The conundrum of the low issue of national bank notes," *Journal of Political Economy*, April.

Janszen, E. 2006. *America's Bubble Economy: Profit When it Pops.* Wiley.

Jastram, R.W. 1977. *The Golden Constant: The English and American Experience, 1560–1967.* Wiley.

Johnson, H.G. 1963. "An overview of price levels, employment, and the U.S. balance of payments," *Journal of Business*, July.

Joplin, T. 1822. *An Essay on the General Principles and Present Practice of Banking in England and Scotland: With Observations upon the Justice and Policy of an Immediate Alteration of the Charter of the Bank of England, and the Measures to be Pursued in Order to Effect It.* Ridgeway & Co.

Kaiser, R.G. 2013. *Act of Congress. How America's Essential Institution Works, and How it Doesn't.* Knopf.

Kane, E.S. 1981. "Accelerating inflation, technological innovation, and the decreasing effectiveness of banking regulation," *Journal of Finance*. May.

———. 2012. "Bankers and brokers first: loose ends in the theory of central-bank policy-making," based on testimony before the Financial Institutions and Consumer Protection Subcommittee of the U.S. Senate Banking, Housing, and Urban Affairs Committee, August 3, 2011.

Kaufman, G.G. 1990. "Are some banks too large to fail? Myth and reality," *Contemporary Policy Issues*, October.

——. 1996. "Bank failures, systemic risk, and bank regulation," *Cato Journal*, spring/summer.

——. 2000. "Comment on Benston and Wood," *Journal of Financial Services Research*, December.

——. 2004. "FDIC losses in bank failures: has FDICIA made a difference?" *Federal Reserve Bank of Chicago Economic Perspectives*, third quarter.

Keen, S. 2006. "The lily, the pond, and the recession we can't avoid," *Centre for Policy Development*, December 14.

Kemmerer, E.W. 1910. *Seasonal Variations in the Relative Demand for Money and Capital in the United States* (National Monetary Commission). US Government Printing Office.

Kettl, D.F. 1986. *Leadership at the Fed*. Yale University Press.

Keynes, J.M. 1923. *A Tract on Monetary Reform*. Macmillan.

——. 1936. *The General Theory of Employment, Interest and Money*. Macmillan.

Khouri, S. 1990. "The Federal Reserve reaction function: a specification search," in T. Mayer, ed., *Political Economy of American Monetary Policy*. Cambridge University Press.

Kinley, D. 1910. *The Independent Treasury of the United States and its Relations to the Banks of the Country* (National Monetary Commission). US Government Printing Office.

Kirshner, J. 2007. *Appeasing Bankers*. Princeton University Press.

Kirst, M.W. 1969. *Government Without Passing Laws*. University of North Carolina Press.

Klein, B. 1974. "The competitive supply of money," *Journal of Money, Credit and Banking*, November.

Klein, J.L. 1997. *Statistical Visions in Time: A History of Time Series Analysis, 1662–1938*. Cambridge University Press.

Klein, L.R. 1947. *The Keynesian Revolution*. Macmillan.

Kolko, G. 1963. *The Triumph of Conservatism: A Reinterpretation of American History, 1900–1916*. Macmillan.

Krooss, H.E., ed. 1969. *Documentary History of Banking and Currency in the United States*. Chelsea House.

Krugman, P. 2009. "The curse of Montagu Norman," *New York Times Blog*, December 18.

Kydland, F.E. and Prescott, E.C. 1977. "Rules rather than discretion: the inconsistency of optimal plans," *Journal of Political Economy*, June.

Lacker, J.M. 2012. "The dangers of the Fed conducting credit policy," *Federal Reserve Bank of Richmond Region Focus*, fourth quarter.

Laughlin, J.L. 1912. *Banking Reform*. National Citizens League for the Promotion of a Sound Banking System.

Law, J. 1705. *Money and Trade Considered with a Proposal for Supplying the Nation with Money*. Andrew Anderson; reprinted A.M. Kelley, 1966.

Leffingwell, R.C. 1921. "The discount policy of the Federal Reserve Banks: discussion," *American Economic Review*, March.

Lent, G.E. 1948. *The Impact of the Undistributed Profits Tax, 1936–37*. Columbia University Press.

Levin, F.J. and A. Meulendyke. 1979. "Monetary policy and open market operations in 1978," *Federal Reserve Bank of New York Quarterly Review*, spring.

Lincoln, A. 1907. *Early Speeches, Life and Works*. Current Literature.

Lindsey, D.E., A. Orphanides, and R.H. Rasche. 2005. "The reform of October 1979: how it happened and why," *Federal Reserve Bank of St. Louis Review*, March/April, pt. 2.

Link, A.S. 1956. *Wilson: The New Freedom*. Princeton University Press.

Lippmann, W. 1933. "Accusations of bad faith," *Today and Tomorrow* newspaper column; reprinted A. Nevins, ed. *Interpretations*. Macmillan, 1936.

Livingston, J. 1986. *Origins of the Federal Reserve System: Money, Class, and Corporate Capitalism, 1890–1913*. Cornell University Press.

Locke, J. 1691. *Some Considerations of the Consequences of the Lowering of Interest and Raising the Value of Money*, 2nd edn. in *Several Papers Relating to Money, Interest and Trade*. A. Churchill and J. Churchill, 1696; reprinted A.M. Kelley, 1989.

Lombra, R.F. 1980. "Reflections on Burns's reflections," *Journal of Money, Credit and Banking*, February.

Lown, C.S. and J.H. Wood. 2003. "The determination of commercial bank reserve requirements," *Review of Financial Economics*, 12.

Loyd, S.J. 1844. *Thoughts on the Separation of the Departments of the Bank of England*. Pelham Richardson; F. Capie, *History of Banking*. W. Pickering, 1993.

Macey, J.R. and G.P. Miller. 1992. "Double liability of bank shareholders: history and implications," *Wake Forest Law Review*, spring.

McCulloch, H. 1888. *Men and Measures of Half a Century*. Charles Scribner's Sons.

McCulloch, J.R. 1858. "A treatise on metallic and paper money and banks," *Encyclopedia Britannica*, 8th edn. Adam and Charles Black.

McGarity, T.O. 2012. "Administrative law as blood sport: policy erosion in a highly partisan age," *Duke Law Journal*, May.

McKinley, V. 2011. *Financing Failure: A Century of Bailouts*. Independent Institute.

McKinnon, R.I. 1973. *Money and Capital in Economic Development*. Brookings.

MacNeil, N. 1963. *Forge of Democracy: The House of Representatives*. David McKay.

Madden, J.T., M. Nadler, and H.C. Sauvain. 1937. *America's Experience as a Creditor Nation*. Prentice Hall.

Madigan, B.F. and W.R. Nelson. 2002. "Proposed revision to the Federal Reserve's discount window lending programs," *Federal Reserve Bulletin*, July.

Madsen, J.B. 2005. 2006. Translated and summarized in D.J. Bezemer, "No one saw this coming: understanding financial crisis through accounting models," *Munich Personal RePEc Archive*, June (2009); and *Boersen*, December 4, 2008.

Maisel, S.J. 1973. *Managing the Dollar*. Norton.

Marshall, J. 1807. *The Life of George Washington*. C.P. Wayne; reprinted Chelsea House, 1983.

Matusow, A. 1998. *Nixon's Economy*. University Press of Kansas.

Mazumder, S. and J.H. Wood. 2013. "The Great Deflation of 1929–33: it (almost) had to happen," *Economic History Review*, February.

Meacham, J. 2012. *Thomas Jefferson: The Art of Power*. Random House.

Meerman, J.P. 1963. "The climax of the Bank War: Biddle's contraction, 1833–34," *Journal of Political Economy*, August.

Meigs, A.J. 1962. *Free Reserves and the Money Supply*. University of Chicago Press.

Meltzer, A.H. 2003. *A History of the Federal Reserve, 1913–51*. University of Chicago Press.

——. 2005. "Origins of the Great Inflation," *Federal Reserve Bank of St. Louis Review*, March/April, pt. 2.

Mill, J.S. 1857. *Principles of Political Economy, with Some of their Applications to Social Philosophy*, 3rd edn; reprinted, W.J. Ashley, ed. Longmans, Green, 1909.

Miller, M.M., ed. 1913. *Great Debates in American History*. Current Literature.

Mints, L.W. 1945. *A History of Banking Theory in Great Britain and the United States*. University of Chicago Press.

Mintz, I. 1951. *Deterioration in the Quality of Bonds issued in the United States, 1920–30*. National Bureau of Economic Research.

Miron, J.A. 1986. "Financial panics, the seasonality of the nominal interest rate, and the founding of the Fed," *American Economic Review*, March.

——. 2009a. "In defense of doing nothing," *Cato's Letter*, spring.

——. 2009b. "Bailout or bankruptcy," *Cato Journal*, winter.

Mishkin, F.S. 2006. *The Economics of Money, Banking, and Financial Markets*, 7th edn. Pearson Addison-Wesley.

Mitchell, B.R. 2007. *International Historical Statistics: Europe, 1750–2005*. Palgrave Macmillan.

Mitchell, W.C. 1903. *A History of Greenbacks*. University of Chicago Press.

——. 1911. "The publications of the National Monetary Commission," *Quarterly Journal of Economics*, May.

——. 1913. *Business Cycles*. University of California Press.

Moggridge, D.E. 1969. *The Return to Gold, 1925*. Cambridge University Press.

——. 1972. *British Monetary Policy, 1924–31: the Norman Conquest of $4.86*. Cambridge University Press.

Morgan, W. 1797. "On the finances of the Bank," *Monthly Magazine and British Register*, October.

Munn, G.G. and F.L. Garcia. 1983. *Encyclopedia of Banking and Finance*, 8th edn. Bankers' Publishing Co.

Myers, M.G. 1931. *The New York Money Market: Origins and Development*. Columbia University Press.

——. 1970. *A Financial History of the United States*. Columbia University Press.

Neikirk, W.R. 1987. *Volcker: Portrait of the Money Man*. New Congdon and Weed.

Nettels, C.P. 1962. *The Emergence of a National Economy, 1775–1815*. Holt, Rinehart, and Winston.

Niskanen, W.A. 1971. *Bureaucracy and Representative Government*. Aldine-Atherton.

Nixon, R.M. 1978. *Memoirs*. Grosset & Dunlap.

North, D.C. 1990. *Institutions, Institutional Change, and Economic Performance*. Cambridge University Press.

North, D.C. and B. Weingast. 1989. "Constitutions and commitment: the evolution of institutions governing public choice in seventeenth-century England," *Journal of Economic History*, December.

Noyes, A.D. 1909. *Forty Years of American Finance*. G.P. Putnam's Sons.

Nussbaum, A. 1939. *Money in the Law*. Foundation Press.

O'Brien, D.P., ed. 1994. *Foundations of Monetary Economics*. W. Pickering.

Odell, J. 1982. *International Monetary Policy*. Princeton University Press.

Orphanides, A. 2003. "Historical monetary policy analysis and the Taylor rule," *Journal of Monetary Economics*, July.

Ostrom, E. 1990. *Governing the Commons: The Evolution of Institutions for Collective Action*. Cambridge University Press.

Page, W. 1919. *Commerce and Industry: A Historical Review of the Economic Condition of the British Empire from the Peace of Paris in 1815 to the Declaration of War in 1914 Based on the Parliamentary Debates*. Constable.

Parker, C.S. 1899. *Sir Robert Peel*. John Murray.

Parliamentary History of England from the Earliest Period to the Year 1803. 1813. T.C. Hansard.

Patterson, J.T. 1967. *Congressional Conservatism and the New Deal*. University of Kentucky Press.

Paulson, Henry M., Jr. 2010. *On the Brink: Inside the Race to Stop the Collapse of the Global Financial System*. Business Plus.

Peltzman, S. 1970. "Capital investment in commercial banking and its relation to portfolio regulation," *Journal of Political Economy*, January/February.

Pepys, S. 1660–9. *Diary*. R. Latham and W. Matthews, eds., University of California Press, 1970–83.

Petty, W. 1682. *Quantulumcunque Concerning Money*; reprinted W. Petty, *Economic Writings*, C. Hull, ed. A.M. Kelly, 1963.

Phelps, E.S. 1973. "Inflation in the theory of public finance," *Swedish Journal of Economics*, March.

Pierce, J.L. 1978. "The myth of congressional supervision of monetary policy," *Journal of Monetary Economics*, April.

Pressnell, L.S. 1956. *Country Banking in the Industrial Revolution*. Oxford University Press.

Ramsey, P.H. 1971. *The Price Revolution in Sixteenth-Century England*. Methuen.

Redlich, F. 1951. *The Molding of American Banking*. New Hafner.

Reinhart, C.M. and K.S. Rogoff. 2009. *This Time is Different: Eight Centuries of Financial Folly*. Princeton University Press.

Reinhart, C.M., V.R. Reinhart, and K. Rogoff. 2012. "Public debt overhangs: advanced economy episodes since 1800," *Journal of Economic Perspectives*, summer.

Ricardo, D. 1816. *Proposals for an Economical and Secure Currency*. 2nd edn. John Murray (*Works*, iv).

——. *Works and Correspondence*, P. Sraffa, ed. Cambridge University Press, 1951–73.

Richards, R.D. 1934. "The first fifty years of the Bank of England," in J.G. Van Dillen, ed., *History of the Principal Public Banks*. Martinus Nijhoff.

Richebächer, K. 2001. "The Richebächer letter," September.

Riefler, W.W. 1930. *Money Rates and Money Markets in the United States*. Harper.

Rist, M.C. 1931. "The international consequences of the present distribution of gold holdings," in Royal Institute of Economic Affairs, *The International Gold Problem*. Oxford University Press.

Robbins, L. 1934. *The Great Depression*. Macmillan.

Robertson, R.M. 1968. *The Comptroller and Bank Supervision: A Historical Appraisal*. Comptroller of the Currency.

Rogoff, K. 1985. "The optimal degree of commitment to an intermediate monetary target," *Quarterly Journal of Economics*, November.

Rolnick, A.J. and W.E. Weber. 1984. "The causes of free bank failures," *Journal of Monetary Economics*, November.

Romer, C.D. 1992. "What ended the Great Depression?" *Journal of Economic History*, December.

Romer, C.D. and D.H. Romer. 1998. "Monetary policy and the well-being of the poor," *NBER Working Paper* 6793.

——. 2002a. "The evolution of economic understanding and postwar stabilization policy," in *Stabilization Policy*, Federal Reserve Bank of Kansas City.

——. 2002b. "A rehabilitation of monetary policy in the 1950s," *American Economic Review*, May.

Roubini, N. 2009. *Global Economics Blog*, in D.J. Bezemer "No one saw this coming: understanding financial crisis through accounting models," *Munich Personal RePEc Archive*, 9, 42.

Salter, A. 1932. *Recovery, the Second Effort*. Century.

Samuelson, P.A. and R. Solow. 1960. "Analytical aspects of anti-inflation policy," *American Economic Review*, May.

Saunders, A. and M.M. Cornett. 2012. *Financial Markets and Institutions*, 5th edn. McGraw-Hill/Irwin.

Sayers, R.S. 1951. "The development of central banking after Bagehot," *Economic History Review*, 1.

——. 1953. "Ricardo's views on monetary questions," *Quarterly Journal of Economics*, February.

——. 1976. *The Bank of England, 1891–1944*. Cambridge University Press.

Scherer, F.M. and D. Ross. 1990. *Industrial Market Structure and Economic Performance*. Houghton Mifflin.

Schiff, P. 2007. *Crash Proof: How to Profit from the Coming Economic Collapse*. John Wiley & Sons.

Schlesinger, Jr., J.M. 1948. *The Age of Jackson*. Little Brown.

Schwartz, A.J. 1992. "Misuse of the Fed's discount window," *Federal Reserve Bank of St. Louis Review*, September/October.

——. 1995. "Why financial stability depends on price stability," *Economic Affairs*, autumn.

——. 2009. "Boundaries between the Fed and the Treasury," Shadow Open Market Committee, April 24.

Selgin, G.A. and L.H. White. 1999. "A fiscal theory of the government's role in money," *Economic Inquiry*, January.

Selgin, G.A., W.D. Lastrapes, and L.H. White. 2012. "Has the Fed been a failure?" *Journal of Macroeconomics*, September.

Shepsle, K.A. 1989. "Studying institutions: some lessons from the rational approach," *Journal of Theoretical Politics*, 1.

Shlaes, A. 2007. *The Forgotten Man: A New History of the Great Depression*. Harper-Collins.

Shull, B. 1971. "Report on research undertaken in connection with a system study," *Reappraisal of the Federal Reserve Discount Mechanism*, Federal Reserve Board.

Smith, A. 1776. *An Inquiry into the Nature and Causes of the Wealth of Nations*; reprinted Random House, 1937.

Smith, V. 1936. *The Rationale of Central Banking*. P.S. King & Son.

Smith, W.B. 1953. *Economic Aspects of the Second Bank of the U.S.* Harvard University Press.

Smith, W.L. 1965. "Are there enough policy tools?" *American Economic Review*, May.

Sorkin, A.R. 2009. *Too Big to Fail*. Viking.

Sprague, O.M.W. 1910. *History of Crises under the National Banking System* (National Monetary Commission). US Government Printing Office.

Sproul, A. 1980. *Selected Papers*, L.S. Ritter, ed. Federal Reserve Bank of New York.

Sraffa, P. 1951. "The ingenious calculator," in D. Ricardo, *Works and Correspondence*, iv, Cambridge University Press, 415–418.

Stanton, T.H. 2012. *Why Some Firms Thrive While Others Fail: Government and Management Lessons from the Crisis*. Oxford University Press.

Stark, J. 2008. "Lessons for central bankers from the history of the Phillips Curve," speech at a Federal Reserve Bank of Boston conference on *Understanding Inflation and the Implications for Monetary Policy: A Phillips Curve Retrospective*, June 11.

Stein, H. 1969. *The Fiscal Revolution in America*. University of Chicago Press.

Stigler, G.J. 1964. "Public regulation of the securities markets," *Journal of Business*, April.

———. 1971. "The theory of economic regulation," *Bell Journal of Economics and Management Science*, spring.

Strong, B. 1930. *Interpretations of Federal Reserve Policy*, W.R. Burgess, ed. Harper & Row.

Sturzenegger, F. 1992. "Inflation and social welfare in a model with endogenous financial adaptation," *NBER Working Paper* 4013.

Summers, L.H. 2013. Speech, IMF Fourteenth Annual Research Conference, November 8.

Sumner, W.G. 1883. *Andrew Jackson as a Public Man*. Houghton Mifflin.

Swanson, E.T. 2011. "Let's twist again: a high-frequency event-study analysis of operation twist and its implications for QE2," *Brookings Papers on Economic Activity*, spring.

Sylla, R., R.E. Wright, and D.J. Cowen. 2009. "Alexander Hamilton, central banker: crisis management during the U.S. financial panic of 1792," *Economic History Review*, spring.

Taleb, N.N. 2007. *The Black Swan: The Impact of the Highly Improbable*. Random House.

Tarr, D.G. 2010. "Lehman Brothers and Washington Mutual show too big to fail is a myth," Ms. New Economic School, July 21.

Taus, E.R. 1943. *Central Banking Functions of the U.S. Treasury, 1789–1941*. Columbia University Press.

Taylor, J.B. 1993. "Discretion versus policy rules in practice," *Carnegie-Rochester Conference Series on Public Policy*, December.

———. 2009. *Getting Off Track: How Government Actions and Interventions Caused, Prolonged, and Worsened the Financial Crisis*. Hoover Institution Press.

Taylor, J.B. and J.C. Williams. 2009. "A black swan in the money market," *American Economic Journal of Macroeconomics*, January.

Temin, P. 1969. *The Jacksonian Economy*. Norton.

———. 1976. *Did Monetary Forces Cause the Great Depression?* Norton.

Temzelides, T. 1997. "Are bank runs contagious?" *Federal Reserve Bank of Philadelphia Business Review*, November–December.

Thomas, R.G. 1935. "Bank failures: causes and remedies," *Journal of Business*, July.

Thomas, S.E. 1934. *The Rise and Growth of Joint Stock Banking*. Pitman.

Thornton, D.L. 2009. "Would quantitative easing sooner have tempered the financial crisis and economic recession?" *Federal Reserve Bank of St. Louis Synopsis*, 37.

———. 2011. "The effectiveness of unconventional monetary policy: the term auction facility," *Federal Reserve Bank of St. Louis Review*, November/December.

Thornton, H. 1802. *An Enquiry into the Nature and Effects of the Paper Credit of Great Britain*. J. Hatchard.; reprinted A.M. Kelley, 1965.

Thorp, W.L. 1926. *Business Annals*. National Bureau of Economic Research.

Timberlake, R.H. 1978. *The Origins of Central Banking in the U.S.* Harvard University Press.

———. 1984. "The central banking role of clearinghouse associations," *Journal of Money, Credit and Banking*, February.

———. 1993. *Monetary Policy in the United States: An Intellectual and Institutional History*. University of Chicago Press, 1993.

———. 2007. "Gold standards and the real bills doctrine in U.S. monetary policy," *Independent Review*, Winter.

Tinbergen, J. 1952. *On the Theory of Economic Policy*. North-Holland.

Tobin, J. 1958. "Defense, dollars, and doctrines," *Yale Review*, March.

Tooke, T. 1838, 1857. *A History of Prices and of the State of the Circulation*. Longmans, Orme, Brown, Green, and Longmans.

Triffin, R. 1960. *Gold and the Dollar Crisis*. Yale University Press.

Unger, I. 1959. "Business men and specie resumption," *Political Science Quarterly*, March.

———. 1964. *The Greenback Era: A Social and Political History of American Finance, 1865–79*. Princeton University Press.

US Bureau of the Census. 1975. *Historical Statistics of the United States, Colonial Times to 1970*. US Government Printing Office.

US Congress. 1789–1824. *Annals of the Congress of the United States*. Gales and Seaton, 1834–56.

———. 1832. *Bank of the United States*, House Report 460, 22nd Cong., 1st sess., April 30.

———. 1877. *Silver Commission Hearings and Report*, 44th Cong., 2nd sess., Senate Report 703.

———. 1908. *Response of the Secretary of the Treasury ... in Regard to Treasury Operations*, Senate Doc. 208, 60th Cong., 1st sess.

———. 1922. *Agricultural Inquiry*. Hearings, Joint Commission of Agri. Inquiry. 67th Cong., 1st sess.

———. 1926. *Stabilization*. Hearings, Committee on Banking and Currency. H.R., 69th Cong., 1st sess., April 8.

———. 1931. *Operation of the National and Federal Reserve Banking Systems*. Hearings, Subcommittee of the Senate Committee on Banking and Currency, Pt. 1. 71st Cong., 3rd sess.

———. 1932. *Stabilization of Commodity Prices*. Hearings, Subcommittee of the House Committee on Banking and Currency on H.R. 10517. *For Increasing and Stabilizing the Price Level and for Other Purposes*. 72nd Cong., 1st sess. March.

———. 1956. *Nomination of Wm. McC. Martin, Jr.* Hearings, Senate Banking Committee, 84th Cong., 2nd sess.

———. 1959. *Public Debt Ceiling and Interest Rate Ceiling on Bonds*, Hearings, House Committee on Ways and Means, 86th Cong., 1st sess.

———. 1964. *The Federal Reserve after Fifty Years*. Hearings, Subcommittee on Domestic Finance of the House Committee on Banking and Currency, 88th Cong., 2nd sess.

———. 1969. *The 1969 Economic Report of the President*, Hearings, Joint Economic Committee. 91st Cong., 1st sess.

———. 1991. *Economic Implications of "Too Big to Fail" Policy*, Hearings, House Subcommittee on Economic Stabilization of the Committee on Banking, Finance, and Urban Affairs.

———. 2008. *U.S. Financial Markets and Sale of Bear Stearns*, Hearings, Senate Committee on Banking, Housing, and Urban Affairs, 112th Cong., 2nd sess.

US Treasury. 1991. *Modernizing the Financial System*, February.

Viner, S. 1937. *Studies in the Theory of International Trade*. George Allen & Unwin.

Volcker, P.A. 1994. "Discussion," in F. Capie, *The Future of Central Banking: The Tercentenary Symposium of the Bank of England*. Cambridge University Press.

Volcker, P.A. and Gyohten, T. 1992. *Changing Fortunes*. Times Books.

Wallace, N. 1990. "A bank model in which partial suspension is best," *Federal Reserve Bank of Minneapolis, Quarterly Review*, fall.

Wallison, P.J. 2009. "Regulation without reason," The Group of Thirty Report. American Enterprise Institute *Financial Services Outlook*, January.

Walsh, C.E. 1995. "Optimal contracts for central bankers," *American Economic Review*, March.

Walter, J.R. 2005. "Depression-era bank failures: the great contagion or the great shakeout?" *Federal Reserve Bank of Richmond Economic Quarterly*, winter.

Walter, J.R. and J.A. Weinberg. 2002. "How large is the federal financial safety net?" *Cato Journal*, 3.

Walters, Jr., R. 1957. *Albert Gallatin: Jeffersonian Financier and Diplomat*. Macmillan.

Warburg, P.M. 1907. "A plan for a modified central bank," *New York Times Annual Financial Review*, November 12. Reprinted in P.M. Warburg, *The Federal Reserve System: Its Origin and Growth*. Macmillan, 1930.

——. 1910. *The Discount System in Europe* (National Monetary Commission). US Government Printing Office.

——. 1930. *The Federal Reserve System: Its Origin and Growth*. Macmillan.

Warburton, C. 1958. "Variations in economic growth and banking developments in the United States from 1835 to 1885," *Journal of Economic History*, September.

Webb, B. 1985, *Diary*, N. Mackenzie and J. Mackenzie, eds., Harvard University Press.

Webel, B. 2013. "Troubled asset relief program (TARP): implementation and status," *Congressional Research Service*, June 27.

Weintraub, R.E. 1978. "Congressional supervision of monetary policy," *Journal of Monetary Policy*, April.

Weintraub, S. 1955. "Monetary policy: a comment," *Review of Economics and Statistics*, May.

Wells, W.C. 1994. *Economist in an Uncertain World: Arthur F. Burns and the Federal Reserve, 1970–78*. Columbia University Press.

Wessel, D. 2010. *In Fed We Trust: Ben Bernanke's War on the Great Panic*. Three Rivers Press.

West, R.C. 1977. *Banking Reform and the Federal Reserve, 1863–1923*. Cornell University Press.

Wettereau, J.O. 1942. "Branches of the first Bank of the United States," *Journal of Economic History*, December.

Whale, P.B. 1944. "A retrospective view of the Bank Charter Act of 1844," *Economica*, August.

Wheelock, D.C. 1990. "Member bank borrowing and the Fed's contractionary monetary policy during the Great Depression," *Journal of Money, Credit and Banking*, November.

——. 1991. *The Strategy and Consistency of Federal Reserve Policy, 1924–33*. Cambridge University Press.

——. 2008. "The Federal response to home mortgage distress: lessons from the Great Depression," May/June.

——. 2010. "Lessons learned? Comparing the Federal Reserve's responses to the crises of 1929–33 and 2007–2009," *Federal Reserve Bank of St. Louis Review*, March/April.

White, E.N. 1983. *The Regulation and Reform of the American Banking System, 1900–1929*. Princeton University Press.

——. 2010. " 'To establish a more effective supervision of banking': how the birth of the

Fed altered bank supervision," for the 100th Anniversary of the Jekyll Island Conference, Federal Reserve Bank of Atlanta.

White, L.H. 1984. *Free Banking in Britain: Theory, Experience, and Debate, 1800–1845.* Cambridge University Press.

Wicker, E. 1966. *Federal Reserve Monetary Policy, 1917–33.* Random House.

———. 1969a. "Brunner and Meltzer on Federal Reserve policy during the Great Depression," *Canadian Journal of Economics*, May.

———. 1969b. "The World War II policy of fixing a pattern of interest rates," *Journal of Finance*, June.

———. 1996. *The Banking Panics of the Great Depression.* Cambridge University Press.

Wicksell, K. 1898. *Interest and Prices*, trans. by R.F. Kahn. Royal Economic Society, 1936.

Willis, H.P. 1915. *The Federal Reserve.* Doubleday, Page.

Wilson, J. 1859. *Capital, Currency and Banking.* D.M. Aird.

Wilson, W. 1885. *Congressional Government.* Houghton Mifflin; reprinted World Publishing Co., 1956.

———. 1914. "Letter to Congressman Oscar Underwood, Oct. 17," in *Papers*, 31.

———. 1966–94. *Papers*, A.S. Link, ed. Princeton University Press.

Wood, J.H. 1967. "A model of Federal Reserve behavior," in G. Horwich, ed., *Monetary Process and Policy.* Irwin.

———. 1975. *Commercial Bank Loan and Investment Behaviour.* John Wiley & Sons.

———. 2005. *A History of Central Banking in Great Britain and the United States.* Cambridge University Press.

———. 2006. "William McChesney Martin, Jr.: a reevaluation," *Federal Reserve Bank of Richmond Region Focus*, winter.

———. 2009. *A History of Macroeconomic Policy in the United States.* Routledge.

———. 2014. "Are there important differences between Classical and twenty-first-century monetary theories: did the Keynesian and monetarist revolutions matter?" *History of Political Economy*, spring.

Wood, J.H. and Wood, N.L. 1985. *Financial Markets.* Harcourt Brace Jovanovich.

Woodford, M. 2003. *Interest and Prices: Foundations of a Theory of Monetary Policy.* Princeton University Press.

Woolley, J.T. 1984. *Monetary Politics: The Federal Reserve and the Politics of Monetary Policy.* Cambridge University Press.

Young, R.A. 1929. *The International Financial Position of the United States.* National Industrial Conference Board.

Index

For Product Safety Concerns and Information please contact our EU representative GPSR@taylorandfrancis.com
Taylor & Francis Verlag GmbH, Kaufingerstraße 24, 80331 München, Germany

www.ingramcontent.com/pod-product-compliance
Ingram Content Group UK Ltd.
Pitfield, Milton Keynes, MK11 3LW, UK
UKHW021001180425
457613UK00019B/770